PRAISE FOR RAV SHMULY

"Rabbi Shmuly Yanklowitz's name has become synonymous with the call for ethical renewal and social justice within the American Jewish community" - Jonathan D. Sarna, Joseph H. & Belle R. Braun professor of American Jewish History, Brandeis University

"Through his essays and articles, Yanklowitz lovingly but firmly gives (rebuke) to his peers. Whether muckraking about the treatment of non-Jewish workers at Kosher meat plants or writing about Jewish responsibility to protect the environment, Yanklowitz calls on Orthodox Jews to think beyond the bounds of their community to engage with the more universal aspects of the Jewish tradition. To read Yanklowitz, then, is to read the social history of a movement wrestling with change, from a leader who knows its tradition well enough to challenge it."– Rabbi Margie Klein, Congregation Sha'arei Shalom

"Shmuly Yanklowitz is a rare young leader who combines brilliance of mind, passion of the heart and spirituality of the soul. He is a great Jewish global leader and activist for the 21st century that calls upon us all to find our callings and to meet our highest potentials. This book challenges us and inspires us all as Jews to support the vulnerable, take responsibility for social problems, and protest the greatest wrongs around the world. – Rabbi Avi Weiss, Hebrew Institute of Riverdale

"Rabbi Shmuly leaves no stone unturned halachically, socially, politically, and religiously" – Mayim Bialik

Bringing Heaven Down To Earth

ALSO BY RABBI DR. SHMULY YANKLOWITZ

Jewish Ethics & Social Justice

Epistemic Development in Talmud Study

The Soul of Jewish Social Justice

Spiritual Courage: Vignettes on Jewish Leadership for the 21st Century.

Bringing Heaven Down To Earth

Jewish Ethics For An Evolving And Complex World

RABBI DR. SHMULY
YANKLOWITZ

© 2014

The pure righteous do not complain of the dark, but increase the light; they do not complain of evil, but increase justice; they do not complain of heresy, but increase faith; they do not complain of ignorance, but increase wisdom.

- Rabbi Avraham Yitzchak HaCohen Kook

Just as something physical can be grasped by holding on it, so one can grasp a soul by calling its name.

- Hasidic proverb

I dedicate this book to my primary Torah teachers and mentors:

Rabbi Avi Weiss,
Rabbi Shlomo Riskin,
Rabbi Nathan Lopes Cardozo,
Rabbi Yitz Greenberg,
and Rabbi Chaim Brovender

May they be blessed with long life and the strength to continue leading and teaching the Jewish people for many more years to come.

For the last decade, I have been on a journey to apply Jewish values and law to the most pressing contemporary moral issue. I have traveled to over a dozen countries to learn and teach, making humble attempts to create social impact.

During my formative years, my involvement with activism was primarily done in the pluralistic Jewish community. I remain indebted to the leaders and educators of these organizations, who provided me with an excellent education, empowered me in leadership, and inspired me with a sense of higher calling and moral conviction. After numerous years serving as the only Orthodox Jew in these pluralistic environments, I became lonely and curious. It was lonely eating kosher food, praying, and learning Torah in remote villages, and I became curious about the potential for attempting to create a unique social justice movement in the Orthodox community.

In the spring of 2007, I founded Uri L'Tzedek, the first and only Orthodox social justice movement in the world. In the last seven years, we have grown tremendously, due to the Herculean (or is it Samson-esque) efforts of many staff members, volunteers, board members, and stakeholders. Uri L'Tzedek has become the American center of Torah social justice thought and leads, inspires, challenges, and supports the Orthodox community to raise our ethical bar to a higher standard. Throughout my life as an activist, I have written scores of articles for newspapers, journals, and blogs. I have compiled some of these writings to create this book, Bringing Heaven Down To Earth. My intention and hope with this work are to foster further discourse, research, and activism around the core issues featured herein. This book addresses a singular issue: how do our traditional Jewish values translate into contemporary Jewish ethical social justice responsibilities? How do the virtues required for each Jew to cultivate become converted into commitments to creating more sustainable and systemic social change for the most vulnerable in our society? Here I offer frameworks to further a broader discourse about these responsibilities.

While I am a moral philosopher and developmental psychologist by disposition and training, I am also a rabbi and an activist by conviction and commitment. While the academic research and insights are implicit within these articles, it is the rabbinic and activist voice that is made most explicit. I believe that there is a greater need for inspiration than for drawn-out analytical essays on these issues and thus I'm more concerned with meaning making than the academic process.

My hermeneutic approach is to show how the Jewish tradition is relevant to our most pressing moral problems. Today, two prevalent trends have emerged. One is to read text with a fundamentalist orientation, with literal application that is ignorant or disdainful of other interpretations and sensitivities. The other is to make text irrelevant and merely confine it to its historical context. One attempts to limit the scope of meaning while the other attempts to nullify any potential for existing relevance. It is my contention that the most complex and meaningful interpretation of text requires intellectual rigor, a concern for the moral consequence of an interpretation, integrity to the meaning of the text, and the consideration of all prior interpretations.

In the following pages, I address issues such as ritual and theology, leadership and community, animals and prisons, business and interpersonal ethics. While there is a constant dance between the parochial and universal, my hermeneutic is clear: the particular informs the universal. It is our Jewish texts, our Jewish values, and, ultimately, our Jewish laws that inform how we are to respond to our greatest moral challenges; it is also clear that we must respond to the inequities that seem to creep deeper into society without a clear path to inhibit them. Therefore, it is my conviction that of the typical and knee-jerk response that the issues are too complex or that only a few are capable of addressing the problems are wholly inadequate. I take a grassroots rather than a top-down approach. This is to say, all Jews must engage in social justice thinking and activism and that all must make their own informed choices on how to proceed. Just as I believe all Jews should be engaged with ritual commitments, so too must be they be engaged with the pressing moral issues of our time.

I would like to humbly offer a *bracha* (blessing) to all my readers, that you continue to search for the true voice of your calling to improve the world and stay focused and earnest in pursuing those goals to create the change that is so sorely needed in our world.

WITH GRATITUDE

These essays have appeared in The Jewish Week, The Jewish Journal, The Jewish Press, The Jewish Forward, HaAretz, Milin Havivin, Conversations, Jewish Educational Leadership, Sh'ma, The Times of Israel, The Washington Post, and The Huffington Post. I am grateful to all of the editors for their support. My intention and hope with this work are to foster further discourse, research, and activism around these core issues.

Through our building the Orthodox social justice movement, Uri L'Tzedek has become the American center of Torah social justice thought and leads, inspires, challenges, and supports the Orthodox community to raise our ethical bar to a higher standard. At The Shamayim V'Aretz Insitute we are working to inspire deeper commitments to animal welfare, veganism, health, and the environment. At the Valley Beit Midrash, we are inspiring, training and funding young Jewish social entrepreneurs to create change whiled educating all who have an interest in Judaism and Jewish intellectual values. I have written this book in response to many of the issues we are addressing to create social change.
This book could not have been written without the core support of family, friends, teachers, mentors, colleagues, and supporters.

I am in gratitude to those who have offered ideas and helped in the editing of articles over the years including: Abraham J. Frost, Dr. Peter Geidel, and Ze'ev Sudry.

Nothing would have been possible at all without the love and support of my family: my father Steven Yanklowitz, mother Sandra Yanklowitz, and brother Scott Yanklowitz.

Most importantly, my lovely wife and partner in life Shoshana Yanklowitz has provided me more support and inspiration than any person could ask for. My sweet baby Amiella Rachel fills me with laughter and wonder. I am so deeply fortunate and full of gratitude.

I thank the Creator for giving me life, hope, and strength to empower me to share my Torah.

Contents

Truth and Theology

Jewish Law: Society And Relationships

Tzedakah, Economy, and Jewish Business Ethics

Moral Education

Conclusion

Truth and Theology

1

The Limits of Reason and the Ethics of Inclusivity

Throughout history, new ideas have emerged and integrated into Jewish thought. Rationalism is an example of this phenomenon, but the countermotion to this mode of thinking is just as well established in our tradition. For example, while Rambam was the great Jewish champion for rational thinking, he also knew its limits:

> I say that there is a limit to human reason, and as long as the soul resides within the body, it cannot grasp what is above nature, for nothing that is immersed in nature can see above it... Know that there is a level of knowledge, which is higher than all philosophy, namely prophecy. Prophecy is a different source and category of knowledge. Proof and examination are inapplicable to it... Our faith is based on the principle that the words of Moshe are prophecy and, therefore, beyond the domain of speculation, validation, argument or proof. Reason is inherently unable to pass judgment in the area from which prophecy originates. It would be like trying to put all the water in the world into a little cup (*Teshuvot HaRambam Veiggerotav*, Lichtenberg, Leipzig ed., 1859, Letter to Rabbi Chisdai, 11 23a-23b).

In the modern world, we have seen spectacular advances due to the development of reason, whether in medicine, food production, and transportation. Nevertheless, at times an extreme dependence on what is perceived to be reason has caused great harm. Some (such as the Thomas Malthus) argued that population would vastly outstrip the ability of people to cultivate food, leading some to argue that the "surplus population" should be allowed to starve. The economist David Ricardo proposed an "iron law" in which wages should never be raised above the subsistence level, and Utilitarians proposed nightmarish prisons and workhouses, in the mistaken belief that people chose to be poor. Charles Dickens sharply portrayed this inhuman philosophy in many of his novels; no passage is more effective than the opening of *Hard Times*, in which the wealthy Thomas Gradgrind expounds on his theory of education, which should discourage all imagination, creativity, or spirituality in favor of reason:

> Now, what I want is, Facts. Teach these boys and girls
> nothing but Facts. Facts alone are wanted in life. Plant
> nothing else, and root out everything else. You can
> only form the minds of reasoning animals upon Facts:
> nothing else will ever be of any service to them. This is
> the principle on which I bring up my own children,
> and this is the principle on which I bring up these
> children. Stick to Facts, sir!

This extreme view of "reason" would later lead to the pseudoscientific of eugenics and "scientific" racism, which led to the deaths of millions in the last century. Today, we see this stress on reason over spiritualism in the views of some political leaders and business executives, who openly espouse the values of Ayn Rand, embracing unlimited greed for a supposed elite while simultaneously opposing altruistic forms of charity for the needy. Fortunately, this tendency has not completely taken hold, as our society values the balance between reason and spiritualism, appreciating the virtues that each affords. Scientists may learn from theologians, and theologians from scientists, in the arenas of the mind and the spirit.

That we have limitations in our reasoning does not cause us to negate our intellectual commitments in the slightest. Nor does it necessitate that we "choose faith over reason." Our faith should, as best as possible, be situated within an intellectual foundation. Proactive doubt can lead to deeper questioning and that questioning can move us toward greater answers. Certainly, we should not shun others who ask big questions and do not come to the same conclusions that we do. Even Rav Avrahom Yeshaya Karelitz (the Chazon Ish), the great twentieth century Ultra-Orthodox thinker, argued for inclusivity in this regard (*Yoreh Deah, Shechitah* z:i6):

[Such laws] only applied at times when the Divine presence was clearly revealed, such as in the days when there were open miracles, and a heavenly voice was heard and when the righteous would operate under direct Divine intervention which could be observed by anybody. Then the heretics were of a special deviousness, bending their evil inclination towards immoral desires and licentiousness. In such days there was [the need] to remove this kind of wickedness from the world, since everybody knew that it would bring Divine retribution onto the world [including] drought, pestilence and famine. But at the time of "Divine hiding," in which faith has become weak in people, there is no purpose in taking [harsh measurements against heretics and violators]; in fact it has the reverse effect and will only increase their lawlessness and be viewed as the coercion and violence [of religious fanatics]. And therefore we have an obligation to try to bring them back with "cords of love" (Hoshea 11:4).

Going even further, Rabbi Judah Loew ben Bezalel (the Maharal), the sixteenth century thinker in Prague, argued that we should not reject others with ideas different from our own but rather take the intellectual freedom to truly learn and discuss with them:

It is proper, out of love of reason and knowledge, that you not [summarily] reject anything that opposes your own ideas, especially so if [your adversary] does not intend merely to provoke you, but rather to declare his beliefs... When our *Rishonim* [the earlier Jewish sages] found something written against their faith, they did not reject it [out of hand], for it stands to reason that [such opposition] ought not to be a cause for rejecting it and silencing a man when it comes to religious matters; for religion is given to all. This is especially so with regard to the written word... should there not have been a reaction against the books of the philosophers who, following their own investigations, repudiated [traditional religious teachings] and asserted the eternity of the universe and thus denied the creation *altogether*? Nevertheless [the Rishonim] read their books and did not dismiss them. For the proper way to attain the truth is to hear [others'] arguments which they sincerely hold, not out of a desire to provoke you. Thus, it is wrong simply to reject an opponent's ideas; instead, draw him close to you and delve into his words (*'Be'er HaGolah*, translated by Dr. Norman Lamm; *Torah Ummada*, Jason Aronson, 57–58).

Jewish ideological camps in the twenty-first century are becoming narrower and narrower. We must remember that there is an incredibly wide range of possibilities for what is a "Jewish idea." And even when something seems to be "outside," it does not mean that the idea should be rejected and certainly not that the person

29

should be alienated. We have to continue filtering the manifest ideas in the world to make very intentional decisions about what we believe. But we must also embrace others lovingly who seem to contradict some of the core ideas and values that we cherish. Of course, there are boundaries and limits, but we must have humility in setting them and always embrace an ethic of sincere inclusivity and deep respect.

2

Spiritual Authenticity: Breaking From Religious Conformity

The fundamental misunderstanding that troubles many today is that there are only two theological viewpoints from which one can understand truth: absolutism (there is one truth) and relativism (there is no absolute truth). These diametrically opposed viewpoints have contributed to fractures in inter-religious as well as intra-religious relations, indeed all of society.

For absolutists, there is one truth, where beliefs and actions are deemed right or wrong, regardless of circumstance. With so many religious commitments, absolutists are unable to create a humble culture of self-critique, doubt, struggle, and reinterpretation. It is certainty and fidelity to unquestioned norms that sustains this community. For relativists, however, there are no absolute morals and truths; instead, these claims are made relative to particular circumstances that may include personal, social, cultural, or religious considerations. David Hume is considered by many to be the founder of moral relativism (although the Baruch Spinoza echoed similar ideas several generations before preeminent Scotsman). Hume distinguished between matters of fact and matters of value, and argued that moral judgments were value judgments, as they do not deal with issues of fact. Thus, he denied that morality had an objective standard of review. Of course, relativism can potentially lead to problematic behavior including intellectual justifications for violence, greed, and misanthropy.

Coming from a position of concern, Rabbi Nathan Lopes Cardozo cautioned against our eagerness to embrace European modern thought, which often stresses absolutism, to address our theological dilemmas:

The history of European thought, even to the present day, has been tainted by a fundamental misunderstanding. It may be termed the Dogmatic Fallacy. The error consists in the persuasion that we are capable of producing notions which are adequately denied in respect to the complexity of relationship required for their illustration in the real world. Canst thou by searching describe the universe? Except perhaps for the simpler notions of arithmetic, even our most familiar ideas, seemingly obvious, are infected with this incurable vagueness. Our right understanding of the methods of intellectual progress depends on keeping in mind this characteristic of our thoughts...

We should remember that many European absolutist movements have led to disaster. Absolute monarchy, literally equated itself with rule by God, and horribly exploited millions of peasants to benefit a small group of wealthy nobles. In reaction, revolutions spun so far in the opposite direction that it tried to create a new calendars and leaders, with everything eventually descending into terror, where everyone had to prove how loyal they were to revolutionary ideals or face death. In view of such historical instances, John Dewey, a twentieth century American philosopher, wrote about the obsessive longing people have for certainty leads to destructive behavior and ways of thinking:

> Such pretensions are known as quackery. But in morals a hankering for certainty, born of timidity and nourished by love of authoritative prestige, has led to the idea that absence of immutably fixed and universally applicable ready-made principles is equivalent to moral chaos...[There is] another manifestation of the desire to escape the strain of the actual moral situation, its genuine uncertainty of possibilities and consequences. We are confronted with another case of the all too human love of certainty, a case of the wish for an intellectual patent issued by authority.

Immanuel Kant, on the other hand, was a well-known relativist, and believed that due to our severance from the objective world we could not know objective truths. Therefore, in his view, people structure the world according to fundamental and universal (and categorical) precepts, which are used to make relative moral judgments. However, since we never know things as they truly are in their essence, we cannot judge them to be moral or absolutely right and wrong, only the individual act. Kant taught that Abraham should have reflected in the wake of God's commandment to sacrifice Isaac (the *Akeidah*), and concluded that anyone who asked him to kill his son could not actually be God. This is compelling, since the mind, shaped by Torah, cannot imagine a malevolent God.

Conversely, there are theological limits to the Kantian approach. When one is in doubt about a moral decision, Kant suggests that we resolve the issue by essentially playing God. His "categorical imperative" is a form of invitation to recreate the world. Essentially, every time one acts morally, one has the opportunity to start the world over by creating a new imperative that all must live by. We seek personal authenticity, as the individual is the arbiter of morality, but also conformity, in that we are all bound to the same universal standards.

Consider how significant Thomas Jefferson viewed the modern era, guided by self-government and privileged with progress of the sciences. Jefferson, ever the patriot, believed that periodic revolutions were necessary so as to restore freedom and independent thinking, shake power structures, and relive the struggle for self-rule so as to be a part of the community and the state:

> May it be to the world the signal of arousing men to burst the chains under which monkish ignorance and superstition had persuaded them to bind themselves, and to assume the blessings and security of self-government. That form, which we have substituted, restores the free right to the unbounded exercise of reason and freedom of opinion. All eyes are opened, or opening, to the rights of man. The general spread of the light of science has already laid open to every view the palpable truth, that the mass of mankind has not been born with saddles on their backs.

We should look at our generation with the same hope and promise that Jefferson did with his. We have been blessed with so much, yet these same blessings have led us to succumb to routine and conventionality. It is time to break from this conformity, religiously and socially, and seek spiritual authenticity. We are in desperate need of deeper moral struggle in religious life today, for individuals to wrestle autonomously, in dialogue with text and community, with moral problems. We must break free from the bondage of spiritual conformity and our routine methods of thinking about and addressing moral quandaries. Religious life that is driven by the social fear of being placed outside the camp has ceased to be an authentic religion of value. We must rebuild a culture of authentic, courageous, honest, encouraged spiritual exploration and service.

There is significant value to having ethical norms respected in society and in our various religious communities. We must not be satisfied with these ethical norms – we must not stop there. Lawrence Kohlberg, the founder of the modern academic field of moral development, taught that conformity to law and societal norms is an average level of moral development. Ultimately, one must live by conscience and principle, which may at times be opposed to social norms and spur a higher level of moral development.

This is the purpose of religious life - to open us to a higher calling. Rabbi Jonathan Sacks elaborated on this point eloquently:

> There is no life without a task; no person without a talent; no place without a fragment of God's light waiting to be discovered and redeemed; no situation without its possibility of sanctification; no moment without its call. It may take a lifetime to learn how to find these things, but once we learn, we realize in retrospect that all it ever took was the ability to listen. When God calls, He does not do so by way of universal imperatives. Instead, He whispers our name—and the greatest reply, the reply of Abraham, is simply *hineni*: "Here I am," ready to heed your call, to mend a fragment of Your all-too-broken world (*To Heal a Fractured World*).

Let us shed the fundamental misunderstanding that has come to plague our theological discourse and divide people. Our world is broken and we must echo that simple, yet profound, reply of Abraham – *hineni*, here I am – and heal the world that we have, undoubtedly, contributed to fracturing. We must realize that religious life is not about absolutes or relatives, but about living the values we have chosen. We cannot look to any outside authority to awaken our own spiritual intensity or to arouse our heart to our own moral and spiritual calling. We must do that work on our own, albeit in community. Our tradition is rich and beautiful yet demanding, and we must faithfully serve others in the way that all those who have come before us have; for this is what spiritual authenticity is about.

3

The Essence Of Judaism Is Obligation: The Foundation For Pluralism

The fundamental commitment of being a Jew is to answer the question, *Ayeka* (where are you?), with *Hineni* (here I am), affirming a sense of responsibility and obligation to the other.

Different Jews feel different kinds of commitments. We come together as a singular people not because we share the same origin of obligation, but because as Jews we all feel obligated. There are many different origins for obligation, but the great majority can be grouped into one or more of the following categories.

- **Traditional Jews** – Obligation originates from the commandments given at Mount Sinai, from an ultimate Authority rather than from the self.

- **Existential Jews** – Obligation originates from an autonomous and voluntary affirmation towards Jewish law and values.

- **Narrative Jews** – Obligation originates from a sense of continuity with the faith and lives of Jewish ancestors.

- **Conscience Jews** – Obligation emerges in the moment of encounter and from moral and spiritual intuition.

- **Gratitude Jews** – Obligation stems from recognition of and gratitude for the gifts that have been provided in one's life.

- **Consequentialist Jews** – Obligation results from the compulsion to ensure that the proper outcomes are achieved from one's actions

- **Social Contract Jews** – Obligation comes from a sense of collective responsibility that binds us together, and affirming mutual obligations.

Of course, there are always alternatives and exceptions to

the rule. One might simply live by social conformity, or by national law, or according to desire, or by rejecting the notion of obligation altogether. This is a departure from the Jewish way to live with intent and to feel charged to improve self and world. Many put each other into boxes based upon the origin of one's commitments, but there are many entry points for Jewish obligation. We should move to a more inclusive and pluralistic paradigm where we differ on the origin and nature of our commitments but unite around our common sense of obligation. It is in this ethical and spiritual framework that we are "called" and that we are responsible; thus, is a fundamental part of being a Jew.

In the modern era, Jews have defined obligation in different ways. Theodor Herzl, the founder of modern Zionism, spent the last decade of his life in an unceasing quest to find a homeland for the Jewish people: "It goes without saying that the Jewish people can have no other goal than Palestine and that, whatever the fate of the proposition may be, our attitude toward the land of our fathers is and shall remain unchangeable."

Lion Feuchtwanger, who grew up in an Orthodox family, expressed his sense of obligation through his novels. In *The Oppermanns* (originally in 1933), Feuchtwanger wrote a chillingly accurate prediction of what would happen to Germany's Jews based on only the first year of the Nazi regime. One of the protagonists, Gustav Oppermann, a retailer of cheap furniture, has admittedly become "indifferent" to his contemporary society. However, as the political situation worsens, he feels uneasy, and dictates a card to himself with a paraphrase of *Avot* 2:16: "It is upon us to begin the work; It is not upon us to complete it." Gustav at first flees from Germany, but eventually (like Feuchtwanger) realizes that his obligation is to document the Nazi atrocities to alert the world about this danger.

Elie Wiesel, through his experience in the concentration camps, has devoted his life to educating the world about the Holocaust and to work toward preventing future instances of genocide. His words ring with Jewish values: "Our obligation is to give meaning to life and in doing so to overcome the passive, indifferent life." On a related note, Albert Einstein, while one of the most noted scientists of the twentieth century, was also noted for his humanistic philosophy, often expressed through Jewish values. His attitude toward obligation fits in well with this tradition: "Many times a day I realize how much my own outer and inner life is built upon the labors of my fellow men, both living and dead, and how earnestly I must exert myself in order to give in return as much as I have received."

In the religious sphere, many leading rabbis have become involved in modern social justice movements. Abraham Joshua Heschel, who famously marched with the Rev. Dr. Martin Luther King, Jr. for the expansion of civil rights, expressed his moral obligation this way: "…there is no limit to the concern one must feel for the suffering of human beings, that indifference to evil is worse than evil itself, that in a free society, some are guilty, but all are responsible." Conservative Rabbi Jill Jacobs, Executive Director of T'ruah: The Rabbinic Call for Human Rights (formerly Rabbis for Human Rights—North America), believes that Jews can work effectively for social justice within their congregation and other Jewish institutions:

> The Jewish obligation for social justice stems from four sources: the historical experience, the legal imperative, a vision of the world to come, and practical considerations about the place of Jews in a diverse society. These four sources should inspire Jews to do social justice work not only as individuals, but also within the specific context of Jewish communal institutions (*Where Justice Dwells: A Hands-On Guide to Doing Social Justice in Your Jewish Community*, 4).

In the political sphere, the passing of Senator Frank Lautenberg of New Jersey in 2013 highlighted another view of obligation. Senator Lautenberg grew up in a working-class neighborhood in Paterson, served in the armed forces in World War II, and later launched a very successful business, Automatic Data Processing (ADP). Unlike many other management figures, Lautenberg was known for treating his employees with dignity, and the company thrived. In the United States Senate, he was responsible for laws regulating smoking and alcohol as well as gun control, along with key support and negotiating skills that won a great deal of revenue for public transportation projects. In spite of this, he always had time to speak with constituents, and would frequently speak to people he had just met for ten minutes or more about their concerns. In other words, he never forgot his roots. Shortly before his death, he confided to his rabbi, Dan Cohen of Temple Sharey Tefilo-Israel of South Orange, NJ, how he wanted to be eulogized: " he wanted to be remembered as a man from humble beginnings who did good and then used those opportunities provided to him to do the same for others." He understood that his success was due to his community support and government policies of the New Deal era, and he worked for the rest of his life to ensure that others would have the opportunity to succeed as well.

Even Jews who (unfortunately) convert to other religious groups often display a sense of obligation consistent with innate Jewish values. Simone Weil, who grew up in a secular Jewish home in France, had a philosophical trip through socialism and anarchism before converting to Christian mysticism. In the years before her early death, she focused her attention on the tremendous suffering of people during World War II: "It is an eternal obligation toward the human being not to let him suffer from hunger when one has a chance of coming to his assistance." Another secular Jewish phenomenon was the "red diaper" babies of the baby boomer generation. These were the children of Jewish parents (many in Brooklyn) who had been Communists during the Great Depression and World War II, when the Party was about the only political faction working for racial civil rights, unionization for unskilled workers, and (with one major exception) opposition to fascism worldwide. Many of these children grew up and took part in the later civil rights and anti-Vietnam War movements, and also connected back to their Jewish roots.

We all exist within this *berit* (sacred covenant) of obligation and shared responsibility. A covenant can be understood religiously, existentially, legally, emotionally, socially, etc., but all of these origins share a commitment to "ought" and not just to "is." We are not merely a descriptive but also a prescriptive people. "To be" Jewish means that "I must do." Judaism is oriented to value over fact .The foundation of our pluralism and shared commitment is our embrace of dreaming of a more redeemed self and world. The origins of our commitments need not inhibit our ability to partnership and thrive together.

4

Prophetic Pluralism: Reaching Higher Truth Together

While epistemic pluralism is generally considered to be a post-Enlightenment phenomenon, we can see the ontological beginnings of this philosophy in the writings of the Prophets. Consider the words of Micah:

> Come! Let us go up to the mountain of the Lord, to the temple of the God of Jacob. He will teach us his ways, so that we may walk in his paths... He will judge between many peoples and will settle disputes for strong nations far and wide... Everyone will sit under their own vine and under their own fig tree, and no one will make them afraid, for the Lord Almighty has spoken. All the nations may walk in the name of their gods, but we will walk in the name of the Lord our God forever and ever (Micah 4: 2-5).

Micah not only imagined, but also advocated for a messianic era, when everyone will "walk in the name of their gods." This does not reduce the prophet's commitment to the one God but he boldly continues to provide space for different relationships to that one God.

This approach to the other is not mindless relativism, but respectful and empowering pluralism. I learned this from my revered teacher, Rabbi Yitz Greenberg:

> Pluralism means more than accepting or even affirming the other. It entails recognizing the blessings in the other's existence, because it balances one's own position and brings all of us closer to the ultimate goal. Even when we are right in our own position, the other who contradicts our position may be our corrective or our check against going to excess ... Pluralism is not relativism, for we hold on to our absolutes; however, we make room for others' as well (*For the Sake of Heaven and Earth*, 196).

There is a certain humility found in this pluralism, where we acknowledge that we cannot see the full picture ourselves and we need others, even those who are different and with whom we disagree, to help us understand the world around us. Rav Yitz continues:

> Relativism... is the loss of capacity to affirm any standards. But the deepest religious response is pluralism – the recognition that there are plural absolute standards that can live and function together, even when they conflict. The deepest insight of pluralism is that dignity, truth and power function best when they are pluralized, e.g., divided and distributed, rather than centralized or absolutized.... The essential difference between pluralism and relativism is that pluralism is based on the principle that there still is an absolute truth.... Pluralism is an absolutism that has come to recognize its limitations (Ibid. 201-203).

We must embrace our own human limitations and acknowledge that God and truth are far more complex than any one individual or faction can grasp alone. Seeing and talking about these big questions in different ways may offend the absolutist's sensibilities, but absolutists can always use some shaking up.

Often we get stuck in language, especially when there appears to be an apparent paradox. Certain language affirmations mean you are on the right track toward truth, while others appear to lead you astray. Hindus say they believe in many gods, but unless someone truly understood the Hindu theology of an ultimate source, this would be totally misunderstood. So, too, some say they believe the "Torah is not from heaven," but mean something very different from might be inferred from the statement. Rabbi Abraham Isaac HaCohen Kook, the first Ashkenazi Chief Rabbi of Israel, explains this well:

There is denial that is like an affirmation of faith, and an affirmation of faith akin to denial. A person can affirm the doctrine of the Torah coming from "heaven," but with the meaning of "heaven" so strange that nothing of true faith remains. And a person can deny Torah coming from "heaven" where the denial is based on what the person has absorbed of the meaning of "heaven" from people full of ludicrous thoughts. Such a person believes that the Torah comes from a source higher than that! Although that person may not have reached the point of truth, nonetheless this denial is to be considered akin to an affirmation of faith. "Torah from Heaven" is but an example for all affirmations of faith, regarding the relationship between their expression in language and their inner essence, the latter being the main desideratum of faith (*Orot Ha'emunah*, 25).

Language is limiting, and that which is used is a function of what people have encountered before; the meaning of the words coming out of someone's mouth often does not match the words coming into your ears. The challenge today is not to slide into blind absolutism (my truth is the *only* truth) or into relativism (there is *no* truth). Pluralism is an approach that enables us to maintain our own truths with complete rigor while honoring the claims of others as dignified and even possible. This allows one to excel with intellectual rigor, expanded human solidarity, and religious humility. May the day come soon when the prophesy of Micah is fulfilled that all people walk together with God in one song albeit with different understandings of the lyrics.

5

Search for Truth, Self and Other: Models of Exclusivity, Inclusivity, and Pluralism

In an era of epistemic confusion and spiritual yearning, many are struggling to own their own journey and to find the language to talk about alternative journeys. The twentieth century English philosopher and theologian John Hick suggested there are three frameworks for religious truth:

- **Exclusivism** – "one particular mode of religious thought and experience (namely one's own) is along valid, all others being false"

- **Inclusivism** – "one's own tradition alone has the whole truth but that this truth is nevertheless partially reflected in other's traditions"

- **Pluralism** – "the great world faiths embody different perceptions and conceptions of, and correspondingly different responses to, the Real or the Ultimate." (*Problems of Religious Pluralism*, 91)

In Judaic doctrine, there exists both support and contestation for each of these frameworks. The following quotes from Jewish leaders and texts explore each model.

Exclusivity

Religious exclusivism is the belief and understanding that only one religion, belief system, or religious practice is true and that it contains all of the truth. Some have suggested that many of the world's greatest injustices including war, genocide, sacrifice, forced conversion, and conquest may be rooted in religious exclusivity and the belief that one's religion alone has the sole truth. In Judaism, religious exclusivity can manifest in particular understandings regarding our status as the Chosen People and from our monotheistic belief system (an example can be seen in the strongest bans against idolatry). Exclusivity, however, is not always necessarily a negative. In 1938, Ogden Nash, in a work titled, *I'm A Stranger Here Myself*, humorously ruminated the subject that tolerance is not always necessarily a virtuous characteristic:

> Sometimes, with secret pride I sigh,
> "How tolerant am I!"
> Then I wonder what is really mine,
> Tolerance or a rubber spine?

My dear teacher Rabbi Nathan Lopes Cardozo further elaborated on the topic of tolerance, taking the position that in fact indifference is often mistaken for tolerance:

> Indeed most of the time it is indifference that makes people believe they are tolerant. It is all too easy to espouse tolerance when one does not really care about values and principles, or about the moral needs of society and one's fellow man. In contrast, the stronger our convictions, the more tolerance we can show when we make the supreme sacrifice of listening to others and respecting their beliefs that we deem as incorrect. But to put up with others because we could not care less about their principles is not tolerance. Quite the contrary, it is a rubber spine," (*Crisis, Covenant, and Creativity*, 38).

Indeed, Rav Kook encouraged us to move away from "cold tolerance." The great rabbi explains that tolerance often is the result of one's difficulty in integrating the spiritual world into the temporal world:

> One must carefully distinguish between a holistic perspective, which succeeds in penetrating the roots of every opinion, enabling it to appreciate every opinion for its intrinsic worth, and the cold tolerance resulting from the difficulty of integrating the spiritual world into life. The later must retreat in its confrontation with the light and energy of life." (Letters of Rav Kook, 79).

In general, the rabbis believed that the Jewish people were unique (either innately or by virtue of the Torah) and that it was our character and values that distinguished us from the gentile world and made us identifiable:

> And God will give you mercy and will be merciful to you,"
> (Deuteronomy 13:18). All who are merciful to other
> creatures, it is known that they are from the ancestry of
> Abraham our father, and all those who are not merciful to
> other creatures, it is known that they are not from
> Abraham (Beitzah 32b).

> The (Jewish) nation is distinguished by three
> characteristics; they are merciful, they are modest (or
> bashful), and they perform acts of loving-kindness
> (Yevamot 79a).

The rabbis pointed to our religious belief as a major distinguishing factor, and the exclusive religious practices of the Jewish people. Our unwavering commitment and dedication to God has set us apart for thousands of years and our covenant makes us unique: "All those who deny idolatry are called a Jew" (*Megillah* 13a). Jews could be identified by what they are not (original *Aleinu* version: *mishtachavim hevel v'rik*) and God would not only protect one's own but punish the other (the idea found in the Haggadah called *shfoch chamatcha*).   In exclusivity, one need not engage with people of other faiths or learn with those of other denominations within one's faith. One is so confident in the truth they hold as the exclusive truth and only engages others in hope of persuading them into their camp of belief. It should be noted that one could, of course, be a compassionate exclusivist. One believes that one has the whole truth, yet still acts kindly toward others who they perceive to be misinformed. Too bad this latter notion is not found enough in the world.

Inclusivity

Religious inclusivism is an approach that asserts that while one's religion is still absolutely true, one can still learn some truths and bits of wisdom from other religions. This approach posits that Jews have much to learn outside of our own people hood and texts. Take for example what we can learn from the natural world:

> Rabbi Yochanan said: If the Torah had not been given, we could have learned about modesty from the cat, honest labor from the ant, marital fidelity from the dove, and good manners from the rooster - who first coaxes his hen and then copulates with her (*Eruvin* 100b).

Rashi, the medieval French rabbi and scholar, explains:

- "Modesty from the cat:" who does not place its excrement before people, but covers it up.

- "Honest labor from the ant:" as it says "Go to the ant, you sluggard; Consider her ways and be wise; Who, having no chief, Overseer or ruler, Provides her bread in the summer, and gathers her food in the harvest," and one does not steal food from another.' (Proverbs 6:6)

- "Marital fidelity from the dove:" who only mates with one partner.

There are also several passages where the rabbis taught that one could best understand the Torah by learning from, and observing, gentiles. "Rabbi Eliezer was asked: how far does the honor of parents extend? Said he: 'Go forth and see what a certain non-Jew, Dama, son of Nethinah by name, did in Ashkelon'" (*Kiddushin* 31a). It is suggested that Jews can learn their own values best at times from non-Jews. The Torah holds the truth, but those same truths can be found outside of the Torah in other manifestations as well.

Another example of the inclusive framework is the proposition that the Divine sees value and favors the other. Maimonides, for example, makes clear that righteous gentiles (*chassidei umot ha'olam*) have a share in the world to come (*Hilchot Melachim* 8:11). Further, the Meiri argued that gentiles must be treated with the same ethical status as fellow Jews:

> Thus, all people who are of the nations that are disciplined through the ways of religion and worship the divinity in any way, even if their faith is far from ours, are excluded from the principle [of the inequality of Gentiles]; rather, they are like full-fledged Jews with respect to their matters, even with respect to lost property and error (*ta'ut*) and all the other matters, with no distinction whatsoever.

This is not just an ethical principle but also an epistemic one. Non-Jews can, and often do, access God and religious truth. Perhaps, most radically, Maimonides argues that Christians and Muslims help straighten the path to the Messianic age and repair the world so all of us can serve God together:

> The founder of Christianity conferred a double blessing upon the world. On the one hand, he strengthened the Torah of Moshe and emphasized that it is eternally binding. On the other hand, he conferred favor upon the gentiles in removing idolatry from them, imposing on them stricter moral obligations than are contained in the Torah of Moshe. There are many Christians with noble qualities and excellent morals. Would that all Christians would live in conformity with their precepts? They are not enjoined, like the Israelites, to observe the laws of Moshe, nor do they sin if they associate other beings with God in worshipping a triune God. They will receive God reward from God for having propagated a belief in Him among the nations that never heard His name: for He looks into the heart (*hilchot melachim u'milchamot* 11). Rabbi Yaakov Emden went further on this point (*Seder Olam Rabbah Vezuta* - letter written by Rabbi Yaakov Emden (1697-1776) to the Council of Four Lands in Poland, 1757, translated by Rabbi Harvey Falk, 1985):

Rabbi Jonathan Sacks, an inclusivist, cautioned us from the exclusivist position, and explained that exclusivity can lead one down a dangerous path:

My argument is far more fundamental, namely that
universalism is an inadequate response to tribalism, and
no less dangerous. It leads to the belief – superficially
compelling but quite false – that there is only one truth
about the essentials of the human condition, and it
holds true for all people at all times. If I am right, you
are wrong.... teaching humanity to make space for
difference. God may at times be found in human other,
the one not like us. Biblical monotheism is not the idea
that there is one God and therefore one gateway to His
presence. To the contrary, it is the idea that the unity of
God is to be found in the diversity of creation, (*The
Dignity of Difference*, 50;53).

Rav Yosef Dov HaLevi Soloveitchik, the twentieth century
thinker, was prolifically adamant about this point that Jews must
embrace not only a covenantal identity but also a human identity:

We Jews have been burdened with a twofold task: we
have to cope with the problem of a double
confrontation. We think of ourselves as human beings,
sharing the destiny of Adam in his general encounter
with nature, and as members of a covenantal
community, which has preserved its identity under
most unfavorable conditions, confronted by another
faith community. We believe we are the bearers of a
double charismatic load, that of the dignity of man,
and that of the sanctity of the covenantal community.
In this difficult role, we are summoned by God, who
revealed Himself at both the level of universal creation
and that of the private covenant, to undertake a
double mission - the universal human and the
exclusive covenantal confrontation (*Confrontation* II:1).

In this thinking, there is something essential for a religious
person outside of one's own tradition that may help them understand
the truth in their own tradition.

Pluralism

Religious pluralism takes the worldview that one's religion is
not the exclusive source of truth and acknowledges that truth and

value exists in other religions, often times leading to interfaith educational efforts, mutual respect, and harmonious co-existence. While the idea of diverse and seemingly antagonistic religions coexisting in society may sound idealistic or even ignorant, religious pluralism has a long history and development that dates from antiquity and offers an extraordinary vision of peace and mutual respect.

Peter Berger and Anton Zijderveld, in their book *In Praise of Doubt: How To Have Convictions Without Becoming A Fanatic*, help explain the concept of religious pluralism:

> By "plurality" we mean a situation in which diverse human groups (ethnic, religious, or however differentiated) live together under conditions of civic peace and in social interaction with each other. The process that leads to such a situation we would call "pluralization." Our thesis here, then, can be succinctly stated: Modernity pluralizes.... The situation we have called "plurality" is more commonly called "pluralism." We eschew this term because the suffix "ism" suggests an ideology rather than (as we intend here) an empirically available social reality... If "plurality" refers to a social reality (a reality that one may welcome or deplore), "pluralism" is the attitude, possibly expanded into a full-blown philosophy that welcomes that reality. (7)

They further explain:

> [T]he modern process of pluralization has been a deinstitutionalizing and existentially destabilizing force. It has enlarged out freedom of choice and thus in a sense our autonomy and self-reliance. Yet, as a visit to any modern supermarket demonstrates, we're confronted by the *Qual der Wahl* ("agony of choice") that we mentioned in the second chapter. In fact, any supermarket can be taken as a metaphor of a fully pluralized society. This pluralization has led to two opposite reactions. There is, on the one hand, a radical return to premodern certainties, such as religious fundamentalism and scientific rationalism, and on the other hand, an often equally radical celebration of allegedly postmodern contingencies, which are propagated as a relativism in which (morally) "anything goes." (93-94).

Some rabbis have even argued that the whole enterprise of Talmudic discourse is premised on the notion of pluralism:

> Rabbi Abba stated in the name of Samuel: For three years there was a dispute between Beit Shammai and Beit Hillel, the former asserting, "The *halakhah* is in agreement with our views" and the later contending, "The *halakhah* is in agreement with our views." Then a *bat kol* issued announcing, "(The utterances of) both are the words of the living God, but the *halakhah* is in agreement with the rulings of Beit Hillel." Since, however, both are the words of the living God, what was it that entitled Beit Hillel to have the *halakhah* fixed in agreement with their rulings?" Because they were kindly and modest, they studied their own rulings and those of Beit Shammai, and were even so (humble) as to mention the actions of Beit Shammai before theirs" (*Eruvin* 13b).

The respect of seeing truth in another's truth can be seen in the touching, and respectful, story of Aher (a teacher who left the tradition) and Rebbi Meir (his student who remained within the tradition):

> Our rabbis taught: It happened with Aher that he was riding on a horse on Shabbat and Rebbi Meir was running after him to learn Torah from his mouth. He said to him: Meir, return from running after me for I have measured the steps of my horse and at this point is the *tehum* of Shabbat (*Hagigah* 15a).

Aher continues to count the steps to the *halakhic* boundary where one cannot leave on Shabbat even though that is no longer his personal boundary. He recognizes and honors his student's epistemic boundaries while rejecting them himself. Consider Rabbi Abraham Joshua Heschel's thoughts on religious pluralism, particularly in regards to Judaism:

> I think it is the will of God that there should be
> religious pluralism. Jewish thinking and living can
> only be adequately understood in terms of a
> dialectical pattern, containing opposite or
> contrasted properties... A central concern in
> Jewish thinking is to overcome the tendency to see
> the world in one dimension, from one
> perspective....

Rabbi David Hartman, the founder of the Shalom Hartman Institute in Jerusalem, discusses the implications that a pluralistic approach to religious thought would have for religious communities and the world:

> The radical particularization of history eliminates the
> need for faith communities to regard one another as
> rivals. Competition between faith traditions arises
> when universality is ascribed to particular historical
> revelations. When revelation is understood as the
> concretization of the universal, then 'whose truth is the
> truth?' becomes the paramount religious question, and
> pluralism becomes a vacuous religious ideal. If,
> however, revelation can be separated from the chain
> of universality, and if a community of faith can regain
> an appreciation of the particularity of the divine-
> human encounter, then pluralism can become a
> meaningful part of biblical faith experiences," (*A Heart
> of Many Rooms*, 165).

Still others have suggested a more integrated, perhaps tempered, approach in the Jewish relationship to the "outside world." Indeed, Rabbi Aharon Lichtenstein wrote:

The contention that a Torah *hashkafah* (a worldview) should sanction scientific studies to the exclusion of the humanities, as only they deal with God's world, blithely ignores man's position as part of that world. To the extent that the humanities focus upon man, they deal not only with a segment of divine creation but with its pinnacle. The dignity of man is not the exclusive legacy of Cicero and Pico della Mirandola. It is a central theme in Jewish thought, past and present. Deeply rooted in Scripture, copiously asserted by Hazal, unequivocally assumed by *rishonim* (medieval rabbis), religious humanism is a primary and persistent mark of a Torah Weltanschauung. Man's inherent dignity and sanctity, so radically asserted through the concept of *tzelem Elokim* (humans created in the image of God); his hegemony and stewardship with respect to nature; concern for his spiritual and physical well-being; faith in his metaphysical freedom and potential—all are cardinal components of traditional Jewish thought...How, then can anyone question the value of precisely those fields which are directly concerned with probing humanity? (*Torah and General Culture: Confluence and Conflict*, 245).

Rabbi Avraham Yitzchak HaCohen Kook wrote a magnificent piece on how Jews should perceive and understand ideas that may contradict Torah and how our response contributes to our spiritual development and growth:

And in general, this is an important rule in the struggle of ideas: we should not immediately feel obliged to refute any idea that comes to contradict something in the Torah, but rather we should build the palace of Torah above it. In so doing we reach a more exalted level, and through this exultation the ideas are clarified. And thereafter, when we are not pressured by anything, we can confidently also fight on the Torah's behalf (*Iggerot Hareayah I*, 163-164).

Ultimately our goal is to "expand the palace of Torah," as Tamar Ross wrote (based upon Rav Kook), and in the words of Maimonides, to "accept truth from wherever one may find it." We add glory to the Torah when it expands to include new paradigms emerging through the evolution of ideas and societies (such as certain versions of feminism, democracy, capitalism, empiricism, etc.).

Though our people have a unique covenant with God and particular ethical obligations that we must follow *halakha*, this does not mandate that we be an inclusive or exclusive people that shun the truth or the value of others and their religious beliefs. We must embrace the diversity that our world has to offer, contribute who we are as people and what we have to offer, and above all seek and accept truth wherever we may find it.

6

Time for A Panentheistic Revolution: An Ethical Theology of Connectedness

Ready to embrace a spiritual revolution to raise the stakes for our social justice impact?

Most monotheistic approaches suggest that God alone created the world but that God is separate and to some degree removed from the world. The resulting view is that either the Divine is "isolated" from humanity or humanity is "alienated" from the Divine. Pantheism, an approach that monotheists reject, suggests that God is everything (or literally all is in God, *pan* = all, *theos* = God). There is, however, a middle ground called panentheism where everything is still a part of, or in, God, yet God created everything and is still greater than everything. Among leading rabbinic thinkers of the last few centuries, Rav Avraham Yitzchak Kook and Rav Shneur Zalman most famously embrace this approach.

Rabbi Hillel Rachmani explains Rav Kook's approach with an analogy:

> Panentheism is fundamentally different from Pantheism in that here, nature is merely a limb of a far greater divine Being, and not an equivalence. There is, explains Rav Kook, a higher divine Source. There remains a spiritual ladder which we must try to climb, a metaphysical hierarchy in which Man is towards the bottom. Only by moving up this spiritual ladder and connecting with God can we enrich our egos... Panentheism is a middle ground between Transcendence and Pantheism: everything that is, is in God; however, God is not everything that is.

Here, there can be real Divine contact. The self (soul) is not distinct from the Godly spirit. But it is not just about humans. Nothing in the world is removed from Godliness.

Oriented this way, how can I harm a human being? How can I kill an animal? How can I destroy nature? When I harm any aspect of existence, I am harming God, because all these beings (and even inanimate things) are also a part of the Divine entity. Our goal as religious people must be to enable all of existence to thrive and flourish. Through a theology of panentheism, we elevate the significance of the non-divine in the world, because to some degree it, too, is divine.

An animal, for example, participates in "being," and "being" is itself divine. As humans, we have the opportunity not only to participate in "being" but also to contribute to the enterprise, to be a part of the revelation of being, to participate in holiness.

In a panentheistic worldview, human autonomy is not jeopardized and we need not get bogged down with issues of theodicy and evil, because it is not necessarily the will of God that permeates all beings but holy energy and purpose. Human responsibility is not diminished when we embrace that we are embedded within the Divine; rather, our responsibility increases because we realize how much more we must care for and attend to. Nothing is insignificant, and to some degree all matters. When our traditional, monotheistic religious leaders and communities are not always the best exemplars of ethical living, perhaps now is the time for a Jewish panentheistic revolution.

7

Who Wrote the Torah? Committed Theology in an Age of Skepticism

It is the question that many wonder but so few investigate, about which we are long on opinion but short on fact: "Who wrote the Torah?" One might think this would be the most basic question in philosophical Jewish learning since of the three primary theological paradigms of religion—creation, revelation, and redemption—revelation most profoundly captivates our human lived experience. It becomes apparent then: how in an age of skepticism can we fully embrace the Jewish tradition?

First we must understand that those who claim our ancient texts are historically flawed cannot succeed at removing the grandeur and beauty of our tradition. Along with the practical obsolescence of the documentary hypothesis, many scholars have found that the arguments that the Torah has multiple authors and a later canonization due to varying Masoretic texts untenable. Further, we do not need to embrace biblical criticism, or that J, E, P, and D were the supposed four main authors, as some biblical scholars have claimed. God speaks in different voices that may appear to be inconsistent or originate from different individuals. Rabbi Joseph B. Soloveitchik explained that the two different accounts of the creation story in Genesis do not mean there were two different authors, but that there is a duality to human experience that these two stories capture: majesty and humility. Contradictions in the text appear very frequently but this should not necessitate the belief in multiple authors.

The rabbis of the Talmud explained that the Torah was not revealed in a perfect Divine language but in an imperfect human language so that it could properly be understood (*dibrah Torah k'lashon b'nei adam*). This inevitably renders perfect interpretation or consistency impossible. This is not a hermeneutical problem unique to Torah. Rather we understand in modernity that our mystical insights and psychological depth can never adequately be captured in language. Human experience is more profound than human language.

Even if the Pentateuch was written down over time, a

position the tradition itself embraces, this does not detract from its Divine origin. Traditional commentators have offered many explanations for how the Torah was written. Rabbi Yochanan argued that the Torah was given scroll by scroll, while Resh Lakish argued that the Torah was originally given in its entirety (*Gittin* 60a-b). According to Rashi's interpretation, even for Resh Lakish the entire Torah was not given all at once on Mount Sinai. Rather, Moses wrote down each passage as it was told to him, and then they were compiled together (*megillah megillah nitnah*). In the thirteenth century, the Ramban explained: "When Moses came down from the mountain, he wrote from the beginning of the Torah until the end of the story of the Tabernacle, and the conclusion of the Torah he wrote at the end of the fortieth year... this is according to the one who says the Torah was given scroll by scroll. But according to the one who says it was given complete, the entire thing was written in the fortieth year" (Ramban, introduction to his Torah commentary).

While traditionally it is understood that God is the author, some traditional scholars believe that there still may have been more than one scribe. Ibn Ezra, at the end of his commentary on the Torah, argued that Moses himself did not write every word since Joshua wrote the last twelve verses of the Torah. "In my opinion, Joshua wrote from this verse on, for after Moses ascended [Mount Nebo], he no longer wrote. Joshua wrote it by way of prophecy, as we see from 'the Lord showed him...' 'The Lord said to him...' and 'He buried him.'" Yosef Albo, the fifteenth century rabbi, explained: "Why was not the entire Torah given in written form? The law of God cannot be perfect so as to be adequate for all times, because the ever new details of human relations, their customs and their acts, are too numerous to be embraced in a book. Therefore Moses was given only certain general principles... by means of which the wise men in every generation may work out the details" (*Sefer HaIkkarim* 3:23).

Earlier, Rambam understood Rav Albo's point that "the law of God cannot be perfect so as to be adequate for all times." Clearly, there are Biblical stories and laws that are morally troubling. Why is slave ownership permitted? Why are multiple chapters dealing with the building of the tabernacle? Are we really authorized to stone rebellious children? Normative Judaism is not primarily a Biblical religion maintaining every particular law crafted for a particular context, but an oral tradition that develops while maintaining its core precepts. The Rabbis actually compare the Bible to lips of a seductive woman (*Tanchuma Teruma* 8). Our loyalty is to the rabbinic interpretive tradition and we shouldn't be tempted to believe that the esoteric Bible is the Jewish authority. The Bible is the revealed wisdom that began our tradition, and countless others, but it also gave license and authority for continued interpretation.

Rav Kook suggests that Jewish law not only evolves, but also expands. He explains that "We should not immediately feel obliged to refute any idea that comes to contradict something in the Torah, but rather we should build the palace of Torah above it. In so doing we reach a more exalted level, and... the ideas are clarified. And thereafter, when we are not pressured by anything, we can confidently also fight on the Torah's behalf" (*Iggerot haReayah* I, 163-164). Rabbi Kook further defended the idea of progress, suggesting, "An evolution marked by constant progress provides solid grounds for optimism" (Ibid., 369).

The Kotzker Rebbe explains that we are to live in this world and outside of it. Embracing both reason and revelation enables us to most fully actualize our values of ethical monotheism. While the Torah comes from heaven, "it is not in the heavens," meaning its continued interpretation, application, and relevance is under human control (Deuteronomy 30:12, *Bava Metzia* 59b). The Torah's applications continue to evolve, while the core truths and values are preserved.

Revelation does not bind us to a destiny of stagnancy but gives us freedom. Kant challenged this point arguing that if revelation were a reality it would be calamitous for man's created freedom. One loses free will and the capacity for reason when encountering Divine truth. Emmanuel Levinas explained why this needed to be so: "The teaching, which the Torah is, cannot come to the human being as a result of a choice. That which must be received in order to make freedom of choice possible cannot have been chosen, unless after the fact" (*Nine Talmudic Readings*, 37). When we received revelation, our freedom was suspended in order that we could be free.

Another barrier to embracing Jewish tradition has been that one should live by reason rather than faith. However, according to the dominant Jewish perspective, one need not take a leap into the irrational when embracing the truth of the Torah. Countless Jewish authorities, such as Rambam, Ralbag, Saadya Gaon, Ibn Tibbon, and the Abravanel, have suggested that reason and revelation are compatible. But why do we need revelation if we have reason? I would further suggest six general categories as to the value of revelation while operating by reason that should be further elucidated:

- **Reinforcing** — Revelation gives the pre-existing reason authority and force

- **Reframing** — Revelation gives one the opportunity to do something rational as a way of serving God

- **Concretizing** — Revelation provides universal reason with particularistic content such as particular stories, narratives, laws

- **Unifying** — Revelation binds a people together into a community

- **Deciphering** — Revelation rejects relativism within the options of reason (choices are made that logic did not necessitate)

- **Evolving** — Revelation is needed to begin a process of rational trans-valuation (the re-reading of texts to consistently provide new meaning and application)

Perhaps the question of "Who wrote the Torah" is not really an important Jewish question anyway. Rabbi Abraham Joshua Heschel once suggested that if we were to find historical proof that the Ten Commandments were indeed revealed from God, few to none would live any differently, for we do not make our daily life decisions based upon historical evidence. Further, we are aware that historical positions of this nature can never be proved. The existence of God and the origin of the Bible are, at best, non-testable hypotheses.

While intriguing, this is not such a problem; history is ephemeral, while meaning is eternal. What matters most in Jewish tradition, much more than historical truth, is the power of values. In assessing the value of historical context in the interpretation of text and law, some Jews are overly dismissive, but others embrace it to the exclusion of all meaning of Jewish core values. Reading ancient texts solely with a historical or scientific lens blocks one from embracing deep moral and spiritual truths. Evaluating the veracity of the literal creation story is much less relevant than the ethical dimension of the narrative.

The *Midrash Sifra*, as explained by Rabbi David Hartman, explains beautifully that it is a principle of faith in the Jewish tradition that God liberated the Jews in an exodus from Egypt (*yetziat mitzrayim*). However, the rabbis go on to explain that the obligation is not primarily a requirement of belief, but of action. The one who truly believes in the miraculous exodus is honest in weights and measures. The one who acts ethically in business has embraced the deepest meaning of this theological value. The truth is not a historical fact merely to be noted, but is rather a value that must transform our character.

I personally believe that God did indeed reveal the Torah to our people. This is primarily an existential, not epistemological, claim. The Torah is the most powerful and persuasive work I have ever read and I feel spiritually elevated from an encounter with Torah unlike anything else. I feel the values of this tradition to be the most ethically poignant and compelling and I'm not alone. All of western religion, adherents making up about half of the world's population, has been built upon the belief of this powerful revelatory experience. The question is not whether one believes in the Torah, but whether one lives it. Further, because one cannot find historical proof that the Torah is from God, this is not a reason to opt out of living by Jewish law and values. Historical ambiguity is no excuse for disengagement. A philosophical agnostic who questions whether human reason can understand anything beyond worldly experience and claims that revelation is merely a myth that cannot be taken seriously risks becoming spiritually numb if tradition is merely dismissed. It is not a leap of faith to embrace that which we understand may not be true; rather one must suspend, or look beyond disbelief in order to find self-actualization. Absorbing revelation may actually represent what is constitutive of our humanity (what makes us uniquely human), since the ability to grasp something phenomenal beyond our own limited experience is what gives man intelligence.

One might ask pragmatic questions: Does living in this community that embraces Jewish revelation enhance my moral responsibility? Does living by Jewish law and values make me a better person? Do I feel closer to the Divine when I learn Torah, pray, and fulfill traditional Jewish requirements? Theology that works, in a sense, is true whether or not it proves to be historically accurate. If one finds that through years of learning and performing *mitzvot*, their moral, spiritual, and intellectual commitments and capabilities grow, this cannot be dismissed as tangential to the goal of religion. True religion must be more concerned with the "good" than the unknowable "true." Judaism is a performative theology; we understand it by doing it. This is why the Israelites say, "*Naaseh V'Nishma* when receiving the Torah, first we will do and then we will understand" (Exodus 24:7). Ritual is spiritual exercise that can facilitate the expansion of one's moral imagination. Torah is like love. You cannot understand it unless you've fully felt it and lived it.

The Pentateuch, written during the second millennium BCE, is a remarkable story of moral and legal teachings, poetry and song, love and tragedy, and dreams of a better world. Today its message is blurred in this age of skepticism, where no commitment is held too tightly, and everything is contingent on what the latest historical evidence seems to indicate. However, if we imagine that God loves us, that a heaven awaits us, that a time of universal peace and justice will come, we can embrace the wisdom of our heritage much more deeply. If we can allow our encounter with God and tradition to be existential rather than historical, we can connect in deep and meaningful ways without having all of our concerns resolved.

When some of the tales told about the Chofetz Chaim were challenged, one leader responded that "I don't know if the story is true or not. But they don't tell stories like that about you or me." In other words, we cannot prove the historical accounts told in the Bible, but there is nothing that compares in the modern world. As Mark Twain said, "If the Ten Commandments were not written by Moses, then they were written by another fellow of the same name."

The wisdom and language of the Bible is unparalleled in its power to inspire idealism and social change. No one claims that the Martin Luther King, Jr., was naïve or unintelligent to root his social activism in the language of the Bible. This revealed tradition has the power to inspire us again and again to transform the world, making a sanctuary where God can dwell. Rather than over-philosophizing as to "Who wrote the Torah," we can spend our time building our character through the deep wisdom it offers enabling us to heal the world.

8

The Torah Does Not Heal

Religion has rightly been criticized for serving as a justification for oppression, but by the same measure it can be the vehicle for truth, justice, and good in the world.

The rabbis taught *Asur lihitrapot b'divrei Torah* – it is forbidden to heal oneself with words of Torah (*Shevuos* 15b). The *p'shat* (literal reading) here is that we should not play with magic and think that reciting a biblical verse will heal a wound. That is not the way God or nature works. At the same time, the rabbis are also teaching a deep lesson about the role of religion in the world. Pray and study can be very transformative and therapeutic. But ideally, we cannot heal people or the world with only religious words and rituals. Rather, pastorally, we must not merely read and quote but inspire and connect. And we must take the lessons of these words and rituals out into the world and physically change it. Prayer must be accompanied by action, study by application, blessing by manifestation, and potential by actualization.

Karl Marx offered the most notable critique of religion's corrupting force. To Marx, religion was created by men (*"Man makes religion*, religion does not make man") to bolster the authority of rulers over their subjects; for the poor, religion offers the false perception that shared religion is the greatest unifying thing, and that there is solace in a world without hope: "Religion is the sigh of the oppressed creature, the heart of a heartless world, and the soul of soulless conditions. It is the *opiate* of the people." To Marx, religion created a false world in which people were prevented from achieving their full potential and happiness, and humanity would not advance without ridding itself of religion: "The abolition of religion as the *illusory* happiness of the people is the demand for their *real* happiness."

The specious argument for the "Divine Right of Kings" (that monarchs were literally God's representative on Earth and could do no wrong) was used by the kings of France and czars of Russia to rationalize their mistreatment of the poor and the terrorizing of dissenters. Eventually, both systems were overthrown in brutal revolutions that rejected the established religion, spanning countless years of war and costing millions of lives. The lesson of Marx and the revolutions of past centuries is that religion should challenge us to be better, not just offering us some of kind of nostalgic satisfaction or spiritual comfort. The Torah cannot allow us to follow a religion that is merely an "opiate of the masses."

Torah does not heal. It is the medicine book and Doctor's ledger but not the actual medicine or Doctor. Even pagans in the ancient world often understood that healing could not be done through religious rite. The staff of Aesculapius image (a snake-like serpent wrapped around a staff), which is still the symbol of the World Health Organization, the American Medical Association, and many other physician groups around the world, originated thousands of years ago. It probably represents an ancient medical practice of extracting parasites from sick people, in which an incision was made in the skin, drawing the parasite to the surface, whereupon the healer turned a stick to extract the parasite by wrapping it around the staff. In eastern religions, meditation and other physical and mental exercises (yoga is one example) are often used to heal, using a theory of balance; we know that blood pressure and the autonomic system can be normalized with regularized breathing. However, even these techniques cannot treat illnesses that may require surgery or other serious treatments. We must do the work to heal, and the Torah will provide us – sometimes clearly, sometimes opaquely – with the inspiration and wisdom on how to do it.

The Rabbis asked a deeply profound question: "Why was the human race created from the offspring of one single person" (*Sanhedrin* 4:5). Three distinct and important answers were given:

- To teach that someone who saves a single life has saved the whole world (life has infinite value)

- For the sake of peace, so that no one should be able to say, "My father was more important than your father" (all are equal)

- So that every person should think that "For my sake the world was created" (all are unique)

The rabbis taught that we must embrace the reality that all have infinite dignity, are equal, and are unique. This means that we must be committed to going out to heal others and the world, that we must cherish each human being with love and care. We cannot allow religion to be used as a means to benefit the wealthy and powerful at the expense of the poor and vulnerable. Words of Torah are healing and sometimes the most appropriate thing to share with another. However, our broader life responsibilities to others require our full self, and our mission as followers of the Torah demands nothing less.

9

Was The Destruction Of The Temple Good For The Jews? A Bold Tisha B'Av Reflection

Have trouble crying for the Temple? Why is it that we mourn on Tisha B'Av? Paradoxically, one of the most tragic events in Jewish history (the destruction of the *Beit Hamikdash*) may also have forced the most generative stimuli that ever propelled the Jewish People forward.

For centuries the Temple in Jerusalem was the singular locus of Jewish life. It was the only way we knew to serve God, and yet at an appropriate time in history we needed a fundamental change, and God supplied it. Rambam famously made the point that the Torah mandate for a Temple with animal sacrifices was not ideal, but God's concession to Israel's needs in an earlier era. Asking the Jews to serve God without offering sacrifices and priests as guides would have been like asking the Jews today to serve God without prayer and rabbis as guides (*Guide for the Perplexed* 3:32).

We cannot simply return to the past or propel a past model into the future. Religion, at its best, is about creative thinking and courageous living in the present. With every paradigm shift (even when that shift leads toward progress) comes some loss—and that's what we mourn. Concurrent with the destruction of the Temple there was a loss of life and a loss of the Divine Presence in this world. Today, in response, we must strive to actively affirm the value of life and find new ways to bring God into the world.   *All God does is for the good*. The destruction of the Temple forced the Jewish people to transition from privileging Judaism's priestly aspect and leadership to its legal ones, from focusing on the pious to focusing on the intellectual, from concentrated authority to decentralized communal empowerment, and from a parochial approach to peoplehood to a global one. Even the dispersion of our people had a positive side to it: Two thousand years of Diaspora life, admittedly riddled with tragedy, have allowed us to refine our ideas rather than focus on power and state building. Also we were able to gain the wisdom of the encounter with majority and other minority cultures, which has enabled us to be in touch with the downtrodden around the globe (*ki gerim hayyinu b'aratzot nokhriyot*). Judaism was able to focus on being a sophisticated religion before focusing on developing as a strong nation. Further, we bring a more enlightened notion of the nation-state than we might have held onto had we never left the land of Israel, where we were stuck in a monarchic-theocratic system. We've seen how horrific dictatorships have been in modernity. Today the modern state of Israel continues to grow and thrive as an open democracy. Even with the all of the religious value and grandeur of our own sovereignty and self-determination, there is still religious value (and for some even an imperative) to living in the Diaspora.

We often have trouble embracing sophisticated change in the Jewish community. One major segment of the Jewish community is willing to toss out traditional major systems to rapidly embrace new realities; another major segment of the Jewish community completely resists change. However, we need to face reality: Just look at the politicization of the Western Wall. Could a single Temple today really serve 13.7 Jews? [1]

We have never been unified as a people (aside from Sinai perhaps) and even when the Temple stood there was great internal fighting between various ideological factions. Perhaps not unlike the Western Wall lately, the Temple, the rabbis taught, had ceased to inspire love and justice and so we needed a new paradigm.

The second Temple, where they engrossed themselves in Torah, Mitzvot, and acts of loving-kindness, why was it destroyed? Because there was baseless hatred (*sinat chinam*) there. This is to teach that *sinat chinam* is equivalent to the three cardinal sins: idolatry, sexual immorality, and murder. They were evil, but they put their trust in God (*Yoma* 9b).

To provide some historical context to the destruction of the temple, the tragic rebellion that led to the Second Temple's destruction was ill-advised at best (based upon messianic fervor) and represented the worst sort of suicidal fanaticism, as Rome had shown for centuries that it would not stop its war making and cruelty until its opponents were completely annihilated. For example, at the battle of Cannae in 216 BCE, Hannibal of Carthage handed Rome its greatest defeat, killing approximately 60,000 Roman soldiers, and

---

[1] http://www.jewishvirtuallibrary.org/jsource/Judaism/jewpop.html

for a decade and a half he continually defeated them on the Italian peninsula, yet he never conquered Rome, and eventually Carthage was completely destroyed by Rome. In 60-61 CE, only a decade before the destruction of our Temple, they crushed the rebellion of the formidable Iceni of East Anglia (modern-day England) led by Boudicca, whose forces had annihilated a Roman legion and massacred several Roman towns, but were themselves mercilessly cut down when they charged headlong into a disciplined Roman legion.

At the outset, the Jews took on Rome at the height of its military power, confronted by Rome's greatest general of the period and his son and future Emperor Titus. The Romans' incomparable siege weaponry, such as siege towers, ramps, and the ballista, completely overwhelmed the Jews. In 69 CE, Titus breached the walls of Jerusalem, while Jewish generals fought and killed each other as often as they fought the enemy, and spent much effort trying to prevent any Jews from escaping. While the Jews fought fiercely and exacted a heavy toll, they were no match for the Romans legions.

Whether by accident or deliberate action, the Temple burned to the ground on Tisha B'Av. Jewish Zealots, Sicarii, and Nationalists committed suicide by throwing themselves into the fire, stabbing themselves, or having others stab them, while the Pharisees understood that the destruction of the Temple did not equate with the destruction of the Jewish people. Indeed, while 10,000 Jews were taken to Rome and sold as slaves, wealthy Jews joined with others in the community to either buy their freedom or help liberate them from their masters; we survived this crisis and many others over the centuries since. We should always remember that our object is not suicide; we are not like the Japanese kamikaze pilots of World War II, and we do not possess the military might to take on the great empires and survive. Our greatness lies in the Torah and living by our core values.

After the destruction, from that day forward, the rabbis understood they must look forward and build Jewish learning institutions and not try to replace the Temple of the past. In his great wisdom, Rabbi Yochanan ben Zakkai foresaw the inevitable future and courageously adapted. He escaped from the Roman siege of Jerusalem, abandoning the Temple while it was still standing to negotiate a deal, allowing him to establish a new center of Jewish learning in the city of Yavneh (*Gittin* 56b). He is our model for courageous Jewish intellectual and spiritual paradigm shifts. He taught us the art of adaptation, that we must chose life over land (even when that land is holy), and that religion often necessitates choosing the pragmatic over the ideal.

With the destruction, the prophets taught us that our people had to move from being transmitters of a parochial, sacrificial religion to practitioners of a universalistic, giving religion: "For I desire kindness, not a sacrifice" (Hoshea 6:6). Much later, the rabbis taught that Rabbi Yehoshua ben Chananyah and Rabbi Yochanan ben Zakkai were walking past the ruined Temple Mount when Rabbi Yehoshua said, "Woe unto us! The Temple, the source of all forgiveness for our sins, has been destroyed." Rabbi Yochanan ben Zakkai replied, "My son, don't despair. We have another source of atonement, and it is acts of kindness"(*Midrash Yelamdeinu*).

Today, we have thousands of diverse synagogues and Jewish organizations around the world; we have been able to do great work in every corner of the earth, not just in Jerusalem. We may not think of Australia as a place with many Jews, but there are more than eighty operating synagogues there. Similarly, we usually consider South America to be a Catholic continent, but there are more than seventy synagogues in Buenos Aires, Argentina, alone[2]. In Hungary, devastated by the Holocaust, there are twenty-six active synagogues in its capital, Budapest.

The fantasy of returning to one centralized monolithic form of Judaism is not only wishful thinking. It's also dismissive of two of the most important aspects of modern Jewish life: diversity and adaptability. Further, in any centralized system of authority, abuses of power and limits of transparency and empowerment have proven to be inevitable. The new paradigm that the Temple's destruction and exile from Israel enabled is one that says, Bring God into your hearts and into the wide world every day and in every way; the Temple was a vehicle for this once, now we have so much more. It is natural to long for past models in a world of uncertainty but we must move forward with courage, creativity, and open hearts to

---

[2] http://www.jewishvirtuallibrary.org/jsource/vjw/Argentina.html

build a world of justice, kindness, and holiness where God can reside. As Rambam taught at the end of his *Mishneh Torah*, we must be humble and not become consumed with what will be in Messianic times. Rather we must be productive and engage in the real religious imperatives and embrace the responsibilities of today.

A core part of the mitzvah of being *mitavel* (mourning) is transforming *aveilut yashana* (old mourning) into *aveilut chadasha* (new mourning). It's the move from history to memory and from distance to relevancy of today. Tisha B'Av is a sustained meditation on the profound brokenness of the world. Only through an honest grappling with the depths of oppression and suffering inside and outside of us can we truly understand what's needed for healing and repair. May we have the courage to sit in the abyss of darkness and then the strength to channel light.

10.)

Praying Mightily For Syria

I know as an Orthodox rabbi I should not struggle with prayer, especially since atrocities occur throughout the world each day, but this feels different.

Unetaneh Tokef, the central prayer on Rosh Hashanah and Yom Kippur that focuses on life and death, always tears upon my soul in the most profound way. In 2013 (5774), it was particularly so, because I could not get the people of Syria out of my mind, especially the gassing of children. At times, I found myself trembling and sweating and simply could not focus on either the joyous or the solemn sections of the prayer liturgy. What if it were my wife, baby and I fleeing for our lives? What if those body bags were full of my friends and family? What if I might find sarin in my next drink? As I struggled to pray, I asked myself "What's the point of prayer at all?"

I do not know how I will rise again with my congregation on Yom Kippur later this week and recite the pinnacle prayer of *Unetaneh Tofek* once again: "On Rosh Hashanah it is written, and on Yom Kippur it is sealed, who will pass and who will be created, who will live and who will die, who in his time and who before his time." I'm afraid that this Yom Kippur I will hear God's intense question of where I've been on the Syria issue.

Is there any way to aid the civilians in Syria without encouraging further military escalation and atrocities? I will leave this question to policy-makers. During Yom Kippur, I entreat God and speak out on behalf of innocent Syrians–though I am not a Syrian. I know this is not the conventional prayer or intention for Yom Kippur. I understand and forgive those among my fellow Jews who find such prayers inappropriate.

However, there is a teaching of Rabbi Heschel that I've never been able to forget at times like these: "Prayer is meaningless unless it is subversive, unless it seeks to overthrow and to ruin the pyramids of callousness, hatred, opportunism, falsehoods. The liturgical movement must become a revolutionary movement, seeking to overthrow the forces that continue to destroy the promise, the hope, the vision."

71

Rabbi Heschel acted on these beliefs when he marched nonviolently with Martin Luther King for civil rights, at a time when standing up for civil rights meant risking your life. I hope that I will have the courage to embrace subversive prayer this Yom Kippur, prayer that spurs me to fight for human dignity.

Many told me that these are not "my people" and even that "these people hate my people." But Rosh Hashanah marks the creation of the world and more specifically day six of creation — the birth of all humanity. On this day, there is no such thing as "my people." We are all brothers and sisters, and the suffering of any one of us, whether in New York or Damascus, is a cause for grief.

We need humility when dealing with such complicated matters. There are a great many actors in Syria and around the world who might respond unfavorably to any American action in Syria. There are a great many potential ramifications for the United States even for a very limited intervention. But we also dare not stand idly by. I have an aversion to war but an even greater disdain for genocide. We know today what President Franklin D. Roosevelt knew in the early 1940s and what he could have done. How dare we say "never again" while it continues to happen time and time again?

Since the violence has escalated, I read every article I could. I have made calls. I have started a petition and got the top rabbinic leadership from Reform to Orthodox to sign on to support a U.S. intervention to protect civilians. I prayed. But nothing feels sufficient. Time is running out.

I am tempted to feel anger toward heaven when extreme suffering or tragedy like this occurs. But this cannot be an excuse for inaction. I'm reminded of the famous quote: "Sometimes I want to ask God why God allows poverty, famine, and injustice in the world when He could do something about it, but I'm afraid He might just ask me the same question."

How can I recite *Unetaneh Tokef* again this Yom Kippur as I know how many are dying each day in Syria, now totaling 110,000 over the past two years? This year, I feel a touch of hypocrisy asking God to seal my soul in the Book of Life, when I myself have not done enough to avert deaths and atrocities in Syria. How can I ask God to save me unless I devote every fiber of my being to saving others who walk in the Valley of Death?

Martin Niemoller, the prominent Protestant pastor who was

transformed from an unthinking supporter to an outspoken critic of the Nazis due to his observation of years of atrocities, ended up in concentration camps, and later wrote the oft-quoted verse:

"First they came for the Socialists, and I did not speak out—Because I was not a Socialist.

Then they came for the Trade Unionists, and I did not speak out—Because I was not a Trade Unionist.

Then they came for the Jews, and I did not speak out—Because was not a Jew.

Then they came for me—and there was no one left to speak for me."

During Yom Kippur, I will pray that the coming year be one of life, in which we cease to be spectators while so many innocent human beings are murdered. I will know if my prayer works if it leads me to stronger and more effective action.

11

An Apology to Jewish Thinkers throughout History Who Have Been Ostracized

Historically, the worst punishment one could receive in the Jewish community was *herem*, or excommunication. One was completely ostracized from the Jewish community, yet – unlike today – generally could not turn to the secular or non-Jewish world for refuge. Many were put in *herem* for immoral actions but many for unpalatable ideological positions, such as Baruch Spinoza and Leon Trotsky. Maimonides, generally thought to be the greatest of Jewish philosophers, had his own books burnt, as did the great legal authority Rabbi Moshe Feinstein.

Distancing thinkers who have strayed from dogma often push them further away from the very ideology the authorities were seeking to protect. It also hurt some of the greatest thinkers. Rabbi Baruch Halevi Epstein, the early twentieth century scholar and son of the Arukh Hashulkhan, wrote:

> This phenomenon, to our sadness, seems to repeat itself in every generation. Whenever people quarrel over matters related to ideology and faith, and a person discovers his more lenient opinion is in the minority, all too often—although his original view differed only slightly from the majority—the total rejection he experiences pushes him over the brink. Gradually, his views become more and more irrational and he becomes disgusted with his opponents, their Torah and their practices, forsaking them completely…. Instead of instructing him (da Costa) with love and patience and extricating him from his maze of doubts by showing him his mistake, they disparaged him. They pursued him with sanctions and excommunication, cursing him until he was eventually driven away completely from his people and his faith and ended his life in a most degrading way… (*Mekor Baruch*, 13:5).

Rabbi Epstein alluded to Baruch Spinoza, the Dutch-Jewish philosopher who was banned by the Amsterdam community, and addressed the earlier tragic case of Uriel da Costa (who died in 1640). Da Costa was born into a family of *Conversos* (Jews from the Iberian Peninsula who had been forcibly converted to Christianity); after a period of religious study, da Costa and his family converted back to Judaism. Upon resettling in Amsterdam, da Costa became disenchanted with Judaism as practiced there, as he believed it was too immersed in the minutiae of ritual to the exclusion of spiritual content. For this, he was denounced, his writings were burned, and after seeking in vain to find a Jewish community to identify with in Europe, he increasingly began to view all organized religion as harmful. On his return to Amsterdam, his synagogue ordered him to be whipped and then to be trampled by the members of the congregation. In his despair, he committed suicide.

Other religions have begun to examine unjust persecutions, even though the process may take centuries. The Catholic Church has started to address some of their past mistakes of distancing intellectuals. In 1633, Galileo was convicted of heresy and forbidden to teach or publish his ideas. In spite of his public denunciation of his supposedly erroneous beliefs (e.g., that the Earth was not the center of the universe), he was kept for the rest of his life under house arrest. It was only in 1992 when Pope John Paul II formally apologized to Galileo on the Church's behalf.

The United States has also apologized for past wrongs. In 1988, President Reagan signed the Civil Liberties Act, which offered a formal apology and $20,000 compensation to all survivors among the more than 100,000 Japanese-Americans who were detained in camps during World War II. In 2005, Congress issued a resolution of formal apology for failing to approve legislation outlawing lynching, which had been used for decades by white Southerners to terrorize the black population[3]. Sadly, the senators from the state with the most recorded lynchings, Mississippi, were not on the list of eighty co-sponsors of the resolution.

Today, the Jewish community must also ask forgiveness from great intellectuals in our past whose reputations were destroyed because they disagreed with the established dogmas. We're sorry because it was just wrong. As we can see from numerous examples from other religions and nations, an unwillingness to even consider any criticism proves to be historically harmful and regrettable. More importantly, we must never destroy another's life because of their theological beliefs and teachings.

---

[3]http://www.washingtonpost.com/wp-dyn/content/article/2005/06/13/AR2005061301720.html

12

All Jews In One Sukkah

Rabbi Avi Weiss often tells his students that one of the most important traits to be an upstanding Jew, and certainly a Rabbi, is to have a deep sense of *Ahavat Yisrael*, love for our fellow Jew. For many, this can be challenging. To cultivate a love for the values of the Torah, for the holiness of Israel, for the Jews we know is one thing, but can we cultivate a deep love and connection to a random Jew we never met or have anything in common with? What is the origin of this love, and is it genuine? In theory, as a historical construct, it sounds beautiful, but what is its emotional foundation?

In the Midrash, Rabbi Shimon bar Yochai (the Rashbi) once taught: "A man in a boat began to cut a hole under his seat. His fellow passengers protested: 'What concern is it of yours?' The hole-maker responded, 'I am making a hole under my seat, not yours.' They replied, 'That is so, but when the water enters and the boat sinks, we too will drown'" (*Vayikra Rabbah* 4:6). Without a consideration that we as the Jewish people are on a ship together, not in the survivalist sense but in the spiritual sense with a shared mission, our ship cannot sail with its full grandeur. With all passengers, in a shared history and destiny, our ship will sail the mighty oceans.

The Gemara says: *"kol Yisrael re'oooim laishav b'sukkah achat,"* that all of Israel is fit to sit in one *Sukkah*; as a community looking to perpetuate peace in the world, we maintain the ideal of living under one proverbial *sukkah* (*Sukkah* 27b). While we as Jews may have different ideologies, ways of serving God, languages, and values, and it may at times seem that we have little in common, we can remember that the "*sukkah* of peace" must house us all. And so we require the *shalom* of a unified *sukkah* with the diverse members of our people. The Midrash teaches that the four species that we wave on Sukkot represent the four different kinds of Jew, and they all unite at this festive time.

Rabbi Shlomo Riskin, the Chief Rabbi of Efrat in Israel, tells a story about Reb Levi Yitzchok of Berdichev, who invited all types of Jews into his *sukkah* – simple people, beggars, even scoundrels. But the more established members of the community, the learned and the wealthy, felt uncomfortable around this motley crew. To address this situation, Reb Levi Yitzchok explained that Jewish tradition records that in the world to come, the holy Jews of all the generations would be gathering inside the *sukkah* of Leviathan, led by Abraham, Isaac and Jacob. Moses would be speaking words of Torah, Aaron would conduct the ritual, and King David would sing the songs of praise. If the doorkeeper demanded to know by what right Levi Yitzchok thought he could enter (because, after all, he was hardly of the caliber of the aforementioned spiritual giants of our nation), then he would answer that since he invited everyone, including the "lesser lights" into his *sukkah*, would not these true masters of our faith open their hearts and invite him into their *sukkah*? In teaching the need to welcome and love all Jews into our *Sukkah* and our hearts at this special time, Rabbi Riskin asks an important question: "What do we say to a great soul who cannot be burdened with the complexity of religious details (as so many of us are committed to)?" He offers the following analogy: On a clear night, I can often manage to see stars hundreds of light years away, but on a cloudy night I may not be able to see anything at all. However, if I learn the laws of optics and build a telescope, I will see much farther and clearer. But acquiring a telescope has its price. There are many facts to learn regarding its proper use, and an object comprising countless details is placed between the eye and the world. But just look at the added vision it provides.

The laws of the Torah are like this telescope (or microscope) into reality. It seems constrictive, but it is really liberating. On Sukkot, we embrace the stargazers who shun telescopes, we open our hearts and invite them into the *sukkah*, but at the same time we know how much sharper our vision is when we look at the stars through the gaps (required by *halacha*) in the roof of the sukkah. As religious Jews we may at times feel at great odds with our secular sisters and brothers, but as an *Am Kadosh* (holy nation), there is an imperative for some type of unity. This unity is not an end in itself, but a means to fulfilling our global role as advocates for love, truth, and justice. Our love is born out of the unique intensity of this holy partnership.

Sefer Kohelet (the Book of Ecclesiastes read on the Shabbat of *Chol Hamoed Sukkot*) teaches: "There is no *tzaddik* on earth (no perfectly righteous person on earth) who only does good and does not sin," (7:20). This sets a foundation for love and tolerance among the Jewish people. From the most to the least learned, from the oldest to the youngest, from the most cultivated to the most reckless, on some level we all err and we all stumble.

As we are continuing our focus on *teshuva* (growth and transformation), which in many ways can feel like a solo journey, we reunite to remember that we are all stumbling and striving for growth. It is for this reason that *Sukkot* must follow these holy days. *Teshuva* cannot happen in pure isolation, but rather in community. The peak of our life commitments and growth must now happen together. May we learn to expand the size of our tent to include a few more within our camp (more religious or less religious, older or younger). Let's expand our hearts to create more room for the *other* as well.

13

Sinai And The Social Contract

The Torah explains that all of us were present to accept the Law at Mount Sinai (Deuteronomy 29:14). How can this be – if I was not physically present, let alone born, in what way was I present? And, barring a satisfying answer to that question, how can I be bound by a covenant that I did not make? The Jewish mystical tradition holds that our souls were present, though our bodies were not. There were three million bodies and souls present at the time, but through reincarnation over time those souls have splintered off and been housed in many bodies. Thus, one may truly have a "soul mate" out there who is the other part of their fractured soul.

If one is not inclined to such a mystical view, one can see an aspirational message in this idea: Of course we were not there on that day, but we should strive to connect, existentially, to the spiritual moment as if we were there and to replicate the Sinaitic experience in our own lives.

For Sinai is not really a singular historical moment. It is a continuing and recurring possibility that every soul can achieve unity with the beneficent Revealer. We all have the potential to stand there. This event is relived every time a committed and properly trained *halakhic* Jew attempts to grasp the Torah using his intellect. Per the Rav:

"He does not search out transcendental, ecstatic paroxysms or frenzied experiences that whisper intonations of another world into his ears. He does not require any miracles or wonder in order to understand the Torah. He approaches the world of *halakha* with his mind and intellect just as cognitive man approaches the natural realm. And since he relies upon his intellect, he places his faith in it and does not suppress any of his psychic faculties in order to merge into some supernal existence. His own personal understanding can resolve the most difficult and complex problems. He pays no heed to any murmurings of [emotional] intuition or other types of mysterious presentiments." (*Halakhic Man*, 79)

Another aspect to the deeper connection to the revelation at Sinai is nostalgia. There is a power to spiritual memory. Religious memory takes on its own inner life: To some extent, to remember an experience is to live it, to return home to a cherished, perhaps only imagined past. When you love someone, you can stand in solidarity with those connected with that person, even if the physical proximity is no longer there. I love my father's mother, and I believe she loves me, but we never met; we are in a chain of solidarity and transcendental love, connected through her hopes, my living relatives' memories of her and my personal story. When I rise to recite *kaddish*, the memorial prayer, I believe there is a connection.

An alternative perspective, perhaps a more important one, is that we the living are partners having and taking responsibility for the evolution of Torah. We have as much responsibility as our predecessors did, perhaps even more, as the great Revealer continues to retract from the world (per the kabbalistic idea of *tzimtzum*). The Jewish interpretive enterprise began in the beginning and continues through time so that the moral and spiritual revelation can continue to be relevant and true in all eras and contexts: "What great praise it is for Israel, that as soon as they heard God's word at Sinai, they began to interpret it." (*Midrash Mechilta*)

A famous Talmudic passage illustrates how Moshe was terrified upon prophesying that Rabbi Akiva would teach Jewish law that he himself didn't understand. Moshe was comforted; however, when he heard Rabbi Akiva state that what he was teaching was also revealed to Moshe at Sinai: A revelatory process was put into place, producing new results to new generations that previous generations could never have fathomed and this enduring connection was solace to the initial recipient of the Torah (*Menachot* 29b).

Lastly, we ought to consider the legal notion of the "social contract." We are bound by the social acceptance established by a founding generation, and we represent the generation that is the continuum of that agreement. We may be most familiar with the social contract in its political sense. One school of thought, Absolutism, theorized that humans in their natural state were in a perpetual state of war, and that only the rule of a strong leader with unlimited power could establish the stability necessary for organized society to prosper; Thomas Hobbes' *Leviathan* in the mid-seventeenth century is the most well-known Absolutist work. We can see this in the god-kings of ancient Mesopotamia, the Pharaohs of Egypt, through various modern tyrants, many of whom encouraged the idea that a spiritual right was given them from on high to rule others without any check or balance on their power.

Another school of the social contract reacted against tyrants, from the Athenian democracy through the early Roman Republic to the later American and French revolutions. This concept, eventually outlined by John Locke in the late seventeenth century in his *Second Treatise on Government* and incorporated into the American Declaration of Independence, presented a very different notion of a social contract. In this interpretation, people gathered in society for the mutual protection of rights; one person's freedom existed so long as it did not infringe on the rights of another. In this social contract, absolute, concentrated power was an abomination.

Jean-Paul Sartre, the noted French existentialist philosopher, experienced Absolutism at its most appalling depths during the Occupation in France during World War II. His great work, *Being and Nothingness*, reflects this rejection of this perverse social contract in which mass murder was normal and resistance to tyranny meant going against the norm. To Sartre, humans come into the consciousness of existence and can either follow the accepted modes of identity for one's profession and class, which is merely the deceiving of oneself, or one can achieve "nothingness" by going outside of these deadening restrictions and take responsibility for one's actions in the world. Sartre suggests that this choice of "nothingness" is a great existential achievement.

This compares in an interesting way with our Sinai covenant. The word for "those not present" (who really are present) at Sinai is *ainenu* (those who are not); with different meaning, the chassidic thinkers call this *bitul-yesh*. Those who were present (but who were not physically present) achieved the spiritual state of nothingness. As we view the social contract in its various forms and interpretations over the millennia, let us reflect on what this concept means to us, and be grateful for our continuing Sinai covenant – with our past selves, our families, and with God above.

14

The Value of Nightmares: A Jewish Approach to Bad Dreams

Humans have long pondered our need for sleep, and the physical and mental harm that sleep deprivation causes. The ancient sages, however, saw a spiritual reason for sleep.

> When the Holy One Blessed be He, created man, the ministering angels mistook Adam for a divine being and wished to exclaim "Holy" before him. What does this resemble? A king and governor were riding together in a chariot. The king's subjects wished to greet their king with cries of "Sovereign," but they did not know which one was the king. What, then, did the king do? He pushed the governor out of the chariot and thereby the subjects knew who the king was. Similarly said Rabbi Hoshya, when God created Adam the angels mistook him (for God). What, then, did the Holy One, blessed be He, do? He caused sleep to fall upon him, and thereby all knew he was a human being (*Bereshit Rabbah* 8:10).

According to this Midrash, sleep was created to differentiate humans from God. It is a sign of our weakness. For hours of the day, every human gives up complete control of themselves. This is to inspire humility. But sometimes, sleep is not so restful. We have all woken up trembling, sweating, and in fear of our lives without any hope of return to sleep. Have you ever wondered why this happens?

Scientists have put forward physical and psychological reasons for why we experience nightmares. Nightmares tend to occur during rapid eye movement (REM) sleep episodes. These REM episodes become more frequent as the night progresses, so nightmares often occur in the latter portions of our sleep, during the early morning for most people. Nightmares frequently concern being unable to escape danger, falling, or reliving a traumatic experience. Unlike night terrors, which occur soon after going to bed and are not experienced as dreams, we do remember our nightmares. Sometimes nightmares can have physical triggers, such as eating just before sleep, or taking drugs such as antidepressants or antihypertensives, or conversely, trying to stop drinking alcohol or sleeping pills. Paradoxically, sleep deprivation can also increase the likelihood of nightmares, as can sleep apnea (where breathing is impeded during sleep, causing episodes of waking while gasping for breath). Finally, nightmare disorder (often hereditary) can cause nightmares. Nightmares may have serious physical consequences, such as an increased risk for obesity and heart disease, while those suffering from depression are more likely to consider suicide.

Psychological explanations for nightmares have also been offered. About a century ago, Sigmund Freud taught that dreams were a way to access our subconscious, and interpreting these was a key element of psychoanalysis. Nightmares would reveal thoughts and desires that we were not aware of in our daily life, but which manifested in such things as a slip of the tongue (where we might says a word that seems totally out of place, which revealed what was secretly on our mind) or a persistent thought (which could be a song or poem that included a key word or concept). Today, many psychological theorists believe that dreams serve the purpose of allowing us to work out emotional or problem-solving issues; nightmares may convey an ongoing, unresolved spiritual conflict.

I have argued previously that nightmares enable us to cultivate compassion for the other we do not understand.

> For example, I believe that nightmares are gifts from God enabling us to access a painful situation without really having to experience the pain of the experience. This helps us to cultivate empathy if we choose to consider our self-improvement after our bad dreams. In fact, Rabbi Zeira taught, "if a man goes seven days without a dream, he is called evil," and Rabbi Huna taught that "a good man is not shown a good dream, and a bad man is not shown a bad dream" (*Berachot* 55b). Perhaps this comes to teach us that, on some level, we need the human vulnerability of bad dreams to remain humble, sensitive, and empathetic. We must actively choose to use our dreams as a vehicle for deepening our spiritual and ethical sensitivities.

Abraham was the first to have a nightmare in the Torah. "And it happened, as the sun was about to set, a deep sleep fell upon Abraham; and behold—a dread! Great darkness fell upon him"

(Genesis 15:12). Rabbi Samson Raphael Hirsch, the great eighteenth century German scholar, interpreted Abraham's experience in a unique way:

> The answer had to experience figuratively the endless night and dread and the exulting awakening therefrom so that it could be grasped more surely and more deeply and be handed down with all the certainty of something that had already been lived through.

This opens up a new way to understand nightmares from a theological perspective. Perhaps God provides us with experiences outside of reality in order to prepare us to handle real situations within our reality. We are more prepared for a negative life experience in our lives since we have already "encountered" it. Further, we are better able to digest a painful situation because we explored it more deeply in the unconscious realm. Hopefully, we will all know as many positive things in our lives as possible, but our dreams and nightmares can be healing tools that prepare us to proceed along more difficult journeys.

15

Understanding God Through Knowing The Self

One of the most timeless and thought provoking questions regarding religion is whether spirituality and religious study is primarily about self-knowledge or other-knowledge? An old Chassidic teaching demonstrates the position that religion is, generally, first and foremost a search for the self:

> A chassid came to visit his rebbi.
>
> The rebbi asked the chassid: "Why have you come here?"
>
> The chassid replied: "I have come to find God."
>
> The rebbi, with a twinkle in his eye, responded: "For that you didn't have to come here, since God, Whose glory fills the entire earth, can be found everywhere in the world!"
>
> Surprised by the rebbi's reaction to his statement, the chassid asked: "Then why indeed do people come here to the rebbi?"
>
> To which the rebbi answered quietly: "People come here to find themselves."

As the Chasidic teaching illustrates, we often seek the guidance of religious leaders and texts to find ourselves. There is, of course, nothing wrong with gaining self-knowledge and growth, in fact this is beautiful, but we cannot lose sight of another important goal of religion: Other knowledge. What can we learn about the world? About God? About humanity?

Society (religion of course included) has markedly turned toward individualism. Many of the effects of this have been positive, as it has increased a sense of autonomy, empowerment, and responsibility. However, a significant, and often overlooked, cost has been the loss of engagement with the Other. One Midrash demonstrates the extent to which we should be engaged with God and ideally focused:

> R. Levi b. R. Hanina said: 'For every single
> breath that a human being takes, he should offer
> praise to the Creator.' What is the reason?
> Scripture says, "Let every soul (*neshamah*) praise
> God' (Psalm 150:6) —let every breath (*neshimah*)
> praise God (*Genesis Rabbah* 14:9).

Of course many of us fall far short of this ideal. We are often too caught up in the mundane tasks and stresses of everyday life, and find it hard, if not impractical, to stop and thank God for every breath we take. However, let us now stop, for just a second, and give thanks to God, as this Midrash commands, for the gift of life and the blessings we have been given. Let us renew our search for God and begin anew our engagement and focus.

A beautiful idea from Rebbe Nachman of Breslov is that of finding the good in our brothers and sisters, and understanding the implications of our actions toward others:

> Know! A person must judge everyone favorably. Even in the
> case of a complete sinner, one must search until one finds
> some point of good within that person. For the verse says:
> "With a little bit [of good], and the wicked will be no more"
> (Psalms 37:10).... Once you judge a sinner favorably you
> actually elevate the sinner to the side of holiness. This can
> help this person return to God. How is it possible that this
> sinner never once fulfilled a mitzvah or did something good
> throughout his entire life? Once a person does even one good
> deed, he becomes part of and attached to God, the source of
> all-good. Every person can sense how another person feels
> toward him. A person's feelings toward another are broadcast
> loud and clear through verbal and non-verbal
> communication, intimations, body language, and gestures.
> Therefore, if one projects and transmits positive feelings
> toward another, the warmth and good attitude that one
> projects can be felt and can literally uplift the other person.
> Once a person feels uplifted and is imbued with a sense of
> self-worth and joy, this happy attitude could motivate a
> person to seek out God and return to Him. If one, however,
> projects negative feelings toward another, this could literally
> kill the other person and cause him to fall completely....

Imagine if we viewed others and interacted with others in such a fashion and how that would affect our own souls and the souls of those around us! A Medieval rabbi used to teach that the way to understanding God is through self-understanding. There is something significant about this - a religious approach that seeks to know God and man by knowing one's self. However, I fear that some sort of solipsism can lead to a religious narcissism that epistemically relegates God and man to the sidelines, simply written off as unknowable and ultimately as irrelevant. This fear though is, of course, not preventative in endeavoring to understand one's self, thereby attempting to understand more profoundly and know God through self-exploration.

Carl Jung once wrote, "The telling question of a person's life is their relationship to the infinite." This meaningful proposition is significant in the depth and complexity of its implications. Our relationship to God and the infinite is inextricably linked to our character, behavior, guiding ethical principles, and relationships with others. Being aware of how our relationship to God affects these important aspects of our life should serve as inspiration to dedicate more time to others, self-improvement, devotion to learning, and on focusing on our relationships with others, as well as God. The Chofetz Chaim told a remarkable story about ceding ones own desires and worries in order to selflessly serve others:

Rabbi Bunim spent his early years of life working as a traveling businessman. On one such journey, he stopped at an inn on a cold, stormy night. The Jewish innkeeper found in Rabbi Bunim a sympathetic ear for his tale of a failing business and they spoke for a while. The peasants no longer came to him, vats of liquor sat untouched in the basement and the landlord was growing impatient for the rent, the innkeeper cried.

In the middle of the night a traveler, drenched and freezing, knocked at the door and begged the innkeeper to admit him, even though he had no money with which to pay. The innkeeper obliged, gave him a change of clothing and a room for the night. The traveler, however, was still shivering. "Could you bring me some vodka, please" he asked.

The innkeeper went to the basement and poured a cup of vodka, then shook his head firmly and smashed the cup to the floor, unaware Rabbi Bunin was watching. Four times he repeated this. Finally, upon pouring the fifth cup, he happily proclaimed, "Now" and brought the vodka to his guest.

The innkeeper explained to the rabbi that he couldn't serve the guest a drink he had poured with disappointment and resentment in his heart. He had been handed a golden mitzvah - a chance to revive a shivering hungry, poor man, yet his financial worries were clouding his ability to appreciate this gift. He tried and tried again, until true loving kindness was within him. Only then could he pour and bring the man his drink.

With this story in mind let us engross ourselves in the pursuit of understanding and loving God and others. Let us attempt to understand and serve God through self-exploration and understanding as the innkeeper did in Chofetz Chaim's story. We must dedicate ourselves to seeing the good and holy in others and with that in mind act selflessly in their service with the joy of understanding that we are also serving God when we serve others.

16

What Wisdom Is Eternal? The Maimonidean Approach To Superstition

There are many cases where the Talmud forbids something because of "demons" or spiritual danger. Rambam merely explains that this concern is for practical reasons (health or safety) and should not be considered literally.

Professor Marc Shapiro of the University of Scranton, in his article *Maimonidean Halakhah and Superstition*, explains:

> When examining how Maimonides treats laws associated with superstition, we must remember that other codifiers also omit some of these laws. Thus, even if Maimonides had believed in the various superstitions, it is unlikely that he would have codified all of the related *halakhot* mentioned in the Talmud...There can be no question that Maimonides distinguished between *halakhah* and prudent behavior, and exercised great freedom in rejecting Talmudic advice, particularly with regard to medical matters. Still, the sheer number of *halakhot* that Maimonides ignored, many of which are recorded in other codes, is sufficient to establish his great originality in the exclusion of superstitious elements from *halakhic* codification... I think the best definition that can be given to what Maimonides regards as superstition is any belief or practice which in his opinion resulted from ignorance, fear of the unknown, trust in magic, or a false conception of causation.

In his *Letter on Astrology*, Maimonides writes that it is not proper to accept something as true unless it falls into one of the following categories:

- It can be proven, such as concepts in arithmetic, geometry, and astronomy

- It can be perceived through the senses

- It is received as tradition from the prophets or the righteous ones of previous generations

Superstition, of course, was not merely a product of a pre-scientific age. According to surveys, more than half of all Americans are superstitious to some degree.[4] We may think it is silly or at least harmless, as when we see a building with a 12th and 14th floor but no 13th floor, or a person who wears a "lucky shirt" to an interview and for some reason feels reassured. However, a gambler who puts his faith in superstition is most likely to lose his lucky shirt, and people who fear certain dates (such as Friday the 13th) might curtail their activities to such a degree that it could increase anxiety and jeopardize their work status. Similarly, women who give credence to astrology columns (much more than men) are in danger of losing opportunities based on this spurious advice. It encourages the idea that we are not in control of our own lives.

Japanese researchers have investigated ways in which national superstition has adversely affected people's lives. An old Japanese superstition relating to the ancient six day lunar calendar is that there are "lucky" days (*Taian*) and "unlucky" days (*Butsumetsu*). Japanese researchers found that people were much more likely to be released from a Kyoto hospital on a "lucky" *Taian* day than an "unlucky" *Butsumetsu* day; significantly, the most discharges occurred on *Taian* and the fewest occurred on *Butsumetsu*. In addition, patients were much more likely to have had a longer stay when they were released on a *Taian* day, strongly suggesting that these patients had extended their stay just to be released on a lucky day.[5] In addition to needlessly taking up hospital beds and adding extra healthcare costs, an extended hospital stay can increase the chance of patients contracting infections within the hospital setting (known as nosocomial infection).

Another Japanese superstitious belief is that the year *Hinoe-Uma* (Elder Fire-Horse), which occurs about every sixty years, will be unlucky for the birth of girls. In its last occurrence, 1966, there was a decrease of 463,000 live births in Japan, and the number of abortions increased by more than a third. In a more disturbing

---

[4] http://www.webmd.com/mental-health/features/psychology-of-superstition?page=1
[5] http://www.ncbi.nlm.nih.gov/pmc/articles/PMC28746/

development, an analysis demonstrated that in 1966 there was a spike in neonatal accidents and violence reports involving girls and not boys born in that year, indicating that parents may have literally injured or killed their infant girls for the sake of their superstitions.

We are accustomed to seeing signs of superstitious beliefs, whether it is a horseshoe over a doorway, a lucky charm carried by the superstitious person, avoiding cracks in a sidewalk when people walk, or some other peculiar sign. We must keep in mind Rambam's teachings that superstitions can be harmful, and avoid the self-destructive behavior that some engage in for the sake of avoiding "bad" luck. The Torah charges us to break from relying upon irrational fears and to embrace our human autonomy to make hard life choices. Then we actualize the most unique human gift of all: free will.

17

A Theology Of Angels: Our Daily Choices

Throughout history, some Jewish philosophers never took the idea of angels literally. Rambam, for example, argued that any textual reference to an angel had to be understood as a prophetic vision and not as an actual occurrence. Even further, the talking serpent in the Garden of Eden should be considered an allegory, and Balaam's experience with a talking donkey should be considered a dream (*Guide*, 2:42). In Maimonidean angelology, contrary to the pop culture flying winged angel in white, angels have form but no matter.

On the other hand, however, many Jewish thinkers have understood angels literally and even considered them to be protectors of the righteous. Other sources describe mitzvot (such as *tzitzit*), in itself, as being angels that protect. Consider this Midrash:

> A person who does one mitzvah, is given one angel. One who does two mitzvot, is given two angels. One who does all the mitzvot, is given many angels–as it says, "He will assign His angels to you," (Psalms 91:11). Who are these angels? They are the ones who guard the person against harm (*Tanhuma Mishpatim*, 19)

Other spiritual leaders teach that angels actually follow human behavior and are vicariously affected by our own leadership and worship. The rabbis teach that what we do in this world is of utmost importance. The Chassidic master Rav Dovber of Mezritch taught, "Know that all that is above–is dependent on you" (*Likutei Amarim* 198). Rav Schneur Zalman, the Alter Rebbe, taught, "In the upper worlds, the preciousness of this world is well appreciated. The ministering angels... would forego everything for one "*amen, yehei shemeih raba*" said by a Jew with full concentration!" (*Hayom Yom*, 17 Adar 1).

It has generally been taught that angels do not have free will and that they are merely the servants of God. One debate that emerged was whether or not one can pray to an angel and if such prayer is acceptable. The kabbalists argued that one can and must pray (not to, but through angels) to reach the highest throne. Some rationalists argued that one must not, as one may only pray to God. The kabbalists generally won this argument, as evidenced by our traditional prayer liturgy, which is replete with prayers to angels. Consider, for example, the opening Friday night dinner song, when we pray to the angels for a blessing.

Still, rabbis, philosophers, and textual sources differ regarding the nature of angels and depth of human characteristics and experiences that angels may share with us. In one source, the angel is considered a virtuous messenger of God to be contrasted with a demon:

> Raba pointed out a contradiction. It is written, "I do speak with him in a dream," and it is written, "the dreams speak falsely." There is no contradiction; in the one case it is through an angel, in the other through a demon (*Berakhot* 55b).

Then again, other sources suggest that an angel can be evil:

> It was taught, R. Jose son of R. Judah said: Two ministering angels accompany man on the eve of the Sabbath from the synagogue to his home, one a good [angel] and one an evil [one]. And when he arrives home and finds the lamp burning, the table laid and the couch [bed] covered with a spread, the good angel exclaims, "May it be even thus on another Sabbath [too]," and the evil angel unwillingly responds "amen." But if not, the evil angel exclaims, "May it be even thus on another Sabbath [too]," and the good angel unwillingly responds, "amen" (*Shabbat* 119b).

Furthermore, angels are generally considered to be outside of human experience and not subject to human temptation, and thus of a completely different nature. One Talmudic passage explores angelic "jealousy" of humans who can serve God through the Torah in a way that they cannot:

When Moshe ascended to the heavenly realms, the angels who served there in the Divine Presence (protested) saying, "Lord of the universe, what is a human being doing among us?" "He has come to receive the Torah," answered God. They responded: "How can You be giving to creatures of flesh and blood this beloved treasure, which You kept to Yourself for nine hundred and seventy-four generations before the creation of the world?" God said to Moshe: "You answer them." Moshe replied: "I am afraid that they will burn me with the fire of their mouths." He told him: "Hold on to My throne of glory and give them an answer." Moshe said to God: "Lord of the universe, what is written in the Torah that You are giving to me? 'I am the Lord your God, who took you out of the land of Egypt.'" He then turned to the angels. "Did you go down to Egypt? Were you Pharaoh's slaves? What good is the Torah to you? What else is written there? 'You shall have no other gods besides Me!' Do you live among the gentiles who serve idols (that you must be warned against them)? What else is written there? 'Remember the Sabbath day to sanctify it!' Do you ever work that you should need a day of rest?...' On hearing these words the angels immediately admitted to the Holy One, Blessed be He, that He was right to give the Torah to Moshe"(*Shabbat* 88b).

While there are angels in heaven, I believe that humans can (perhaps just for a moment) act as angels, as pure emissaries of God. When one transcends one's own self-interest and truly fulfills the will of God by helping another, in the deepest altruistic sense, perhaps for that moment they have transcended their own humanity. One might suggest that there are angels inside each of us (the angel who told Abraham not to sacrifice his son Isaac, the angel Jacob wrestled with, the angel who helped guide Joseph when he was lost, etc.) and that when we bring our will in accord with that purest side of the self we can actualize our holy potential.

Throughout scripture we find that angels are often given different unique attributes (Michael, angel of mercy; Gabriel, angel of justice; Raphael, angel of healing; and Uriel, angel of illumination). So too, it follows, that when one masters a Divine attribute one has realized the angelic component of their purest nature.

When we struggle each day with moral choices, which internal angel will say, "May it be even thus on another Sabbath [too]"? We make the choice each day to live as angels or demons. Let's choose each day to sanctify the heavens by living with compassion and empathy as we actualize our inner angelic side.

18

Happiness Is A Life-Death Issue

For many people, happiness is not a simple goal to achieve. Within all of us, we must choose to cultivate happiness in our lives. Achieving and living with happiness is not just about experiencing personal enjoyment, but survival.

A long-term study of seniors[6] has shown that those who enjoy life are better able to handle the physical activities required to live a healthy life, whereas the unhappiest people were 80 percent more likely to experience physical difficulty with basic routines.
Scientific and medical researchers have long explored the connection between mood and health. Harvard University School of Public Health Professor Laura Kubzansky's research has demonstrated, in long-term studies, that individuals who maintained an optimistic attitude and had the ability to focus on a single task had far fewer health problems over a thirty year period than those who did not demonstrate these qualities. In addition, optimistic people had a 50 percent risk reduction for heart disease. Professor Kubzansky believes that while close to half of attitudinal demeanor and outlook seems to be hereditary, treatments for depression initiated at any stage of life will help the physical health of patients.

Conversely, Harvard Professor Jack P. Shonkoff has found that adverse experiences in childhood – such as long-term neglect, living with violence, or living with a guardian who has mental illness – can trigger "toxic stress." Toxic stress is defined as the body's response to stress that leads to a spike in stress hormones, faster heart rate, and high blood pressure. This bodily reaction can lead to hypertension, cardiovascular disease, and, ultimately, premature death.

In addition, depression has been shown to shorten lifespan. It had previously been proven that those being treated for depression developed cardiovascular disease at a younger age,[7] but

---

[6] http://consumer.healthday.com/senior-citizen-information-31/misc-aging-news-10/life-enjoyment-linked-to-more-active-old-age-in-studyer-seniors-are-more-active-seniors-study-finds-684014.html

[7] http://www.research.va.gov/news/features/depression.cfm

since depressed people tend to adopt unhealthy lifestyles and behaviors, such as smoking and lack of exercise, than those not being treated, it was not possible to confirm that depression alone was the cause. However, a Department of Veterans Affairs study published in 2012 demonstrated significant differences in longevity between VA patients with diagnosed depression versus patients without a diagnosis. In this large study (700,000 patients with diagnosed depression in a population of nearly five million, with 167,000 deaths recorded during the year-long study period) the researchers found that patients with depression died at an average age of 71.0, versus 75.9 years for patients who had not been diagnosed with depression. Thus, patients with depression died, on average, five years earlier than those who were not depressed. This difference was noted in all thirteen separate causes of death studied (including heart disease and cancer; it was all noted in accidents, suicide, and homicide). Thus, depression has been confirmed as a literal killer.

In Jewish thought, happiness is not the goal of life, but a tool toward actualizing our potential. We labor not to be happy but rather, we are happy in order to labor. Even though there is a mitzvah to be happy on holidays (*simchat yom*), the purpose of this mitzvah is for one to elevate that joy in a closer relationship with God, Torah, family, and community, not to singularly enjoy oneself. We should all be blessed with happiness and should do our best to help those around us, and beyond, experience the joys of life as well. Achieving true internal happiness requires cultivating rich spiritual, emotional, and relational lives filled with giving and love.

19

Am I Too Late? Seeking Forgiveness From Someone Who Has Passed Away

We all know that there is necessary, albeit difficult, work to ask others for forgiveness. But what do we do when they have already passed away?

Rambam taught:

> One who commits a wrongdoing, and the victim dies before he has a chance to request a pardon – he should bring ten people with him and stand by the victim's grave. There he should say before all of them, "I have sinned before Hashem, the God of Israel and before this individual in that I did such and such." If he owes the victim money he should pay it to his heirs. If he doesn't know who the heir is, he should give it to the Beit *Din* and confess (*Hilchot Teshuva* 2:11, *Yoma* 87a).

Other Jewish teachings reinforce Rambam in stating that one should offer public confession and if money is owed to the deceased, it should be given to the deceased's heirs (*Bava Kamma* 103a). There have been many famous cases of important Jews publicly going to graves for forgiveness. One of the recent publicly known cases is of Rabbi J.J. Schachter going to the grave of Rabbi Yechiel Yaakov Weinberg (Sreedei Aish) for publishing his private letters. It was a great lesson about the value of restrained privacy over scholarship and *yirat shamayim* (fear of God) over career advancement.

There have been many prominent cases of people asking for forgiveness for a deceased person who was wronged. For example, in 2009 British Prime Minister Gordon Brown publicly apologized for the mistreatment of Alan Turing, a brilliant mathematician who was persecuted and driven to suicide for being a homosexual. Turing had played a pivotal role in cracking the German Enigma machine code during World War II, which greatly helped Allied intelligence by exposing the location of German submarines and battle plans. After the war, he worked to help create modern computer science, working on the one of the first true computers. However, in 1952 he lost his government job and security clearance when he was convicted of "gross indecency" for having had a homosexual relationship. Faced with a sentence of forced chemical castration (female hormone injections usually reserved for men with prostate cancer), Turing committed suicide in 1954. After a long-term campaign to redress this injustice, the British leadership agreed to publicly acknowledge its mistreatment of Turing and many other gay men who had served the nation well. Prime Minister Brown's apology read in part:

> This recognition of Alan's status as one of Britain's most famous victims of homophobia is another step towards equality and long overdue.
>
> But even more than that, Alan deserves recognition for his contribution to humankind … It is thanks to men and women who were totally committed to fighting fascism, people like Alan Turing, that the horrors of the Holocaust and of total war are part of Europe's history and not Europe's present.
>
> So on behalf of the British government, and all those who live freely thanks to Alan's work I am very proud to say: we're sorry, you deserved so much better.

Prime Minister Brown's public apology illustrates many of the aspects addressed by the Rambam and other Jewish teachings. He apologized for a wrong that had been committed against Turing and other homosexuals, he acknowledged the tremendous service that Turing had given to his nation, and in doing so he made it clear that these injustices would not be repeated.

There is a very important *mitzvah* of sincerely asking others for forgiveness. It is complicated when one has passed away already. The most important moral act is to repair any damage that is left and to improve one's ways. Spiritually, there is also the opportunity for public statement at the grave. This would require a great deal of courage, but we must ensure that the wrong is not perpetuated.

20

The Western Wall: Do Objects Contain Holiness?

I have always felt something exceptional at the Kotel (the Western Wall), but I have generally had to work to achieve that feeling and it remains unpredictable. There is something holy that I cannot yet fully grasp about that place in the heart of Jerusalem. It may seem counterintuitive to think that our religion (consumed with the heart, mind, and soul) could find holiness[8] in objects or places, but Jewish law is unequivocal in the proposition that there are, in fact, holy objects and places. Rabbi Natan Lopes Cardozo explained:

> Like love and beauty, we can only really tell what it is when we experience it. While the Torah itself fails to give us a definition, we could perhaps make the following suggestion: Holiness is that which a person experiences when he or she lets God into their thoughts, feelings, and actions. The experience is ineffable but highly recognizable for those who undergo it. A powerful encounter with the Creator. It leads to an internal transformation that brings with it both elation and elevation.

To me, what is holy about the Kotel is that millions of people, for thousands of years, have poured their spiritual energy upon those stones. That for thousands of years have worshipped, prayed, thought, cried, sung, celebrated, commemorated, mourned, dreamed, placed notes of prayer, made pilgrimage, and emptied their souls and spiritual energy upon the Kotel. That energy can be accessed today. All spiritual energy is Divine and so it's really a collective multi-generational human energy that has morphed into a transformational Divine energy.

We do not worship the stones themselves, for that would be idolatry. But we may embrace (from a panentheistic perspective, see the earlier chapter on the topic) that there is Divinity within the rocks themselves. Our human nature craves a connection to the physical world and religion cannot ignore that craving. Spirituality

---

[8] http://www.jewishjournal.com/socialjusticerav/item/is_all_of_jewish_leadership_work_holy_the_not ion_of_meta-holiness

can be most powerful when our connection to the spiritual world is channeled through physicality. One might even suggest that the soul is accessed through the brain.

We can access some of the most powerful collective aspirations, dreams, prayers, and hopes at places where people have cried from their heart to move the "heart of God." Holiness is about connecting above but also below. Levinas took the vertical theology (looking up) and made it horizontal (where embracing the Other includes, in its deepest sense, embracing the other). Levinas writes: "Holiness represents the moment at which, in the human...the concern for the other breaches concern for the self."

The Kotel survived the Roman Empire and many succeeding dynasties that sought to degrade it, in a profound misunderstanding of what the holy is. Professor Moshe Halbertal has argued that the holy is that which cannot be instrumentalized (i.e., used for political gain), rather the holy is good for its own sake. The Kotel cannot be used for political gain either by the ultra-Orthodox or by the activists-feminists. When both see that it is not only God that we honor but also the dignity of the other, we will reach agreement. People access spirituality differently, and gender has a major role in spiritual energy. We should honor those different human needs to achieve something synergistic and more powerful than what we started with.

We may see a normative model for this potential outcome in philosophy. Hegel argued that thought can progress in a three-stage process: From thesis to antithesis and then, out of conflict, we create synthesis. One of his classic examples was that one may contemplate "being" and then "nothing" and ultimately can come to a place of "becoming." Marx went further, suggesting that each stage of society creates the very forces that also destroy it. A new status quo emerges from clash and destruction. So too, a new paradigm shift will come from all of the spiritual energy being poured upon the rocks of the Kotel. But the Wall will only remain holy if we honor the spark of Divinity.

21

Learning to Trust: Our Relationship to Government and Heaven

There was a lot of wisdom in the psychoanalytic revelation that our relationship with our parents is interconnected with our relationship with God. Perhaps there is a connection between our relationship toward the government and toward heaven as well?

The sages actually teach us that our relationship to our government is not totally removed from our relationship toward heaven. Consider the following Talmudic passage:

> Rabbi Abbahu was bereaved. One of his children had passed away. Rabbi Jonah and Rabbi Yose went up (to comfort him). When they called on him, out of reverence for him, they did not express to him a word of Torah. He said to them, "May the rabbis express a word of Torah." They said to him, "Let our master teach us." He said to them, "Now if in regard to the government below, in which there is no reliability, (but only) lying, deceit, favoritism and bribe-taking, which is here today and gone tomorrow (if concerning that government) it is said, 'And the relatives (of the felon) come and inquire after the welfare of the judges and of the witnesses, as if to say "We have nothing in our hearts (against you), for you judged honestly" (*Sandhedrin* 6:6)' in regard to the government above, in which there is reliability, but no lying, deceit, favoritism, or bribe-taking, and which endures forever and to all eternity, all the more so we are obligated to accept upon ourselves the just decree (of the heavenly government)," (*Talmud Yerushalmi, Sanhedrin* 6:12).

The rabbis are teaching that the relatives of one who is executed must eventually testify that they have come to terms with the verdict and punishment (that they remain bought in to our imperfect human courts of justice). At the appropriate time, the relatives should greet the judges and witnesses involved with the case and declare that they do not hold a grudge toward them and that they have accepted the verdict and meted out punishment. This can be compared with the statement of *Baruch Dayan Emet*, the declaration that God is the true judge stated after one's loved one has been taken from this world.

The rabbis intuited that in learning to trust and accept our government, we would become more open and able to do so with God as well. Consider the God as King metaphor used throughout the High Holiday liturgy. Often times, we come to relate to the all Powerful through our experiences with the earthly powerful. This, of course, does not mean that there is not struggle, questioning, or even protest. It does mean, though, that some things cannot be changed. If we are to live in the present and in the future we cannot be stuck in the past. We have to work hard to remove certain pains from our past and to move forward with audacious hope. All of creation is dependent upon a God above. So too, justice and order in this world relies heavily upon our nation-states and governing bodies. Although they fail too often, we must continue to be an integral part of the solution and work diligently, and with perseverance, toward building more just societies.

It is all too common notion, printed in newspapers and magazines, heard on the radio, and voiced on nearly every televised news program, that our government is completely broken; that it has become paralyzed by partisan gridlock; that our elected officials have become slaves to corporate interests. These claims are substantiated by the remarkably low approval ratings for our government and elected officials today. During the government shutdown of 2013, hundreds of thousands of federal workers were furloughed, the District of Columbia was forced to delay Medicaid payments, North Carolina ended its monetary and food assistance to the poor, Michigan was on the verge of doing the same,[9] and many other states would have been forced to follow this lead if they were unable or unwilling to foot the bill without federal aid. This reprehensible political brinkmanship cost the economy 120,000 jobs and $3.1 billion in gross domestic product from lost government services; still, the lasting effects to businesses and workers, many of whom will not receive back-pay, has yet to be determined.

We must be optimistic to defeat the cynicism in our hearts and keep our sacred dreams alive. Sometimes it is nearly impossible

---

[9] http://www.washingtonpost.com/blogs/wonkblog/wp/2013/10/10/nine-ways-the-shutdown-will-get-more-painful-as-it-drags-on/

and the brokenness penetrates my heart and brings me to tears - the divisiveness of our moral discourse (manifest in broken politics), the destructive clashing of values among my people (manifest in power struggles and war), the oversight of those suffering the unbearable (manifest in deepened loneliness when they are left to bleed and die alone) – but we must endure and continue this holy struggle. Good Lord, if only all humans would sit with this pain and empathize with their brothers and sisters for a single minute each day. Let us have strength. Our investment in human justice may affect our relationship to Divine justice.

22.)

The Genius Fetus

The rabbis teach that as a fetus we were much more actualized than we could ever imagine. In fact, we were geniuses!

(During the period of gestation) a light burns
above the fetus' head, and it gazes and is able to
see from one end of the world to the other...
There is no time during which a person abides in
greater happiness than during those days... It is
taught the entire Torah, all of it... But as it comes
into the air of the world, an angel comes, strikes it
on its mouth, and makes it forget the entire Torah
(*Niddah* 30b).

This is a remarkable teaching, reminding us that we do not just learn Torah as humans but relearn it from our fetal days. Further, it reminds us that while the details and applications of Torah are very complicated, the essence of the word of God is very simple. All people can learn just as every fetus was capable of mastering our tradition.

The gestational development is a fascinating biological process, but it is non-linear. First, there is an embryonic stage for ten weeks during which there all essential organs begin to form.[10] During the fetal period (staring with week 11), the fetus begins to produce red blood cells, make active movements (including sucking motions), hear sounds, and has defined gender, although the fetus' brain makes up half its size, its eyes remain shut from weeks 11 until week 28, and the lower lung, while developed, will not be capable of air exchange until about week 30. During weeks 31-34, the fetus rapidly stores fat and minerals, and begins rhythmic breathing with immature lungs. By the final weeks of gestation, the fetus has fully grown fingernails, breast buds, and some hair on top of the head. The fetus is now ready to be introduced to the world.

---

[10] http://www.nlm.nih.gov/medlineplus/ency/article/002398.htm

While we see that from a biological perspective a newborn brings a genetic makeup, from a spiritual perspective an infant is a *tabula rasa*. While a fetus is not considered a full life (and thus the mother's life takes precedence if God forbid there are complications) that this potential life still has immense value. If one, God forbid, has a miscarriage, we can see that the potential life had great virtue and spiritual value (knew the whole Torah).

Biologically, what abilities do we have when we are born? Anecdotally, many believe that the fetus in the womb is helped by (and reacts favorably to) music, particularly classical music (and Bach and Mozart, at that). This theory lacks hard scientific proof.[11] On the other hand, another trait from birth may have been proven. Recently, Finnish researchers[12] published the results of a study to determine whether babies can remember things they heard before birth. During the final weeks of pregnancy, pregnant women listened to a recording of a nonsense word played repeatedly with an uncharacteristic drop in pitch at one point. Then, on an average five days after birth, the same recording was played for the babies (with a control group that had not been exposed to the recording). Significantly, all the babies who had heard the recording before birth reacted when they heard the pitch drop in the recording, while the control group did not react. While the sample size was small (seventeen pregnant women and their children plus a control group), the findings do appear to confirm that the babies retained a memory of something they heard in the womb, although this memory appears to disappear some time after birth. Some learning remains, but the Torah is gone.

Interestingly, these findings fit well with the teachings of the rabbis. Perhaps most significantly, though, the rabbis teach us something about how we learn. Torah is about dependence (between the fetus and mother, human and God, people-to-people). We truly learn most appropriately when we learn through humble dependency.

Religion and science appear to indicate that when we are born, our hearts and minds are still wide open and we have the

---

[11] http://www.early-pregnancy-tests.com/music.html

[12] https://www.sciencenews.org/article/babies-learn-words-birth

innocence to truly engage in transformative learning. But as the fetus is struck by the angel and forgets all of her Torah, so as time goes on we have a tendency to close our minds to learning. This reminds us that the constant journey for self-discovery, God discovery, and ethical growth is what is most important. Mastery and perfection is just for the fetus.

23

Jews and Halloween: To Trick or Not to Treat?

I grew up with this funny custom of knocking on strangers' doors once a year to ask for free candy. By the end of the night, I had enough sugar to last a lifetime. We do not intend to send our children door-to-door. Purim will be our time for costumes and gift exchanging, but we will always open the door, greet children with a smile, and provide them with their requested trick-or-treat (I fear my tricks would disappoint).

Jews have always been nervous about Halloween due to its presumptive pagan roots. Some have even argued that it is forbidden by Jewish law to have any involvement at all. I can understand why we do not dress up and go door to door, but there is no need to turn off our lights and close us off from the community. It is a nice opportunity to meet new people in the community and spread goodwill.

Appropriately, the roots of Halloween are murky. Some say with confidence that the holiday's roots go back to the Celtic festival of Samhain (November 1), where on the eve it was believed that the spirits of the dead arose and caused mischief,[13] so people disguised themselves to blend in with the spirits. Later, they claim, when the Romans invaded that they brought their holidays, including one honoring the dead, and another honoring the fruits and trees (Pomona), symbolized by the apple. Finally, the Christians sought to incorporate some of the pagan customs and created All Saints Day, the eve of which in Middle English was All-Hallows Eve, which eventually became Halloween.

Skeptics, on the other hand, have noted that Samhain was celebrated on different dates in different regions, and that some people have employed a pick and choose method for matching the customs to Halloween. As for the Christian attempt to usurp the pagan holiday, there is no proof that there was any intention to replace Samhain or to adopt any of the supposed customs. Even without an examination of history, it should be obvious that many

---

[13] http://www.huffingtonpost.com/2009/10/30/the-history-of-halloween_n_321021.html

customs are of modern origin. For example, pumpkins (and thus Jack-o-lanterns) were native to the Western Hemisphere, so they were not present in Europe until long after the Celtic period. As for giving apples, we do not need the Romans to tell us to give a fruit that is in season during a harvest festival. In addition, it stands to reason that cheap and plentiful candy is also a modern development; so modern trick-or-treating is a modern custom.

What we do know is that in the nineteenth century Halloween was marked by the telling of ghost stories and youths engaging in mischievous activities. Later, there was a concerted effort to transform the holiday into a family-oriented, secular harvest festival. The heyday of trick-or-treating took place in the post-World War II period, when the growth of suburbia and its safe neighborhoods, the huge emerging baby boomer generation emerged (and this was also the pinnacle of the low-budget, campy horror movie), many women raising children were at home to answer the door and give children individual bags full of different candies, and society embraced the custom. Strangely, however, the baby boomers seemed to have taken Halloween with them as they grew up. Instead of putting on an old sheet and a cheap mask bought at a local candy store, adults now began to buy increasingly elaborate costumes and decorate their homes for parties. In October 2012, for example, two million people came to Greenwich Village in New York City for the annual Halloween Parade, and about 9 of 10 were adults. This trend has been accompanied by a period when people have been increasingly afraid to allow their children out, and so trick-or-treating has declined.

Incredibly, Halloween has become the second-leading holiday for decorating in the United States, and one would be hard-pressed to find any Christian or idolatrous elements. According to the National Retail Federation,[14] about 158 million Americans (nearly 44 percent) were expected to participate in Halloween activities in 2013. Annual spending on decorations, costumes, and candy has averaged about $75-$80 recently, with total spending expected to be $6.9 billion this year. In a trend that began with the baby boomers, there will be more spent on adult costumes ($1.22

---

[14] http://www.nrf.com/modules.php?name=News&op=viewlive&sp_id=1668

billion) than children's costumes ($1.04 billion). (Incredibly, Americans are expected to spend $330 million on costumes for their pets.) In terms of activities, 72 percent will hand out candy, 47.5 percent will decorate their property, 44.2 percent will carve a pumpkin, 31.7 percent will take their children trick-or-treating, and nearly 31 percent will attend or host a party. Modern costumes, far from ghosts and witches, are more likely to be movie characters or actors, political figures, and even inanimate objects, not very different from Purim costumes.

Oddly, people tend to worry about things that are not true and ignore the true risks of Halloween. In nearly all cases, allegations of poison laced candy or apples with razor blades inside, and other candy tampering have proven to be urban legends. However, children are four times more likely to be struck by an automobile on Halloween than on any other day of the year.

Youths have a tradition of causing some minor vandalism on Halloween (the "trick" threat). In certain areas of the north and northeast, the evening before Halloween is still knows as "Mischief Night," or "Goosey Night," or some variant. Those unfortunate enough to have to park their car on a street may find their car pelted with eggs, and homeowners may find their trees have toilet paper in their branches, but it rarely gets more destructive. However, in Detroit, the evening before Halloween was called "Devil's Night," which for decades was marred by many incidents of arson that burned down buildings.[15] In 1984, for example, arsonists lit 297 fires, earning Detroit the dubious title of "arson capital of the world." After strong efforts to reduce the level of arson, it flared again to a similar level in 1994, leaving many injured and homeless people. Eventually, Detroit succeeded in changing "Devil's Night" into "Angel's Night," with far less destructive activities. This illustrates that a community can take hold of a holiday and redirect it to a more constructive purpose.

Even more than meeting new community members and offering goodwill, there is some benefit to be gained from embracing Halloween and a time for us to reconsider the mystical questions

---

[15] http://www.nytimes.com/1994/11/01/us/hundreds-of-fires-light-up-devil-s-night-in-detroit.html

some raise about guests, demons, and spirits. It is a time for us to look back at our Jewish mystical and philosophical literature to better understand approaches to angels, spirits, providence, and miracles. Everything around us provides an opportunity for learning and Halloween is no exception. There is a human need and desire to understand our spiritual existence. Halloween is one of the ways that Americans have created to grapple with this. Let us not squander the opportunity with demon costumes and candy but use it as an intellectual and spiritual opportunity for spiritual growth.

24

Job Opening: Prophets Needed

We have great pragmatic leaders today for whom we should be grateful. We, however, have a dearth of prophetic leaders inspiring the masses to a higher level. Consider how Biblical scholar Walter Brueggemann thinks of the role of the prophet:

> [One of the prophet's tasks is] to bring to public expression those very fears and terrors that have been denied so long and suppressed so deeply that we do not know they are there…The prophet must speak evocatively to bring to the community the fear and the pain that individual persons want so desperately to share and to own but are not permitted to do so…The prophet does not scold or reprimand. The prophet brings to public expression the dread of endings, the collapse of our self-madness, the barriers and pecking orders that secure us at each other's expense, and the fearful practice of eating off the table of a hungry brother or sister. It is the task of the prophet to invite the king to experience what he must experience, what he most needs to experience and most fears to experience, namely, that the end of the royal fantasy is very near. The end of the royal fantasy will permit a glimpse of the true king who is not fantasy, but we cannot see the real king until the fantasy is shown to be a fragile and perishing deception (*The Prophetic Imagination*, 45-46).

Brueggemann, Professor Emeritus of Old Testament at Columbia Theological Seminary, is also an ordained minister in the United Church of Christ and a former president of the Society of Biblical Literature. He frequently relates today's political and economic choices to those of Biblical figures such as Solomon or Jeremiah. His writings have a particular value in pinpointing the timeless qualities that true leaders and prophets possess, and the shortcomings that lesser leaders and false prophets possess.

The leading Jewish thinker of the twentieth century on the topic of the modern prophet was Abraham Joshua Heschel, who wrote a book fittingly called *The Prophets*. He suggested: "[A] prophet's true greatness is his ability to hold God and man in a single thought." The prophet is both deeply concerned with God's demands and with the human condition. The prophet also serves as a spokesperson for the Divine: "To extricate the people from despondency, to attach meaning to their past and present misery, was the task that the prophet and God had in common."

Heschel explained that the prophet experiences the world at a deeper level, with a sensitivity adjusted to manifest social injustices:

> Indeed, the sort of crimes and even the amount of delinquency that fill the prophets of Israel with dismay do not go beyond that which we regard as normal, as typical ingredients of social dynamics. To us a single act of injustice—cheating in business, exploitation of the poor—is slight; to the prophets, a disaster. To us injustice is injurious to the welfare of the people; to the prophets it is a deathblow to existence: to us, an episode; to them, a catastrophe, a threat to the world... Our standards are modest; our sense of injustice tolerable, timid; our moral indignation impermanent; yet human violence is interminable, unbearable, permanent. To us life is often serene, in the prophet's eye the world reels in confusion. The prophet makes no concession to man's capacity. Exhibiting little understanding for human weakness, he seems unable to extenuate the culpability of man (*The Prophets*, 4;10).

Heschel points out how much more attuned prophets are to injustice. Think about how easy it is to look at another culture or time period and point out aspects of society that are wrong. On the other hand, if we grew up in a society that condoned slavery, or polygamy, or the abuse of women, would we have the vision and courage of a prophet to denounce these practices? Probably not. Continuing on, Heschel notes that to a prophet, injustice is not only a moral outrage but also a completely different epistemic foundation to how meaning is made:

> Prophecy, then, may be described as exegesis of existence from a Divine perspective. Understanding prophecy is an understanding of an understanding rather than an understanding of knowledge; it is exegesis of exegesis (ibid, xxvii).

113

There is profound intellectual and spiritual depth for one who has tapped into one's own soul, indeed the entirety of the human condition. Yet tragically, the Prophet can never be loved because of her role in society.

> The prophet is intent on intensifying responsibility, is impatient of excuse, contemptuous of pretense and self-pity. His tone, rarely sweet or caressing, is frequently consoling and disburdening, his words are often slashing, even horrid—designed to shock rather than to edify (Ibid., 8).

The Prophet is also not loved, because he or she is an extremist:

> The prophet hates the approximate, he shuns the middle of the road. Man must live on the summit to avoid the abyss. There is nothing to hold to except God. Carried away by the challenge, the demand to straighten out man's ways, the prophet is strange, one-sided, an unbearable extremist... Others may suffer from the terror of cosmic aloneness, the prophet is overwhelmed by the grandeur of divine presence. He is incapable of isolating the world. There is an interaction between man and God which to disregard is an act of insolence. Isolation is a fairy tale (ibid, 19).

Rabbi David Hartman felt the conflicting emotions of one deeply wrestling with society but also transcending it. He wrote of the prophet:

> The aspiring prophet must transcend this
> egocentric dependency on society, so that his
> assumption of political leadership will not be
> grounded in the longing for power. The disdain for
> the community, then, is the condition of the
> prophet during his ascent, i.e., when he is
> struggling to transcend the political leader's
> dependency on the community.... Disdain for the
> community characterized the prophet during his
> ascent; in exact contrast, love for the community
> becomes his characteristic quality during his
> descent (*Maimonides: Torah and Philosophic Quest*, 198).

The Prophet innately struggles through his paradoxical hyper-connection to what exists above and what exists below combined, with his radical separation from everything but his truths and ideals. Heschel continues to teach that the Prophet seeks not only to repair the outer world but also the inner world of humanity:

> Yet the purpose of prophecy is to conquer
> callousness, to change the inner man as well as to
> revolutionize history. It is embarrassing to be a
> prophet. There are so many pretenders,
> predicting peace and prosperity, offering cheerful
> words, adding strength to self-reliance while the
> prophet predicts disaster, pestilence, agony, and
> destruction. People need exhortations to
> courage, endurance, confidence, fighting spirit,
> but Jeremiah proclaims: You are about to die if
> you do not have a change of heart and cease
> being callous to the world of God. He sends
> shudders over the whole city, at a time when the
> will to fight is most important (*The Prohets*, 20).

One must be careful not to misunderstand radical passion, misinformed absolutism, or fanaticism with authentic prophetic leadership. There have been many false prophets in the modern world, ranging from the comic to the deeply tragic. One of the most peculiar and recurrent false prophecies is that the end of the world is near. Among these bizarre predictions are these examples:[16]

- In 1806, some briefly believed that a hen in Leeds, England, laid eggs with a message indicating that the end of the world was near.

- New England farmer William Miller convinced thousands of followers that, through his study of Biblical predictions, the end of the world would occur in 1843. This began the cultish group called the Millerites, who are now more or less extinct as a viable religious entity.

- The San Diego-based cult Heaven's Gate committed mass suicide in the belief that the world was nearing its end and that the 1997 Hale-Bopp comet was accompanied by an alien spaceship that would rescue them at the moment of their death.

- Harold Camping, a California evangelist, has made a career with his "end of days" predictions, including claims that the world would end on September 6, 1994 and (after acknowledging that he may have miscalculated the first estimate) May 21, 2011. Sadly, a retired transit worker spent $140,000 for subway and bus ads in New York warning people of the alleged cataclysm, which was supposed to start in Jerusalem. Camping suffered a stroke not long after his prediction failed to materialize.

- Proving that not only Biblical fundamentalists can give in to miscalculation, many people subscribed to the belief that the Mayan calendar predicted that the end of the world would come on December 12, 2012. It didn't.

There are also false prophets who believe that change, which frequently entails uncertainty, will result in disaster. In 1957, segregationist Arkansas Governor Orval Faubus claimed that "blood will run in the streets" if there was an attempt to implement racial integration in Little Rock schools. In 1965, just before the passage of Medicare, Ronald Reagan made the following prediction if

---

[16] http://www.livescience.com/7926-10-failed-doomsday-predictions.html

Medicare passed: "one of these days you and I are going to spend our sunset years telling our children and our children's children what it was like in American when men were free." Obviously, we have survived.

A true modern prophetic leader may be seen in the life of Rachel Carson. She worked for years for the U.S. Fish and Wildlife Services, and wrote several works about the oceans before she became alarmed by the indiscriminate use of pesticides, such as DDT, which was literally sprayed on people in an effort to eradicate malaria. In her paradigm shifting work, *Silent Spring* (1962), she set forth a choice that fulfills the criteria set forth by Heschel:

> We stand now where two roads
> diverge.... The road we have long been
> traveling is deceptively easy, a smooth
> superhighway on which we progress with
> great speed, but at its end lies disaster.
> The other fork of the road — the one less
> traveled by — offers our last, our only
> chance to reach a destination that assures
> the preservation of the earth

For this, she was heavily criticized by many politicians and the powerful chemical companies. When she was struggling with breast cancer, she testified before Congress in 1963 to ask for changes in legislation to protect the environment. She was vindicated after her death when the environmental movement took off. The pesticide DDT was banned in 1972, and in the ensuing twenty-five years the bald eagle, the nation's symbol, increased its population by ten times over, and many other species have enjoyed a similar increase. Perhaps a new prophet will emerge to finally bring climate change to a similar place in the mind of the world's people.

Today, we have many great thinkers, manager, leaders, and writers that affect contemporary society in tangible ways. But we also need prophets: those who can touch the human core and create change on a systemic level because they see the bigger picture and are willing to sacrifice their best interests at times in order to move the world toward progress.

25

Mordecai Kaplan's Social Justice Thought

In early 2014, I was fortunate to be invited to join a Georgetown University panel on the social justice thought of Rabbi Dr. Mordecai M. Kaplan (1881-1983). In preparation for this panel, I had the opportunity to study the writings of Rabbi Kaplan more thoroughly than I ever had before.

Mordecai Menahem Kaplan was born in Lithuania, received early traditional education in Vilna, and later his family moved to New York while he was still a child. Shortly after moving to America, Kaplan began his education, religious studies, and practical leadership in the Orthodox community. In fact, at one point during his illustrious career he was the rabbi at Kehillath Jeshurun (Upper East Side), at the Jewish Center (Upper West Side), and was an instrumental founder of the Young Israel movement, although he was ordained at the [Conservative] Jewish Theological Seminary. Kaplan moved away from the Orthodox community in 1922, when he founded a synagogue called the Society for the Advancement of Judaism. In one of his first books, the seminal *Judaism as a Civilization* (1934), he advocated a reconstructed Judaism that would continually evolve to meet the needs of Jews in the modern world. Among these changes were voluntary membership within the synagogue, mutual respect for those with differing views, and a focus on egalitarianism for women in the synagogue, including the modern introduction of bat mitzvah[17] into the synagogue. Perhaps out of a desire to maintain democratic ideals, Kaplan also believed that no people were "chosen." and thus denied that Jews had a unique status in the world. Kaplan's movement continued, and grew momentously, after his death, and his primary legacy is the development of the Reconstructionist movement, which today comprises perhaps two percent of American Jews.

Reconstructionist Judaic theology differs from traditional Judaism in a number of ways, among them: the highlighted significance of different aspects of the Torah, prayer and ritual, and mitzvot. Reconstructionist Rabbi Lester Bronstein wrote that

---

[17] http://jwa.org/encyclopedia/article/reconstructionist-judaism-in-united-states

Reconstructionist Judaism offers beliefs "different from traditional Judaism, but surprisingly close to the spirit of that tradition." Specifically, the theology regards the Torah as being written by Jews in response to the presence of God, a way for Jews to see the sacred in their daily lives. Thus, while Jews wrote the Torah, "God is everywhere in the details of it." Furthermore, Reconstructionist ideology stresses the purpose of prayer as a way to remind the people reciting the prayers of their obligation to carry out God's values, not a way to address or appeal to God. Finally, mitzvot are seen as "our people's way of bringing that universal sacredness to the minutiae of daily life in our own specifically Jewish context," and not as direct commandments from God.

Though I greatly respect the work and legacy of Rabbi Kaplan, there are many aspects of his thought that do not resonate with me. To name a few:

- **Naturalist Theology** – I believe in versions of liberation theology and process theology and a God that intervenes in the world (albeit in ways we cannot expect to understand).

- **Revelation** – Kaplan came to reject Divine revelation and the centrality of Jewish texts. Obligation is primarily derived from civilization and shared history, not from God and revelation.

- **Chosenness** – Kaplan rejected the unique nature of the Jewish people and our mission.

Still, on the other hand, there are parts of Kaplan's theology that *do* resonate with me, particularly in my social justice work. For example, Kaplan advocated for a more democratic framework for decision-making in Jewish communities (i.e. elected leadership) rather than top-down leadership. I find this idea very important in social justice work and leadership and it is a framework I strive to adopt and utilize.

Kaplan also believed in the importance of cleaning up our own shops before those of others:

> The Jewish community in our day should
> organize the participation of Jews, in cooperation
> with other communities, in the struggle against
> poverty, disease, ignorance, oppression and war.
> But to qualify for participation in this struggle,
> Jewry must set its own house in order. The Jewish
> community is not free from the evils that beset
> society in general, and must accept full
> responsibility for carrying out the fight against
> them on its own sector of humanity's front....
> When the synagogues, schools, and other cultural
> and social agencies of Jewish life conform to such
> ethical norms, it will be within their power to
> influence the ethical behavior of Jews in their
> other relations as well." (*Future of the American Jew*,
> 54;349)

This ethically rigorous approach should be considered again. Another inspiring idea from Kaplan is his belief that Jewish education was not for the purpose of survival, but about thriving in our worldly mission. He suggested we must radically innovate in our pedagogical approach:

> In all specifically Jewish instruction, whether in
> the traditional sacred texts, in Jewish history, in
> the languages and literatures of the Jewish people,
> or whatever else is Jewish, it is not enough to
> convey that information for the sake of satisfying
> intellectual curiosity, or bolstering Jewish pride, or
> perpetuating Jewish ritual, or even developing
> certain skills that may contribute to Jewish
> survival. All these achievements have their place
> in Jewish education as subordinate purposes. But
> the primary purpose must always be to qualify the
> Jew for such participation in the life of both the
> Jewish and the general community as will make
> for a better world. Jewish education, that fails to
> extend the young Jew's spiritual perspective and
> to link his personal life with the life of mankind, is
> wasted effort. (Ibid., 488-489)

One of Kaplan's most important ideas, and one that I passionately share with him, is that our relationship with God, through prayer, ritual, holidays, text, and community offer a strong foundation to have a universalistic impact, and achieving the destiny of the Jewish people in collaboration with other nations. While my religious framework looks very different from Kaplan's, I gain inspiration from his approach and think that it can be a model that may work for others today. It is crucial that we provide more, not fewer, entry points into Jewish life to actualize our spiritual and ethical potentials, and I find certain aspects of the work of Rabbi Mordecai Kaplan to be both accessible and inspirational.

26

On Free Will And Revelation

The ancient rabbis taught that free will was suspended at the time of revelation. "The Holy One held the mountain over them like a bucket and warned them: If you accept the Torah — good. And if not — here you will be buried" (*Shabbat* 88a). There is an interesting Talmudic debate regarding how the Israelites responded to the intensity of this revelation at Sinai:

> And Rabbi Yehoshua ben Levi said: With every single statement that emanated from the mouth of the Holy One, Blessed is He, the souls of the Jewish people departed (from their bodies), as it is stated: "my soul departed as He spoke." Now, since their souls departed after the first statement, how could they have received the second statement? (God) brought down the dew with which He will resurrect the dead in the future, and He resurrected them, as it said: "A generous rain did You lavish, O God, when Your heritage was weary You established it firmly" (*Shabbat* 88b).

However, the rabbis continue and a contrasting encounter is described:

> And Rabbi Yehoshua ben Levi said: With every single statement that emanated from the mouth of the Holy One, Blessed is He, the Jewish people retreated twelve miles, and the ministering angels helped them to totter back, as it is said "The angles of legions totter, they totter. Do not read this *yidodun* (they lead) but as *yedadun* (help others to lead) (ibid.).

There is a distinct paradox evident in the dialectical account of the Israelites approaching the Divine. The first narrative tells a story of love (a return to God); the second relates more to fear (backing away with awe).

Perhaps the most interesting and pertinent dynamic that

reveals itself in this exploration is that of human essence vs. human will. In the first case, human nature does not allow for a full encounter with God; the experience would be far too overwhelming and the implications/responsibilities would be exceedingly vast. In the second case, the Israelites do not die, but they back away willingly – the encounter with God is simply too overwhelming to bear. Furthermore, in the first narrative, the Israelites have lost free will as they are being forced to accept the Torah. In the second narrative, there is a clear demonstration of free will.

Amidst revelation and the intensity of encountering the Divine, most commentators suggest that the Israelites experiencing revelation either died during it or that they continued to back away (as we saw). Ramban, suggested that God forced intimacy at the giving of the Ten Commandments:

"And the nation saw the thunder…and they said to Moshe 'You speak with us, and we will listen, but let God not speak with us, lest we die.'" The opinion of the commentators is that this is after the giving of the Torah…But this is not my opinion, since it says here "Let God not speak with us," and it doesn't say "again." …And what appears correct in my eyes, regarding this section and the order of events, is that this verse is before the giving of the Torah…. And the order of the events is that "in the morning there was thunder and lightning…and the sound of a shofar quite loud" (19:16) and Moshe strengthened their hearts "and took them out towards God, and they stood at the foot of the mountain" (19:17). When they were there at the foot of the mountain looking and standing, God descended on to the top of the mountain in fire (19:18) and the mountain itself trembled, (19:18) and the sound of the shofar grew exceedingly great (19:19) then "the nation was afraid, and was shaken backwards and stood from afar" (20:16). Farther (back) than the border. Then they said to Moshe that God should not speak to them at all lest they die. But Moshe strengthened them, and said to them, "don't be afraid" (20:17) and they listened to him, "and then stood far off" (20:18) and Moshe approached the thick darkness (20:18). But he didn't enter. And then God spoke the Ten Commandments. And after the Ten Commandments, (as it says in Deut. 5:20), the heads of the tribes and the elders drew near to him, and said to him "If we again hear the voice of the Lord, our God, we will die…. You should draw close, and hear all that the Lord our God will say, and speak to us all that the Lord our God will speak to you, and we will hear and we will do (5:24). And God agreed to their words, and said, "They have said well, and all that they have spoken."

From Ramban, it seems that God forced an intense intimacy with the Israelites that surpassed human capacity. However, this imposed intimacy was not inflicted as a lover (for forced intimacy would be violent) but is comparable to the intimacy experienced with a parent (where a parent longs for closeness at times more than a child can handle). During the overpowering and intense revelation of the Torah the Israelites still retained their faculties and ability to exercise their will, however, in the presence of the Divine they were overcome with fear and only strengthened through the encouragement of Moshe.

Consider a teaching from Rabbi Eliyahu Dessler on the topic of free will:

> When two armies are locked in battle, the place where the struggle takes place is called the front line. This line is drawn at the place where the two forces meet. On either side, there is territory that belongs to that side and is thus not the location of battle. The front line moves and changes, but battle, generally speaking, occurs only where the two sides meet. Our moral choices can be thought of in a similar way. There are decisions that we have made in our lives so many times that they are no longer decisions. It is obvious to us that we will respond in particular ways to particular events. Those choices are within our territory. There are also choices we have never had to make and likely will never have to make. They are beyond the realm of our experience. They are firmly out of our territory. The place where these territories meet is the place of choice – bechirah. On the spectrum of what we know to be ethical and what we know to be unethical, we make choices only at the bechirah point. This is the point where our values come into conflict and thus the choices are not obvious. Each individual's bechirah point is unique, and it moves as we grow and change. By recognizing the bechirah points in our lives, we are able to set our sights on expanding our moral territory and thus becoming better people" (*Strive for Truth*, 52-57).

Rabbi Dessler's teaching explains eloquently that an individual's moral choices are uniquely his or her own and eventually become so commonplace throughout life that they no longer become decisions, but instincts. However, Rabbi Dessler continues and discusses the limits of individual free will when he explains there are choices that are beyond our dominion of understanding and that we have never made these choices nor will we ever have to. These types of choices are beyond our realm of experience and surely can relate to the Israelite encounter with the Divine on Sinai. Though the Israelites possessed free will, their encounter with God was unlike anything they had experienced or could comprehend and thus their decision was not made freely, as we understand free will to operate.

For a different perspective, consider Levinas and his understanding of free will as it relates to the Divine. Levinas suggested that the first thing God does after creating humanity is create human limits (law). Through this order, humans are able to give meaning to the world; ethics precedes meaning. The command allows for ethics since one is already obligated prior to the making of meaning. Here, Levinas suggests that after God created man he commanded and taught him limits, influenced his understanding and interaction with the world, and thus enabled man to give meaning to the world and the beings that occupy it. So through Divine education and ethical instruction man was able to make informed decisions regarding moral choices and ethics, still, though, of his own volition.

There are times we must encounter truth in a transformative way (as if we were compelled) before we can truly choose it. We seek out moral transformation in this way to maximize the potential of our free will. Further, we should embrace a sense of obligation that precedes our own will and understanding. Our impulses should be cultivated to make service and giving a core part of our being. We move it from volition to nature, from choice to instinct.

Clearly, the issue of free will amidst revelation and the intensity of encountering the Divine, most aptly illustrated through the Israelites encounter with God on Sinai, will never be completely understood. Nor is there a consensus, as has been demonstrated, regarding the Israelite experience. However, as Levinas writes, *halakha* provides Divine guidance, through which we are empowered with free will, and enables us to give meaning to the world and seek out the holy. Let us be inspired by the greatness and intensity of God's relationship and become better people so as to fulfill our ethical responsibilities.

27

Unity Of Religions?

I recall at a global interfaith gathering in Davos, a faith leader stood up and claimed "we are all brothers and sisters since our faiths are really the same." I recall feeling shocked by the simplicity; that type of unity can be terrifying. We can respect each other while honoring differences in values. The Dalai Lama has argued, "[T]he essential message of all religions is very much the same."

Boston University Professor Stephen Prothero, however, in his book *God Is Not One* argues that religions are in fact very different. How can we pretend that the various scriptures, dogmas, ethics and rituals all lead to one universal truth? Only one not well versed in various religions could be so oblivious of the vast differences. God is found in the details of our religious lives, not in abstract universals. Not only is it not meaningful to conflate different traditions and value systems, it can be dangerous. The universalist impulse may be a "lovely sentiment," Prothero writes, "but it is dangerous, disrespectful, and untrue."

Anyone who is slightly familiar with comparative religions will immediately realize that there are core differences, even outside of technical theological doctrine. For example, Islam and Judaism prohibit the eating of pork, while in some Christian cultures a pork meal is integral to their holidays. Islam bans alcohol, unlike Judaism and Christianity, which incorporate wine in religious rituals. Judaism and Christianity practice monogamy exclusively, as opposed to Islam, which allows polygamy. Most Christian sects accept and patronize religious imagery (think of Michelangelo), while in Islam it is forbidden, and even in recent years people have been murdered over the issue of giving prophets a human form. If we raised the question of the status of women within religion, it is doubtful that a consensus could be derived even within individual religions.

Many atheists dismiss "religion" as if it were a singular entity. Actually, the sophisticated approach requires that we contend with each religion and its claims. Religions have much in common, and we should come together and learn from each other. But we cannot pretend that our truths are identical. Rabbi Jonathan Sacks writes:

> There is a fundamental difference between the
> end-of-days peace of religious unity and the
> historical peace of compromise and coexistence.
> The attempt to force the former can sometimes be
> the most formidable enemy of the latter.... It is
> time we exorcized Plato's ghost, clearly and
> unequivocally. Universalism must be balanced
> with a new respect for the local, the particular, the
> unique" (*The Dignity of Difference*, 10, 20).

Rabbi Sacks continues:

> My argument is far more fundamental, namely that
> universalism is an inadequate response to tribalism, and
> no less dangerous. It leads to the belief – superficially
> compelling but quite false – that there is only one truth
> about the essentials of the human condition, and it holds
> true for all people at all times. If I am right, you are
> wrong.... teaching humanity to make space for
> difference. God may at times be found in human other,
> the one not like us. Biblical monotheism is not the idea
> that there is one God and therefore one gateway to His
> presence. To the contrary, it is the idea that the unity of
> God is to be found in the diversity of creation, (Ibid., 50,
> 53).

History has proven that people who wish to create a universal
religion frequently resort to suppression. The Egyptian Pharaoh
Akenhaten[18] (reigned ca. 1352-1336 BCE) created a religion
dedicated to a single deity, the sun disk Aten, but he also spent vast
sums building a new city to his new religion and punished those who
maintained old beliefs. When he died, his monotheistic experiment
was abandoned. (Such a thing also happened on *The Simpsons* when
the character of Mr. Burns attempted to create his own cult. It
flamed out before it could spread to the masses). Shortly after Islam
was founded, there followed centuries of warfare against Christian
areas as well as within nations with Islamic rulers. For their part,
beginning in 1095 through 1291, there were Crusades[19]

---

[18] http://www.pbs.org/empires/egypt/newkingdom/akenhaten.html

[19] http://www.metmuseum.org/toah/hd/crus/hd_crus.htm

launched by Pope Urban II in 1095 and carried on sporadically until 1291, that sought to take Jerusalem and other areas of the Middle East back from Muslim control. Participants were promised that their sins would be forgiven in exchange for fighting. While Jerusalem was initially taken (as well as Constantinople in the 13th Century), Muslim rulers ultimately regained these territories; we are still dealing with this terrible legacy today.

The best approach appears to be one of coexistence, and one of the most interesting examples involved a Muslim ruler and a majority Hindu population, as unlikely a pairing as can be imagined. Islam is monotheistic and forbids religious imagery, while Hinduism is polytheistic and embraces religious imagery. Islam adheres to the doctrine of an individual soul, while in Hinduism there is a belief in reincarnation, so there is a reverence for animals (especially cattle), who are seen as the reincarnated spirits of people. Akbar the Great, who ruled India from 1556-1605, expanded the Muslim Mughal Empire. Nevertheless, he participated in festivals of other religions, married several Hindu princesses, abolished a special tax on Hindus, and did not press for the conversion of Hindus. Later, he built a temple in which he received Hindu, Zoroastrian, and other religious scholars, allowed the Christians to build a church, and curried respect for Hinduism by discouraging the slaughter of cattle. Eventually, he attempted to form a cult that incorporated Islam, Hinduism, and other religious beliefs. Unfortunately, he centered the new belief system on himself, and so his experiment died with him. Ultimately, the profound religious differences could not be blended without losing the values of each religion.

Perhaps the best religious policy is one that appreciates the good points of all religious traditions, while not pretending that a universal religion can be created or imposed on all. In the 20th century, Mohandas Gandhi was an eloquent spokesman for religious toleration, but even he could not prevent the creation of India and Pakistan as separate Hindu and Islamic states. He rejected the idea that everyone should belong to one religion: "My effort should never be to undermine another's faith but to make him a better follower of his own faith." He specifically deplored the kind of coercive proselytizing that missionaries frequently employed. In a piece published in his own *Harijan* newspaper in January 1937, he wrote:

It is impossible for me to reconcile myself
to the idea of conversion after the style
that goes on in India and elsewhere today.
It is an error which is perhaps the greatest
impediment to the world's progress
toward peace ... Why should a Christian
want to convert a Hindu to Christianity?
Why should he not be satisfied if the
Hindu is a good or godly man?

We must be tolerant of other religion; that is not up for debate. Even further, we should collaborate and learn from one another but not in such a way that shows honor and dignity to other's beliefs and does not merely pretend that we have no differences and that we do not have a unique contribution to make through our religious tradition.

28.)

God Prays but Do We? Reflection on Creation

In one Talmudic narrative, God asks humans for a blessing (*Berachot* 7a). The rabbis go even further and teach that God prays:

> R' Yochanan said in the name of R' Yosi ben Zimra: "How do we know that God prays? Because it says: 'I will bring them to My holy mountain, and I will gladden them in My house of prayer.' It does not say 'the house of their payer,' but 'the house of my prayer.' This teaches that God prays. What does He pray? 'May it be My will before Me that My mercy will suppress My anger, and that My compassion will prevail over My (other) attributes, and that I will deal with My children with compassion, and that I may treat them beyond the strict interpretation of law (*Chullin* 60b).

Another passage suggests that God even wears *tefillin* (*Berachot* 6a). Of course, some commentators do not take these teachings literally (and neither are we). After all, whom would God pray to? Besides, God does not have a corporeal body to wear *tefillin*. It does not matter, however, as the teaching is still valuable. We learn that prayer is not a sign of weakness but of strength. It takes courage and humility to pause and reflect upon the self and existence. God "prays" and thus praises creation and reflects upon existence. We learn that God intentionally made the world imperfect in order that humans could be partners in creation.

> A certain philosopher asked Rebbi Hoshaya and said to him: If circumcision is so beloved (by God), why wasn't the first man created circumcised? ... Everything created during the six days of creation requires further work. For example, mustard seeds must be sweetened, legumes must be sweetened, wheat must be ground, and man must be improved (*Midrash Genesis Rabah*, 11:6).

The first humans were the last of creation to show that they had no part in the initial stages.

> Our Rabbis taught: Adam was created [last of all beings] on the eve of Sabbath. And why? — Lest the heretics say: The Holy One, blessed be He, had a partner [Adam] in His work of creation. Another answer is: In order that, if a man's mind becomes [too] proud, he may be reminded that the gnats preceded him in the order of creation. Another answer is: That he might immediately enter upon the fulfillment of a commandment, the observance of the Sabbath. Another answer is: That he might straightway go in to the banquet. The matter may be compared to a king of flesh and blood who built palaces and furnished them, prepared a banquet, and thereafter brought in the guests. So too, Adam was created in a world that was already prepared. (*Sanhedrin* 38a)

Humans had no part in the creation of the world, but we have a huge part in the future of the world. For millennia, humans have turned to prayer for their own needs and those of others. Recent research has tended to indicate that Jews may be less likely than many others to pray. The Pew Research Survey showed that overall, 55 percent of Jews (albeit nearly all Orthodox Jews) viewed religion as very or somewhat important in their lives, versus 44 percent who viewed it as not too or not at all important, versus 79 percent of all Americans who viewed religion as very or somewhat important. However, an earlier study was even more telling. According to the Pew Research Center's 2007 U.S. Landscape Survey,[20] 58 percent of Americans prayed daily, ranging from 80 percent among black Protestants, 71 percent among Muslims, 58 percent among Catholics, 53 percent among mainline Protestants, and (last among major religions) 26 percent among Jews.

The question of the efficacy of prayer has been put to scientific trial on a number of occasions with mixed results. A Mississippi study[21] of patients (nearly all of whom were women)

---

[20] http://www.pewforum.org/2011/04/28/prayer-in-america/

[21] http://www.ncbi.nlm.nih.gov/pubmed/20391859

concluded that direct person-to-person prayer sessions improved the depression and anxiety scores, although they did not affect cortisol levels. On the other hand though, it is worth noting that a three-pronged study of Christian prayers[22] for strangers undergoing heart surgery found that there was no effect on the outcome regardless of whether the patient knew about the praying, and that there was an increased chance of complications following surgery among those who had been prayed for. We do not consider prayer to be magic where we simply receive all of our needs and wants asked for. Rather prayer, when done well can, among other things, ground us and improve us and provide us inspiration and positive energy to fulfill our life missions.

On a personal health level, prayer seems to be on the rise. According to National Health Interview Survey data based on more than fifty thousand interviews, the number of people who prayed about their health increased from 43 percent in 2002 to 49 percent in 2007. Those who exercised less were depressed or had dental pain, or whose health had changed dramatically were most likely to have reported that they prayed. The self-reported results indicated that those who prayed thought that it had helped their health.

Søren Kierkegaard, the nineteenth century Danish thinker, taught: "Life is not a problem to be solved, but a reality to be experienced." One of the great values of religious life is the charge to experience existence more deeply. Rather than merely analyze our existence we must immerse ourselves in the deepest and highest form of living. Often times we can solve problems, but at other times we must merely humble ourselves amidst the challenges. As the union was crumbling, Abraham Lincoln said: "I have been driven many times to my knees by the overwhelming conviction that I had nowhere else to go."

Today, we are surrounded by myriad global challenges. There is still so much necessary work to be done. Even though we are capable of much, we must humble ourselves through prayer and introspection. God can create or destroy the world in a moment, yet God is found in God's own prayer immersed in truth, hope, and love. So, too, we can achieve much (and we must!), but we must also

---

[22] http://www.nytimes.com/2006/03/31/health/31pray.html?pagewanted=all&_r=2&

pause to consider the correct path.

29

Proud To Be Open Orthodox

In the last decade and a half I have been fortunate to study in a great variety of *yeshivot* and to have forged deep connections with many types of Jews: I have happily lived in Washington Heights and studied at Yeshiva University, where I encountered some amazing minds and souls in the *beit midrash* and in the academy. I deeply enjoyed my years in Religious-Zionist *yeshivot* in Efrat and Jerusalem, learning with my revered teachers Rabbis Shlomo Riskin, Chaim Brovender, and Nathan Lopes Cardozo; I have also grown immensely in my time studying in ultra-orthodox *yeshivot* both in Jerusalem (in Mea Shearim) and America (in a Lakewood Kollel). Through these experiences I feel an expansive connection, having significant relationships in the "yeshivish" community, in Chabad, in Ultra/Centrist Orthodoxy, in Modern/Open Orthodoxy, and of course even among those outside of Orthodoxy and Judaism. I appreciate the diversity of Orthodoxy, of Judaism, and of humankind.

In concert with these experiences, my four years of rabbinical training at Yeshivat Chovevei Torah Rabbinical School (YCT) transformed me in ways I could never imagine through some of the most critical, immersive, and introspective Torah analysis I have encountered. As a result of my experiences to date and especially because of my study with and learning from such compassionate mentors and luminary *talmidei chuchamim*, I am proud to tell the non-Orthodox that we are committed to *halakhah*, *talmud torah*, and to the welfare of the entire Orthodox community. And I am proud to tell the Centrist and Ultra-Orthodox communities that we deeply value our relationships with non-Orthodox Jews and non-Jews, our secular studies, our Zionism, and our support for increased leadership for Orthodox women. We strive to be Torah-true and integrated Jews, and to recognize and admire the diversity of Jewish life in general and Orthodox life in particular.

As Open Orthodox Jews, we affirm that Orthodox Judaism is stronger when we embrace our diversity. In the Open Orthodox conception, diverse people committed to *halakhic* life come together to learn, pray, lead, and celebrate in an inclusive and expansive manner. I have deep appreciation for kabbalist thought and rational thought, Israeli Judaism and Diaspora Judaism, masculine spirituality and feminine spirituality, outreach campaigns and in-reach campaigns, Kollel learners and philanthropists, those content and those agitated. Rabbi Jonathan Sacks put the diversity of Orthodoxy well:

> Orthodoxy is not a denomination. It encompasses astonishing variations… different groups evolved widely different responses to modernity…Orthodoxy, then, is diverse…. To what might we compare it? Perhaps the best analogy is a language. A language is determined by rules of syntax and semantics. But within that language an infinite number of sentences can be uttered or books written. Within it, too, there can be regional accents and dialects. Orthodoxy is determined by beliefs and commandments. These are its rules of syntax and semantics. But within that framework lies an open-ended multiplicity of cognitive, emotional, spiritual, and cultural styles (*One People?*, 92-93).

In *Confrontation*, Rav Soloveitchik cautioned that: "[t]he Westernized Jew maintains that it is impossible to engage in both confrontations, the universal and the covenantal, which, in his opinion, are mutually exclusive" (II:1). The Rav rejected that one must either be solely human, American, and secular or solely Jewish, religious, and separated.

Today, sadly, many Jews have pulled back into the isolation of spiritually constructed ghettos or into full assimilation. To truly affirm both the Torah and an open approach to the world has become increasingly challenging for the twenty-first century Jew. Rav Kook taught us that simple party affiliations or language affirmations do not reveal true beliefs:

There is denial that is like an affirmation of faith,
and an affirmation of faith akin to denial. A
person can affirm the doctrine of the Torah
coming from "heaven," but with the meaning of
"heaven" so strange that nothing of true faith
remains. And a person can deny Torah coming
from "heaven" where the denial is based on what
the person has absorbed of the meaning of
"heaven" from people full of ludicrous thoughts.
Such a person believes that the Torah comes from
a source higher than that! Although that person
may not have reached the point of truth,
nonetheless this denial is to be considered akin to
an affirmation of faith. "Torah from Heaven" is
but an example for all affirmations of faith,
regarding the relationship between their
expression in language and their inner essence,
the latter being the main desideratum of faith
(*Orot Ha'emunah*, 25).

I have met many perceived to be "liberal" who possessed the
deepest of faith and many considered to be "more traditional" with a
gap between their garb and their heart. I have learned (and continue
to strive) not to be judgmental of others' religious lives, but to partner
with others in our collective aspiration to live a life of integrity.

To me, the great contribution of Open Orthodoxy is that we
are committed to a Judaism that holds the fundamental incongruity
of being simultaneously particularistic and universal. Our
commitments are not solely to the ten percent of Jews in America
who identify as Orthodox, but to the entire community, to all of *klal
Yisrael*. We are fully committed to Jewish law, supporting Jews and
the State of Israel, and celebrating the uniqueness of Orthodox Jews
and Judaism. And we are also fully committed to partnership with
non-Jews, fighting global injustice, and celebrating our differences
and commonalities with other peoples. I have found through the
building of the Orthodox social justice movement (Uri L'Tzedek)
that the latter can be just as Jewish as the former when it is rooted in
Torah and Jewish ethics. Open Orthodoxy, to me, does not just
mean that we are a little bit more open on this issue or a little bit
more inclusive on that issue (as important as openness and inclusivity
are). To me, rather, Open Orthodoxy means that we are

committed to Judaism and to the world, to Jews and to all humanity. We are Torah Jews and global citizens, and those identities inform and inspire each other.

To have true faith in the Torah is to believe that it has – and we as its guardians, interpreters, and transmitters have – a message for the world. If this is the case, then the totality of our study cannot be an occasional or even regular sermon, class, or *beit midrash* study session. Rather, these core values must be manifest in many ways throughout our lives. This is what I find so compelling in an Open Orthodox approach to *halakhah*, that it strives to integrate our entire lives—even those parts frequently labeled secular—into a life of Torah. We understand that God's presence is in the history we are living, and so we do not hide from the present, from the world around and within us. For me, *halakhah* is not about blind irrational submission but about intentional transformation (*tikkun atzmi, tikkun kehilla, tikkun medina, tikkun olam*). *Halakha* literally translates as "progress." While it's deeply rooted in the past and guided by core Torah values, it's primarily future looking to help solve societal problems, bring holiness into our lives, and cultivate the ethical personality.

There are those who are concerned by the expansion of Open Orthodoxy. Sometimes they have offered constructive critique. This we welcome, in the spirit of genuine *machloket l'shem shamayim*. All people have the right—and, for those of us in positions of leadership, the responsibility—to teach their approach to Torah in an open marketplace of ideas. But sometimes concern about Open Orthodoxy has given way to being threatened by it. Sometimes Orthodox leaders have publicly, and more often privately, defamed and hurt the professions of Open Orthodox rabbis. I see nothing noble in such actions. I do not think we should be in the business of defining others' identities for them.

Torah, and the Orthodox community, is strongest when we positively keep our eyes on the prize, when we stay out of political infighting, when we eschew demeaning and invalidating others. I have faith in the religious community as an astute and perceptive body. I believe religious people will gravitate toward truth wherever they find it, and not be persuaded by angry polemics that seek more to destroy than to build, to compete rather than to collaborate.

If one observed major segments of the Orthodox

community, one might come to think that following blogs of who is in or out of Orthodoxy is the central activity of religious Judaism, more important than Torah learning, supporting Israel, spending time with family, and acts of loving-kindness. God forbid this becomes the norm, and those of us in Jewish leadership must constantly steer the community back to the central tenets and commitments of our faith.

I admit my bias. I love Rabbi Avi Weiss like a father and Rabbi Yitz Greenberg like a grandfather. I admire Rabbi Asher Lopatin moving about the community, and Rabbi Dov Linzer teaching and learning in the *beit midrash*. I trust their judgment on how they guide our community. I felt my Yeshivat Chovevei Torah teachers and friends are like intimate family and my classmates have become my rebbes. I pray that our community will grow because I love God, Torah, and Israel, but also because I love my partners in building a more open, inclusive, and rigorous Jewish community. I feel challenged and liberated in a dynamic Orthodoxy that touches my spiritual core on a daily basis.

I am so proud to be Orthodox and also to "expand the palace of Torah" (as Rav Kook taught) to engage more creatively in secular study, to increase our engagement with and support for Israel, to increase women's roles in Orthodox leadership, to expand our solidarity work for justice outside of Orthodoxy, and to engage in deeper spiritual practices. My teachers, colleagues, and I will be critiqued because we are on a radical mission to take responsibility for the Torah and defend the tradition in the post-modern era, but those critiques will not deter us. In fact, they strengthen our resolve for this supremely critical mission. We will always welcome *tochacha*, constructive feedback, when given with wisdom and proper good intentions. But we must dismiss destructive, mendacious, and unsophisticated public attacks. Our role is to serve God, to increase the awareness of God among *klal Yisrael* and *kol yoshvei tevel*, and to mend the brokenness in the world. Those striving to serve God cannot be governed by fear. True religious leadership requires both enormous humility and enormous courage. We have too much holy work to do in such a short period of time to give any time or attention to those demanding our obedience to their specific norms and ideologies.

30

Standing in Solidarity with the Filipino American Community

In late 2013, I went to a Filipino Church. Why would an Orthodox rabbi and his family go to church on a Sunday morning? The answer is simple: in times of crisis we must cross faith-based and ideological divides to foster human solidarity and love. At the Filipino-American church I was privileged to meet Pastor Joel Padilla, who preached and prayed for the hundreds of thousands of victims living through the horror in the Philippines. While listening to Pastor Padilla I thought about those victims who had lost family members, homes, all of their belongings. I thought about those victims who are soaking wet, injured, and seeking refuge for their surviving children. Where will all these people turn? The thoughts pained me as I grieved with community members in Pastor Padilla's church.

That particular Sunday also marked seventy-five years since the events of Kristallnacht. I was not sure how to engage the solemn occasion in a meaningful way. Somehow, standing with others who were mourning felt most appropriate. In a world full of so much darkness, we desperately need collective acts of light to heal the world. This is ever more pertinent with Chanukah nearly here. As I stood with my community in mourning I tried to prepare my heart and soul to kindle and disseminate some illumination, some contribution of light to a world all too frequently plagued with darkness and sorrow.

Consider the words of Rabbi Yitz Greenberg:

> The only way to wholeness is to heal the world and to work to take the poison out of absolutism without eroding all values and truth in the process. Post-Shoah.... the yearning for perfecting finitude, properly harnessed, can fuel the drive for *tikkun olam* (mending the world), politically and economically as well as religiously and philosophically (*Theology after the Shoah*).

To some people, the Philippines is the nation that invented the yo-yo, and is famously noted for its colorful jitneys that serve as mass transportation in large cities such as Manila. However, there are many features of this beautiful land and its history that bear witness to what President Barack Obama termed the "incredible resiliency" of the Filipino people.

Typhoon Haiyan (known as Yolanda to Filipinos) hit the island of Leyte with sustained winds of nearly two hundred miles per hour and gusts up to 235 miles per hour (the equivalent of a category 5 hurricane, and possibly the highest winds ever recorded in the Philippines), and tidal surges that eyewitnesses claimed were as high as trees (nearly twenty feet tall). This super typhoon extended well beyond a thousand in diameter. In short, its ferocity, magnitude, and impact easily surpassed Hurricane Sandy, the deadly storm that hit the east coast in 2012, and had wind speeds greater than what the gulf experienced during Hurricane Katrina in 2005.

The Philippines, with a population of 97 million, are hit by about twenty typhoons annually, but never one of this magnitude. The hardest hit location was the Leyte city of Tacloban (the city where the Fillipino government was restored in 1944 when the United States liberated the islands from the Japanese). Current estimates are that over 10,000 of its 220,000 residents were killed during the typhoon. The airport and telephone lines were knocked out, and it has taken days for relief efforts to reach the area, so it is still difficult to accurately assess the damage.

Super typhoon Haiyan is unique in that the destruction and deaths were not caused by the usual accumulation of hours of severe torrential rain that leads to mudslides and river flooding. The storm surge caused by Haiyan came rapidly, and the destruction and carnage was similar to that normally associated with a tsunami. Photos of the aftermath show wide swaths of incredible devastation and even a cargo ship that had been swept ashore, reminiscent of the Japanese tsunami of 2011.

Describing the situation around Tacloban, Defense Minister Voltaire Gazmin said: "There is no power, no water, nothing. People are desperate." Unfortunately, since no one has anything, people tend to grab anything and everything they can, from the few remaining stores or from relief convoys that may be sending materials to other afflicted areas. President Obama offered American military help in bringing in relief supplies and in aiding search and rescue operations, but the immediate need is still great. While Tacloban has garnered the most attention, people have noted that there are many fishing communities to the north that border the seafront, and that no reports had been received from any of these areas. There is great concern that these communities were completely destroyed. Symbolically, a huge tree in Mabolo that had withstood every typhoon to strike the area for more than one hundred years was blown over in this typhoon.

The history of the Philippines has at times mirrored the fury of its typhoons, with various powers vying for control. Islam was introduced to the southern area of the Philippines in the 14th century, and in the 16th century the Spanish conquered the islands, naming them after the Spanish King Philip II. Later, the United States seized the Philippines from Spain in the Spanish-American War of 1898, after which it fought the Filipinos for several years in a guerrilla war. As the Philippines prepared for independence, the Japanese invaded the islands in 1941. The Japanese brutalized the Filipino people during their reign, massacring over 90,000 people as they retreated from the invading Americans in 1944-1945. In Lipa, Japanese soldiers threw four hundred Filipinos to their deaths in a well, with the murderous rampage claiming over 1,000 lives. One Japanese soldier recalled: "In the beginning, we could not kill even a man. But we managed to kill him. Then we hesitated to kill a woman. But we managed to kill her, too. Then we could kill children. We came to think as if we were just killing insects." However, the Filipino people withstood the brutality mercilessly reigned down on them and emerged from the Second World War and claimed their independence.

After independence in 1946, the Philippines, unfortunately, continued to experience difficulty. Ferdinand Marcos, who maintained centralized power from 1965-1986, faced Marxist and Muslim rebel factions, and in part used these political threats to justify martial law for much of his rule. In 1983, when opposition leader Benigno Aquino returned to the Philippines from exile, he was murdered immediately after exiting the plane, a shameless assassination by the Marcos regime. Eventually, Aquino's widow Corazon ran for President in 1986, and after trying to fix the election results, worldwide pressure forced Marcos out of power (he was then granted asylum in the United States). However, political corruption, scandal, and poverty still continue to plague the nation.

Recently, President Benigno S. Aquino III won a victory over Muslim separatist rebels in the South, and has also done much to reduce the rampant corruption that has adversely affected the lives of Filipinos for so many years. In addition, only a month ago the Philippines was struck by a severe earthquake from which the nation is still recovering. In response, Filipino-Americans have spearheaded relief efforts through groups such as the National Alliance for Filipino Concerns to try to deal with the nearly 800,000 Filipinos that were left homeless after the earthquake. Today there are 2.5 million Filipino-Americans, the second-largest population among Asian Americans. The Filipino-American population is generally devoutly Catholic, strongly devoted to family, and comprises a large number of health care workers (particularly nurses). While we come from cultures halfway around the world from each other, we are both strong peoples of resiliency, faith, family, and service.

We should always consider donating our resources to help at difficult times, but we must also be sure that relief agencies provide transparency. When I was in Haiti, I realized the extent of this problem as there was much malfeasance and ineptitude in trying to provide basic goods and services to those suffering great hardships. If you are ever in a position to help, please consider helping one of the many well-vetted organizations that are aiding in recovery efforts.

In a world rife with poverty and ubiquitous suffering, we often retreat to narrow truths. But in times of crisis, we must allow our hearts and souls to expand with compassion for the needs of the vulnerable. Sometimes we can help with our wallets and hands, and other times simply with our hearts and expressions of love and solidarity.

31

Thriving, Surviving, and the Dangers of Peoplehood

While Jews have often been described as "a people of the book" (making the book the locus of religious interaction), others have described us simply as "a people" (making peoplehood primary). In the post-Enlightenment era, where more Jews are secular than religious, peoplehood has taken on a much stronger emphasis. The Holocaust, the murder of six million Jews in countries that they considered home, has also contributed to the understanding of Jews as a separate and distinct people. However, while Jews have been collectively persecuted for millennia due to our status as "others," in modernity many influential thinkers have been more embracing. Consider how highly some gentiles in modernity have viewed the Jewish people.

Lyman Abbott, a famous Congregationalist theologian and author of the late nineteenth and early twentieth century, wrote:

> We gentiles owe our life to Israel. It is Israel who has brought us the message that God is One, and that God is a just and righteous God, and demands righteousness of His children, and demands nothing else. It is Israel that has brought us the message that God is our Father. It is Israel who brought us the Divine law, has laid the foundation of liberty. It is Israel who had the first free institution the world ever saw. It is Israel who has brought us our Bible, our prophets, our apostles. When sometimes our own unchristian prejudices flame out against the Jewish people, let us remember that all that we have, all that we owe, under God, is due to what Judaism has given us (*Problems of Life, Vol. 4*, 152)

The historically prominent French mathematician, physicist, inventor, and writer Blaise Pascal wrote:

> It is certain that in certain parts of the world we
> can see a peculiar people, separated from the
> other peoples of the world, and this is called the
> Jewish people.... This people is not only a
> remarkable antiquity but has also lasted for a
> singularly long time... For whereas the peoples of
> Greece and Italy, of Sparta, Athens, and Rome,
> have perished so long ago, these still exist, despite
> the efforts of so many powerful kings who have
> tried a hundred times to wipe them out... They
> have always been preserved, however, and their
> preservation was foretold.... My encounter with
> this people amazes me (*Pensées*, 171, 176-77).

The notion that the survival of the Jewish people is purely miraculous is frequently cited throughout history. Consider the words of Nicholai Berdyaev, the Russian religious and political philosopher:

> ... remember how the materialist interpretation of
> history, when I attempted in my youth to verify it by
> applying it to the destinies of peoples, broke down in
> the case of the Jews, where destiny seemed absolutely
> inexplicable from the materialistic standpoint .... Its
> survival is a mysterious and wonderful phenomenon
> demonstrating that the life of this people is governed
> by a special predetermination, transcending the
> processes of adaptation expounded by the
> materialistic interpretation of history (*The Meaning of
> History*, 86-87).

Miraculous as our ability to persevere in the face of destruction has been, too often survival has become the goal of our religion. This can be considered a form of "idolatry," where self-preservation takes priority over core values. *How* we survive takes precedence over the more important question of *why* we should survive. How can we unite often comes to trump the diversity of our people. These are the inherent dangers of peoplehood, fundamental flaws in a singular definition of Jewishness.

Many Jews, and gentiles, assume our status as a people to be a given, rooted in our covenant with God, socio-political definitions of nationhood, or even philosophical understandings of peoplehood. However, this blind acceptance of our peoplehood often entails a failure to examine what exactly makes us a unique people. Some suggest peoplehood is based upon being a "family" that one cannot opt out of. Philosopher and author Michael Wyschogrod explains this position:

> The foundation of Judaism is the family identity of the Jewish people as descendants of Abraham, Isaac, and Jacob. Whatever else is added to this must be seen as growing out of and related to the basic identity of the Jewish people as the seed of Abraham elected by God through descent from Abraham.... The house of Israel is therefore not a voluntary association defined by acceptance or rejection of a set of propositions. (*The Body of Faith*, 57)

Others, however, suggest that we choose, voluntarily, whether to be a part of the Jewish people or not. Rabbi Yitz Greenberg writes:

> As long as the covenant was involuntary, it could be imposed from above in a unitary way.... In the new era, the voluntary covenant is the theological base of a genuine pluralism...[This] is a recognition that all Jews have chosen to make the fundamental Jewish statement at great personal risk and cost (*Voluntary Covenant*, 22).

Yet there have been others who have suggested that in a post-Holocaust era, we our obligated to maintain our commitment to peoplehood in addition to keeping our religious traditions. Consider the arguments of philosopher Emil Fackenheim: "The authentic Jew of today is forbidden to hand Hitler yet another, posthumous 'victory' by failing to survive as a Jew." Fackenheim refers to this as the 614th commandment – "the commanding voice of Auschwitz." He argued, "the authentic Jewish agnostic and the authentic Jewish believer are closer today than any previous time."

While the root of what makes us a people will certainly be debated in perpetuity, the majority of Jews, and gentiles, have unquestionably accepted our status as a unique people. This peoplehood label has often led to conceptions of oneness and equivalency among world Jewry.

The conception of Jews as a single, unified people emerged with fiery conviction and ubiquity in the immediate aftermath of the Holocaust. Jews were considered to be a singular nation in Diaspora; it did not matter that we were separated by thousands of miles, by oceans, by languages, and by culture; we were one people. This was also what made the land of Israel so important–the promise of a country where Jews could gather, live, and become a unified people with the same language, culture, religious practices, and identity. However, this idea of oneness seems to be just that, an idea, or more precisely, an aspiration for unity in a time of constitutional turmoil.

Rabbi Jonathan Sacks writes about the subject thusly:

> Jewish Unity: The phrase is deceptively simple. It is easier to invoke than to understand, and is beset by irony. The idea that Jews are "one people" has emerged as a, perhaps the, dominant motif of post-Holocaust Jewish reflection. It is a constant presence in the public rhetoric of contemporary Jewry. It evokes passion and conviction, but seldom clarity. Set against the reality it seeks to describe, it is an aspiration, not an achievement; a myth rather than a reality. Not since the first and second centuries CE have Jews been less united. Rarely has it been harder to state what constitutes them as "one people." That, in itself, should not surprise us, because demands for unity surface only at times of great internal conflict (Preface to *One People?*)

Today, we may be inclined to perceive ourselves as part of one people due to a shared language, a shared history, a shared tradition, a shared land, shared values, or for other commonalities, but it is not our membership in a peoplehood that unites us. It is the values we cherish that unite us (as *am kadosh*) not some inexplicable tribal-bonding affiliation. When we prioritize our mere existence – our survival over our values – we depreciate that very existence, we make our survival less significant. I encourage our unity to be based on *halakhah*, common values of justice, ethical responsibility, truth, and peace, not a singular conception of national peoplehood. We must not only survive as a people but also thrive as a people. To do that, we must redirect our orientation beyond ourselves toward the other, the realm of ideas, and back into the dream.

Jewish Law: Society And Relationships

1

To Bet or Not to Bet: Jewish Concerns with Gambling and the Lottery

Judaism presents us with a rationalist tradition that embraces free will, critical thinking, and the importance of the intellect. Most endeavors that mandate irrational and overly chancy behavior are forbidden by the Jewish tradition. Gambling is one of the prevalent modern activities that may make for fun sport in moderation, but when treated as a primary source of income it borders on the irrational.

The rabbis taught that a gambler cannot be considered a valid legal witness (*Sanhedrin* 24b-25a) and that his gambling is either considered theft or as a lack of commitment to doing real work. The Rambam teaches that even those types of gambling that do not create great harm and are not strictly forbidden by law should be avoided because they produce no benefit to society and is a waste of time (*Hilchot Gezeilah v'Aveida 6:1*).

I recently made the case against gambling and I also made the case for why we should not rely upon "signs" to make life decisions. But the problem today continues to get worse. Consider these numbers from the National Council on Problem Gambling:

- About 50 million people around the world participate in online gambling at least once a month, and 6 to 9 million Americans have had a gambling problem at some point in their lives.

- Addicts typically have a gambling debt twice their yearly income.

- More than 313,000 people called the National Council on Problem Gambling's hotline number last year, the highest yearly number on record.

- When problem gamblers finally seek help or treatment, three quarters have already committed embezzlement or other types of fraud to finance their habit, and almost half have attempted or seriously contemplated suicide.

Research also appears to show a correlation between the degree of gambling addiction and tobacco use and nicotine dependency, illustrating a relationship between different kinds of addiction.

Gambling in the United States has traditionally been an illegal activity, and criminal organizations have earned a great deal of money from it, especially after the period of Prohibition ended. However, spurred by organized crime in the second half of the last century, gambling casinos began to proliferate, especially in Las Vegas, which is still the casino capital of America. In spite of the continuing economic stagnation of the past few years, in 2012 the major casinos on the Las Vegas strip had a gross income exceeding $6.2 billion.

The legal gambling industry exploded in the last twenty-five years, increasing in value from $17 billion in 1974 to $482 billion in 1994. By the end of the century, gambling was taking in more money than the film, cruise ship, recording music, amusement park, and spectator sport industries combined. Today, gambling interests contribute heavily to state political candidates (most regulation of the industry takes place at the state level), further expanding their influence. In the meantime, organized crime has migrated from the open involvement in casinos to Internet gambling, where they have set up foreign websites to preserve the inflow of gambling revenue. In the futile pursuit of easy money, nearly twenty percent of pathological gamblers eventually declare bankruptcy due to their addiction.[23]

Today, the overwhelming majority of gambling revenue comes from state lotteries. In 2010, Americans spent more than $50 billion on lottery tickets. The titan of lotteries is the Powerball game, played in forty-three states, the District of Columbia, and the Virgin Islands. When the jackpot grows to hundreds of millions of dollars, the media flock to publicize the story, filling people's minds with the prospect of winning more money than an ancient king. However, in addition to the jackpot being slightly more than half the jackpot listed (for example, $230 million is the cash the winner would take home from an announced $400 million jackpot), the odds of

---

[23] http://www.ncbi.nlm.nih.gov/pmc/articles/PMC2824911/

winning the Grand Prize in the Powerball game are 1 in 175,223,510; there are few things you can name that a player has less of a chance of winning than Powerball. The government plays off the dreams of the poor by furthering impoverishing the vulnerable when they consistently purchase lottery tickets. *The Week* reported, "Americans spent 50.4 billion on state lottery tickets and video kiosks in 2009. Households with take-home incomes of less than $13,000 spent on average of $645 a year on lottery tickets – about 9 percent of their income. Eleven states raise more from lotteries than from corporate taxes." Some have shown how the government preys upon the vulnerable poor with the lottery and how the lottery is really another form of regressive tax.

Valuing hard work and not relying on luck is ingrained in the Jewish tradition. In fact, the rabbis stipulate that people may not rely upon miracles but must operate in the rational world, working hard to achieve results. The gambling industry is not one that we should seek to support (beyond perhaps moderate occasional sports gambling for those who find rare, controlled, and modest enjoyment in it). In a time when many in our community have been blessed with financial resources, we should make sure to use those resources to take care of our families and communities. To throw it away irrationally is to reject many Jewish values, and to engender a deeply unhealthy habit.

The Torah mandates "You shall be holy," (Leviticus 19:2) and that we must affect society for the good. We must work to remove the potency of this negative force that pulls many below ground (financially and emotionally). The power and corruption of the gambling industry must be exposed and we must educate others to value work, healthy forms of leisure, and to trust in rational approaches to improving their lots.

2

Adultery and Marriage: A Jewish Approach to Monogamy

It is well known that one of the Ten Commandments is the prohibition of adultery. Extramarital sex has historically been a man's game, since the male sexual desire is stereotypically assumed to be nigh uncontrollable. A recent survey by the National Opinion Research Center has shown, however, that the number of married American women having adulterous affairs has nearly doubled over the last decade. Today, 21 percent of men admit to having such affairs while 14.7 percent of women now admit to having them.

Sociologists explain that women today are more willing to cheat since they have stronger careers and are not as worried about the financial loss they would incur in a divorce. A recent Pew Research Center poll showing that working mothers are now the primary "breadwinners" in 37 percent of American homes (up from 11 percent in 1960) seems to bear this out, as these numbers roughly match the proportion of men and women having affairs. Most of these breadwinning women are single mothers, but 40 percent of them are married and earn more than their husbands. Perhaps it is true that when women began to enter the workforce in greater numbers and rise in the corporate world, they learned from and now emulate corporate male behavior.

In *What Do Women Want?*, Daniel Bergner noted that women may be no different from men in their struggle with monogamy and desires for sexual novelty, although there may be differences depending on the situation. For example, research on rhesus monkeys demonstrated that males initiated sexual relations when the monkeys were kept in smaller cages, but in larger spaces the females initiated sexual relations. Significantly, this and other findings have occurred at the same time that the number of women in scientific research has soared. We hope that science has passed the era when scientists could claim that women suffered from "hysteria" (based on the Greek term for uterus), irrational behavior supposedly caused by disturbances in the uterus.

One might think that monogamy was considered to be against the norms of evolution, since a male biologically wants to have as many offspring as possible. Analysis of various animals living with their brood show that anywhere from 10 percent to 70 percent of their offspring have a father different from the male animal currently staying with the brood. Professor David P. Barash of the University of Washington famously quipped, "Infants have their infancy; adults, adultery." Even among primates (which include humans), more than two hundred species are not monogamous. However, British scientists have found that in the three species of primates in which monogamy evolved, it did so after a period where males had earlier committed infanticide. In reaction, fathers began to remain by their children and mothers to protect them from rival males, thus establishing the monogamous nuclear family. The virtual universality of this system among humans, and its staying power across civilizations, argues for its value.

Even among other species from beetles to baboons, while exogamous sex occurs, one mate will often react with a ferocious jealousy if it observes the other straying. Promiscuity may be necessary among some species for survival, but that does not mean that these creatures like it.

Marriage is one formal marker and arrangement for monogamy. In the Jewish tradition, marriage is a central institution, and Rabbi Joseph B. Soloveitchik wrote about this unique commitment:

> On the one hand, the great covenant [of marriage] has been compared by the prophets time and again to the betrothal of Israel to God; on the other hand, the ordinary betrothal of woman to man has been raised to the level of covenantal commitment. Marriage as such is called *berit*, a covenant. Apparently, the Bible thinks that the redeeming power of marriage consists in personalizing the sexual experience, in having two strangers, both endowed with equal dignity and worth, meet. And the objective medium of attaining that meeting is the assumption of covenantal obligations, which are based upon the principle of equality. Hence, we have a clue to the understanding of the nature of matrimony. All we have to do is analyze the unique aspects of covenantal commitment and apply them to the matrimonial commitment (*Family Redeemed*, 41-42).

Knowing how hard it is to find the perfect partner, the Rabbis taught: "It is [as] difficult [for God] to match up [a man and a woman for marriage] as it is to split the sea (*Sotah* 2a)." Elsewhere in the Talmud, the rabbis debate whether the primary (and primal) goal of marriage is to produce offspring or about the marriage itself:

> Rav Nachman said in the name of R. Shmuel that even though a man has many children, he may not remain without a wife, as it says: "It is not good that man be alone." But others say that if he does have children then he may abstain from procreation and he may even abstain from taking a wife altogether (*Yevamot* 61b).

But even those who subscribe to the latter position, that it is not obligatory to get married, must agree that it's still desirable and good (i.e., not legally required but clearly very good and important) to marry. Rav Soloveitchik further explains:

> Within the frame of reference of marriage, love becomes not an instinctual reaction of an excited heart to the shocking sudden encounter with beauty, but an intentional experience in reply to a metaphysical ethical summons, a response to the great challenge, replete with ethical motifs. Love, emerging from an existential moral awareness, is sustained not by the flame of passion, but by the strength of a Divine norm whose repetitious fulfillment re-awakens its vigor and force. The marriage partners, by imitating God who created a world in order to be concerned with and care for it, extend the frontiers for their communal living to their offspring, and by questing to love someone who is yet unborn, defy the power of erotic change and flux. The ethical yearning to create and share existence with someone as yet unknown redeems *hedone* by infusing it with axiological normative meaning and thus gives it a new aspect — that of faith. Since our eternal faith in God is something, which defies rationalization, the mutual temporal faith of man and woman united in matrimony is just as paradoxical. History does not warrant our unswerving religious faith; likewise, utilitarian psychology denies the element of faith in the marriage institution (*Family Redeemed*, 42).

No one claims that creating a strong societal commitment to loyal monogamy will be easy. Humanity as a whole is still struggling to actualize this value commitment. We know from psychological studies that young people often have cognitive skills that are still evolving, and it is difficult to tell whether two people can grow compatibly over decades. The choice of a partner is a serious matter. Honest and loving marriage is central to the Jewish faith. We must do all we can to collaboratively preserve the holy covenant that strengthens our families and societies.

We must protect our own marriages and the institution of marriage. Adultery, as one of the many causes of failed marriages, must be rejected through ethical conviction and spiritual commitment. We must all have personal moral accountability, legitimate caring for our spouses and children, and Jewish commitment to the pledge of monogamy and shared covenant of love and devotion.

3.)

Drinking and Driving: Raising the Bar?

The National Transportation Safety Board (NTSB) recently suggested lowering the legal threshold assessing drunk driving – the blood-alcohol content (BAC) level – from the current level of 0.08 to 0.05. A 160-lb. man can reach that level of 0.05 with two beers or a single martini; a 120-lb. woman can reach that level with one glass of wine. With current regulation, drunken driving accounts for around ten thousand accidents a year in the United States. The hope is that lowering the legal limit will prevent even more of these tragic deaths; one study shows that this move can save more than five hundred lives a year.

Yet even with a BAC of 0.05, it is shown that one is still 38 percent more likely to get into a car crash. And some show that one's driving skills are impaired with a BAC as low as 0.01 percent.

Before the legal BAC was lowered to its current level, alcohol-related deaths accounted for 48 percent of all highway fatalities. In 1980, when alcohol-related highway deaths reached 20,000, the standard state BAC was 0.15. Over the next two decades, by 2004, all states lowered the legal limit to a BAC of 0.08, thanks in large part to Mothers Against Drunk Driving and other grassroots organizations. By 2011, the number of alcohol-related highway deaths had fallen by more than 50 percent. If the NTSB succeeds in lowering the BAC to 0.05 in every state, the United States will join more than a hundred nations that already have this BAC level or lower. Even with this impetus, it took federal legislation to ensure that every state lowered the BAC. In 2000, President Clinton signed legislation that withheld state highway construction funds from states that did not lower their BAC levels to 0.08. This economic persuasion worked, and all states soon complied. It would be helpful if our current Congress dragging its feet on creating all issues changed its ways and spurred this reform through similar legislation, which would almost certainly be signed by President Obama. Even with these advances, drunk driving remains a serious problem. It is estimated that each year, police stop about four million drivers in America, but half manage to avoid arrest. Attempts to get drunk drivers to use interlock devices and other methods to monitor their drunk driving have met with minimal success. Relying upon a "designated driver" is not always the solution: University of Florida researchers found that 40 percent of those designated as the drivers had also been drinking, with half of those having levels that impaired their driving.

Jewish law mandates that we take extreme measures for *pikuach nefesh* (the saving of life). The simple solution of drinking less, relying upon a trustworthy designated driver, or of paying for a cab or car service is not too difficult to do and it saves life. I have made the case that it is forbidden by Jewish law to text while driving and this is of course all the more so with drinking. In the meantime, the government should continue to regulate BAC levels, even if it means a few more DUIs need to be issued, frustrating those who think they "can hold their liquor."

Significantly, the NTSB recommendation for a lower BAC coincided with the twenty-fifth anniversary of the worst drunk driving accident in history, when a man drove his pickup truck the wrong way on an interstate road in Carrollton, Kentucky, and hit a school bus at high speed, killing twenty-seven people (mostly children) and wounding thirty. This is a dramatic, compelling example that we must be as strict as possible with drunk drivers. Jewish law and our conscience demand action.

4

Are Watches Forbidden? When *Halakhic* Prohibitions Go Too Far

In 2012, eighty-five-year-old Ultra-Orthodox *posek* Rabbi Chaim Kanievsky ordered his followers to burn their iPhones. According to Rabbi Kanievsky (indeed many Haredi rabbis), the outside world, especially the Internet, must be kept out of consciousness, and anyone who has a cell phone with Internet and video capabilities should be shunned. Not only did he forbid owning one, on grounds that a Jew cannot sell weapons (which iPhones are) to a non-Jew, he also forbade owners from selling it – instead one must "burn it!"

Rabbi Kanievsky is undoubtedly a tremendous Torah scholar in his own right, and his rabbinic pedigree is illustrious: His father, Rabbi Yaakov Yisrael Kanievsky (the Steipler), and his uncle, Rabbi Avraham Yeshayahu Karelitz (the Chazon Ish), are counted among the most respected and influential Haredi figures of the last century. He is revered within the Haredi community, receiving thousands of visitors in Bnei Brak, offering advice and blessings. He has also published many books and rulings in Talmud and Jewish law.[24] His recently promulgated position, however, that a wristwatch is *beged isha* (a woman's garment and therefore biblically prohibited for men) raises concerns. Tangentially, some ultra-Orthodox authorities have also argued that women cannot serve in the army because a gun is a *"beged ish"* (man's garment), and that a woman may not touch a weapon in the presence of a man. Every rabbi has the right to his own rulings and every observant Jew has the option to follow whichever rabbi they want, but the community must be cautioned. Two concerns emerge here regarding the watch ruling.

Firstly, men and women are mostly the same. As human beings, we share much more in common than the minor differences that separate us. For example, men and women have the same hormones; while there are certain differences in levels, the endocrine system operates in nearly the same way for both sexes. In addition, the brains of men and women are far more similar than different.

---

[24] https://www.rabbimeirbaalhaneis.com/Rabbi%20Chaim%20Kanievsky.asp

The prohibition of *beged isha* sought rightfully to remind us that there are some boundaries to help maintain our distinct gender identities. Nevertheless, we need not strengthen or expand these categories to further divide the sexes, particularly when history shows that women suffer considerably more than men when we divide society along these lines.

Secondly, a rejection of the wristwatch seems like a rejection of something fundamental to the modern human condition. Let me explain: to be a part of the world, one attends meetings, drops children at school, fulfills time commitments, etc. To reject the wristwatch, a primary tool for keeping a schedule, is in a sense to reject this world altogether. Historically and ironically, watch-making owes its existence to a religious prohibition. In 1541 in Geneva, the Protestant leader John Calvin banned the wearing of all jewelry. In order to maintain a living, the skilled jewelers of the city turned to making clocks, at first long clocks (later given the name "grandfather" clocks) and smaller table clocks. From this period until the last century, the pocket watch steadily became more popular. One of the first wristwatches was made in 1812 for the Queen of Naples, and within a century, by the end of World War I, the wristwatch became dominant as synchronized military timing required soldiers to wear the less cumbersome wearable clock. Since then, countless men have worn wristwatches while performing historic achievements, including Charles Lindbergh, who wore one during his transatlantic flight from New York to Paris in 1927, and Neil Armstrong, who wore one during the first landing on the moon. Among American Presidents, Franklin D. Roosevelt may have been the first to wear a wristwatch regularly. Even Israel's current Prime Minister, Benjamin Netanyahu, wore a wristwatch when he spoke at the United Nations in November 2012.

The final irony about this series or rulings by Rabbi Kanievsky is that the one device that may make the wristwatch obsolete is the cell phone, one of whose functions is to tell time. Some technology companies have been known to disqualify potential hires because they wore a watch instead of using their cell phones to check the time. To burn a device that would require men to wear the also-proscribed wristwatch presents a peculiar dilemma.

The great power of religion is the capacity to transform our world, not to escape from it and ourselves. Forbidding things that should not be forbidden not only hurts the followers who dedicate their lives to being the best observant Jews they can be, but hurts Judaism itself.

5

Bangladesh: We Must Prevent Future Industrial Disasters

In late 2013, over seven hundred Bangladeshis[25] tragically perished in the collapse of a building housing several garment factories. It appeared that the owners of the Rana Plaza factory building illegally added three floors to the structure and installed generators and machines that caused the vibrations that led to the structural collapse. While this is the highest death toll in a single garment factory, the death of workers in this region is not uncommon, as hundreds of Bangladeshi garment workers, women and men, have been badly burnt, suffocated or crushed to death.

In a country responsible for around $18 billion in clothing exports each year, there are more than 3.5 million Bangladeshi workers – 80 percent of them women – who toil in clothing factories. While the minimum wage is the equivalent of only $37 a month, this is much better than what farmers and maids in this region are making. Thus, many are forced to choose between starvation wages and working in factories that are little more than death traps.

Americans have seen this before. On March 25, 1911, a fire at the Triangle Shirtwaist Company in New York caused the deaths of 146 workers, mostly young Jewish immigrant girls. The employees, especially those on the ninth floor faced terrifying, shameful safety conditions like a locked door, a rickety back fire escape (which collapsed), and the choice of leaping to their deaths or burning to death inside the factory. At one of the memorial services, labor leader Rose Schneiderman compared the workers' conditions to a torture chamber of the Inquisition:

---

[25]   http://www.nytimes.com/2013/05/08/world/asia/bangladesh-death-toll-in-collapse-of-garment-factories-passes-700.html?src=rechp&_r=1&

...the thumbscrews are the high-powered and
swift machinery close to which we must work,
and the rack is here in the firetrap structures
that will destroy us the minute they catch
fire... Every week I must learn of the untimely
death of one of my sister workers. Every year
thousands of us are maimed. The life of men
and women is so cheap and property is so
sacred!

Incredibly, in 1911 the Triangle factory owners were
acquitted of wrongdoing and made a $60,000 profit from their
insurance payout in contrast to the meager amount they paid to the
families of the victims.[26] The public outcry eventually led to
legislation that achieved vast improvements in workers' conditions
and factory safety. Fast-forward and the owners of the Bangladesh
factory may face the death penalty for what they have done. We
shall see whether this tragedy leads to improvements in conditions
for the millions of garment workers in Bangladesh and other nations.

A commitment to safety can have dramatic results. The
American workplace has improved tremendously since the late
nineteenth and early twentieth century, when thousands were
maimed and killed on the railroads and up to two thousand miners
died every year. Since 1970, the federal government (through
Occupational Safety and Health Administration) has helped bring
the number of worker fatalities and injury rate down by about two-
thirds. Nevertheless, in 2011 more than 4,600 Americans died in
accidents in the workplace, and about 4 percent of workers still
sustain an injury or contract an illness while on the job.

Some companies have pledged to offer some compensation to
families who have lost loved ones, and others that do business in
Bangladesh have begun to talk about how to improve factory safety.
Even with the laudable increase in expressed concern over this issue,
there has not been enough action. As western companies are now
buying more and more goods produced by Bangladeshi factories, we
consumers must be more proactive in urging better conditions.
Major American clothes outlets (Gap, H&M, Wal-Mart, etc.) buy

---

[26] http://www.dol.gov/shirtwaist/aftermath.htm

their garments from Bangladesh, and we must urge them to demand better health and safety conditions for workers. We must take our national experience and act to avoid future disasters around the world.

We cannot imagine that our religious lives are separate from our consumer lives. Many today think that religion can be relegated to occasional prayer experiences or at most to local acts of good will. Scottish philosopher Alasdair MacIntyre described this phenomenon more elaborately:

> Any contemporary attempt to envisage a human life as a whole, as a unity ... encounters two different obstacles... The social obstacles derive from the way in which modernity partitions each human life into a variety of segments, each with its own norms and modes of behavior. So work is divided from leisure, private life from public, the corporate from the personal... The philosophical obstacles derive from . . . the tendency to think atomistically about human action and to analyze complex actions and transactions in terms of simple components...[as well as the tendency to make a] sharp separation ... between the individual and the roles that he or she plays."
> (*After Virtue*, 204).

We know from rabbinic sources, for example, that the consumer is held accountable for wrongs done by the producer. If there were no buyer there would be no producer and thus no wrong done (*Kiddushin* 56b). Today we all wear clothing made in developing countries by workers under very trying and often less than humane circumstances. Each day as we make the morning blessings of *malbish arumim* and *ozer Yisrael bi'gvura* when we are getting dressed (*Brachot* 60b), we should consider how we could improve conditions for global workers producing our clothing. Just as a century ago we mourned "our own" that perished and acted to prevent future tragedies, so today we should act to prevent these disasters throughout the world. Let's make the events in Bangladesh as a teachable moment to not allow the world to forget tragedy before essential safety measures are put into place.

6

After the Postville Immigration Raid: Revisiting Immigration Reform

It feels like yesterday that Rabbi Ari Hart and I were in Postville, Iowa speaking with workers to learn about their suffering and to offer our solidarity. The tears and pain of the immigrant women and children we encountered will always be with me. But now it has been years since the kosher scandal and the immigration raid shook the Jewish community and the world. What has changed since then?

On May 12, 2008, the largest immigration raid in American history took place, with 389 workers from the Agriprocessors slaughterhouse and meat packaging plant in Postville, Iowa being arrested. The U.S. Immigration and Customs Enforcement (ICE) officials raided the plant (the main producer of kosher meat in the United States), handcuffed hundreds of immigrants, and bused them to the National Cattle Congress in Waterloo, Iowa. Most of the detainees were charged with identity theft and were sent to prisons all over the country where they spent five months before being deported out of the country. Postville was severely damaged and hundreds of lives were torn apart. Immigration raids were incredibly destructive to all.

The town of Postville was destroyed,[27] with 20 percent of its population detained and hundreds of families torn apart. Half the population left within months, stores and restaurants formerly owned by Mexican immigrants closed, and business in many other places also dropped by 50 percent. Ironically, among the few allowed to stay and work were women who had filed sexual harassment charges at the plant, who stayed to be witnesses and were then given U-visas, as they were victims of crime within the United States.

The aftermath exposed several myths about undocumented residents, such as that they are criminals or are taking jobs away from Americans. The military-style raid was an extreme

---

[27] http://news.yahoo.com/blogs/lookout/years-immigration-raid-iowa-town-feels-poorer-less-133035414.html

overreaction to the situation: the workers offered no resistance, and American citizens did not flock to fill the open jobs. Instead, the owners had to import workers from locales as diverse and remote as Palau (since its workers can work here legally) and Somalia (undocumented alien refugees). Unfortunately, even Hispanics who have United States citizenship find it difficult to work in this field, as plant owners are afraid of further raids. Low wages, long hours, and a high accident rate make the jobs unpalatable to most Americans. The pay may be slightly higher than before, but it is still very low and, because the plant is non-unionized, workers are not able to band together to negotiate protections for themselves.

What is true is that immigrants contribute a great deal more to our nation than they receive. A 2006 analysis by the non-partisan Congressional Budget Office concluded that a Senate bill promoting immigration reform (similar to current proposals) could raise gross domestic product (GDP) from between 0.8 percent to 1.3 percent from 2012-2016, for an estimated $134 billion a year. In this tight economy, who would not want to implement a policy that could appreciably improve the GDP?

On the other hand, we need not resort to theory to show the beneficial effect of immigration on the economy. A 2012 report titled *Open for Business: How Immigrants Are Driving Business Creation in the United States* by the Partnership for a New American Economy,[28] noted that immigrants now start new businesses at more than double the rate of native-born Americans. Other highlights of the report include:

- Ten percent of American workers are now employed in companies owned by immigrants

- During the past decade, immigrant business income has grown at more than four times the rate of native-owned business income

Immigrants now start more than a quarter of all businesses in seven of the eight sectors of the U.S. economy that are expected to grow the most over the next decade

---

[28] http://www.renewoureconomy.org/sites/all/themes/pnae/openforbusiness.pdf

Immigrants and their children are also very important in large American corporations, and are an integral part of the Fortune 500:

- Immigrants founded ninety of these companies, and their children founded 114, for a total of 40 percent of all Fortune 500 companies
- If these companies comprised a country, their combined revenues would qualify as the fourth largest in GDP
- Seven of the ten most valuable brands (including Apple and Google) were founded by immigrants or their children.

Today, many of our immigrant workers come from Latin America, Asia, and Africa. This was not always the case. More than a century ago, Upton Sinclair's 1906 novel *The Jungle* described an America where nearly all meatpacking industry workers were European immigrants. In this searing indictment of the ill-treatment of immigrant slaughterhouse workers in Chicago, a Lithuanian family headed by Jurgis Rudkus faces exploitative employers, hazardous work environments for adults and children, miserable housing conditions, and hostility from the authorities. Unfortunately, the American public took interest mostly in the unsanitary conditions of the meat packing factories; ironically, the novel helped spur the first generation of laws ensuring more healthful food and drug processing, but did not immediately improve the lives of immigrant workers. Only during the New Deal did factory workers throughout America unionize and improve their condition, thus achieving the American Dream for many immigrants and their children, who were able to enter and strengthen the growing middle class.

Today, long hours, low pay, high injury rates, and exploitation of child labor are still problems facing undocumented aliens in the meat processing and other industries. We can give in to hatred and ignorance by regarding them as enemies and criminals, or we can understand how valuable immigrants have always been to our society and welcome them. At this time of Pesach, as we remember the days of our slavery in the land of Egypt, we should especially remember the command: "You shall not wrong a stranger or oppress him, for you were strangers in the land of Egypt" (Exodus 22:20).

More than half a decade ago, Uri L'Tzedek launched a national boycott against Agriprocessors after all of the abuses emerged since it is against Jewish law to buy products that were produced against the mandates of Jewish law. Around two thousand rabbis and Jewish leaders signed on to the boycott within the first two weeks. After company representatives met with us and agreed to our demands for ethical and legal transparency, we called off the boycott. Since then, the ethical *kashrut* movement has blossomed with tens of thousands of followers but we have a long way to go still. The damage done to the reputation of the kosher industry has been immense and we are yet to take full responsibility for the conduct within the industry. The Tav HaYosher has been one serious response to ethical abuses (worker injustices) in *kashrut* but segments of the Orthodox community still reject the problem and deny our collective responsibility. Much more needs to be done. We must continue to call for immigration reform and stand in solidarity with all workers and immigrants that encounter abuse.

7

Russian Jews, Women Of The Wall, and *Zera Yisrael*: The Jewish People Consists of More than Just *Halakhic* Jews

The typical discourse in the Orthodox community suggests that the world consists of a dichotomy between the "Jews" and the "Non-Jews." Most of the time this makes sense, but at other times it inevitably leads toward unnecessary exclusion. Instead, I'd like to propose that there are three categories: Non-Jews, Halakhic Jew, and Members of the Jewish people.

The Kedushat Levi, Rav Levi Yitzchak of Berditchev, taught that the Jewish People who left Egypt (*Am Yisrael*) consisted of Jacob's descendants (*Bnei Yisrael*) and the other people who joined as part of the *Am* (*erev rav*) (*Balak* 300). Even though this was a pre-Sinaitic reality, this teaches that non-Jews who join Jews in their identity and mission are also part of the Jewish people; the Kiddush is another reminder that Shabbat is also for non-Jews, because, at times, they are part of the nation.

In the United States, undocumented residents are not considered legal, official residents of our country. But at the same time, they are American in a deep way: they live, learn, serve, work, and socialize in America, becoming an integral part of the fabric of America. That they do not have full legal status does not deny their identity as Americans. No person is "illegal," as our own historical experience teaches us. The Kabbalah already teaches a category called *Zera Yisrael*, Jews of patrilineal descent who are not legal Jews but have the sparks of Jewishness in them. Another idea holds that all proselytes were destined to convert, since they were Jewish souls trapped in non-Jewish bodies.

Rav Azriel Hildesheimer gave an interesting ruling about whether or not boys with non-Jewish mothers and Jewish fathers should be circumcised:

> And I would also like to point out that these children who
> have Jewish fathers, even though they are not Jewish
> according to *halakha*, we still see that they are called
> "sacred children." For Ezra rebuked Jewish men who
> intermarried because they were spreading "sacred
> children" amongst the nations… And in our case,
> [circumcising this son] would not only open up the door
> for him to become Jewish, it would also make it easier for
> the father to do *teshuva*…And even if the father doesn't do
> *teshuva*, nevertheless he is right in trying to strengthen his
> children's Jewish identity and when they grow up it will be
> easier for them to convert because they will know that it is
> in accordance with their father's wishes. And some of these
> children might end up being Jewish leaders for the rose
> blossoms out of the thorns" (Responsa, *Yoreh Deah* 229).

While, according to Jewish law, Jews by patrilineal descent are not considered "*halakhic* Jews" they are still, on a mystical level, deeply connected to the Jewish people and should be brought closer. Further, in the Orthodox community, it is common not to count a Jew who has undergone a non-Orthodox conversion in a *minyan*, in line with established *halakhic* principles, but exclusions that are not mandated by *halakhah* must be reconsidered.

Today in Israel, the struggle between exclusion versus inclusion continues to rage. For example, while founded primarily by secular Jewish leaders, Israel does not allow the performance of civil marriages, only Orthodox marriages. Those who cannot prove they have Jewish conversion or parentage by Orthodox standards cannot be married in Israel. Thus, many Israelis go to Cyprus to marry, after which this foreign "civil" marriage is recognized in Israel. This is complicated further by the Law of Return, which states that anyone with a Jewish grandparent is entitled to immigrate to Israel and be granted citizenship. This has saved many from persecution, particularly the approximately million Jews who emigrated from the former Soviet Union. Ironically, about a third of these Jews are not considered to be Jews under current Israeli standards and cannot be married, in spite of serving in the Israel Defense Forces and being (politically active) Israeli citizens. This anecdote[29] explains the issue:

> "Alex Kalmikov's family, which lives in Holon, came
> to Israel out of Zionist beliefs. Even so, as a Russian,
> he 'was beaten and spit on' in school. For Michael
> Yoshpa, that's not unique. 'Kids always pick on each
> other,' he said. But even by the time Kalmikov entered
> service in an elite army program, one woman still
> called him a 'stinky Russian.'" Lily Galili, a journalist
> and immigration expert, said of Russian Jews in Israel:
> "They feel Jewish. They were raised Jewish. They
> have Jewish names. They once suffered for being
> Jewish in the Soviet Union. Now they suffer for being
> Russians in Israel."

Even if one is not a Jew according to the standards of *halakhah*, they may still be Jewish in their social identity and that should be accepted and respected. As the Kedushat Levi taught, *Am Yisrael* (the broader nation) is greater in number than *Bnei Yisrael* (those who are Jewish according to *halakhah*). Non-*halakhic* Jews are also part of the holy nation (a "social Jew" rather than a "legal Jew")

American Jews, more than two-thirds of whom are Reform or Conservative, live in a country where there is no established religion. Many also have had female rabbis for decades, and often feel friction from Orthodox control of religious practices in Israel. For twenty-five years, the Women of the Wall sought to pray alongside men at the Kotel in Jerusalem. This enduring symbol of Judaism, which many associate with the iconic photograph of Israeli soldiers standing in awe before the Kotel after its liberation in 1967, has more recently seemed to be a symbol of religious strife. The women, carrying the Torah[30], singing, and wearing of *kippot* and *tallitot* deeply offended the ultra-Orthodox men (and some women) who prayed there, were spat upon, beaten, had bags of excrement thrown at them, and arrested. In a 2010 incident, for example, a group of Haredi men yelled "Nazi!" and "You caused the Holocaust!" at the women. Fortunately, after increased world

---

[29] http://www.algemeiner.com/2012/03/13/russias-jews-rebuild-communities-after-exodus/

[30] http://womenofthewall.org.il/about/history/

attention (including petition campaigns by American Jewish groups), it appears that a solution achieved through negotiations with the government has been found, and the recent instances of women praying at the Kotel did not result in arrests or beatings, although some bystanders spat on the women.

One of their WOW petitions to the government says: "Sadly, however, in Jerusalem, a woman can be verbally assaulted, physically assaulted, arrested and treated as a criminal for wearing a *tallit* or holding a Torah Scroll or reading from a Torah Scroll at the Kotel and its surrounding areas."

We must be careful not to alienate those who believe themselves to be part of the Jewish people by claiming that they are not Jewish (and not Jewish like us). Even if they do not fit into our legal standards and are not included in certain ritual acts for technical reasons, they can still be viewed as Jews and as a holy and essential part of the Jewish people to be loved, cherished, and brought closer. It is true that embracing this reality makes it more difficult for *halakhic* Jews in some ways, but it is no longer an option to impose a pre-modern form of government on a modern nation-state. Today, the only option is to create an open, tolerant, and pluralistic society. We must not fear losing our religious values and culture. Truth can and must prevail within an open marketplace of ideas and others' self-identities must be valued as we strive to see the dignity in all people.

8

A Growing Divide: The Ultra-Orthodox In The Army and Workplace

As one who has lived and learned among the Ultra-Orthodox, I have a great respect and affinity for the community. I feel, as a religious Jew, that I stand in solidarity with this community in the absolute commitment to Torah and Torah values. With every love, however, comes concerns and I am not alone in being deeply worried about Ultra-Orthodox spiritual intemperance, isolation, and, unfortunately, poverty.

The pinnacle achievement for an Ultra-Orthodox Jewish man is to learn Torah full-time in Kollel. In Israel, the growth in the number of these institutions has made this possible, but it has also created a host of growing problems: overburdened wives and mothers, a culture of poverty (over 55 percent live below the poverty line), disappointment with unfulfilled promises, a lack of integration into and widening divide with Israeli society, and growing resentment from the rest of the country. The growing divide between the extreme religious and frustrated secular camps is perpetuating a very unhealthy national culture.

Many in the Ultra-Orthodox do not serve in the Israeli army, out of a belief that the military is a secular (i.e. not Torah-true) entity and that dedicated, full-time Torah study, rather than military power, is what ultimately protects the Jewish people. When Israel was founded, David Ben-Gurion helped secure the support of Ultra-Orthodox eastern European rabbis by exempting about four hundred Ultra-Orthodox students from military service,[31] under the Torato Omanuto arrangement, so they could study the Torah and Talmud on a full-time basis. Israel's leadership at the time, which was composed of almost only secular people, saw the number before them and anticipated that in the future only a small number of Israelis would be engaged in full-time religious studies.

Today, however, the Ultra-Orthodox are the largest growing group in Israel, comprising 10 percent of the population, and a crisis

---

[31] http://www.jpost.com/Features/In-Thespotlight/Pressure-on-to-end-draft-exemption-for-haredim

is looming. Now 60,000 male students are exempt from military service, and estimates for the annual cost of supporting Haredim and their large families stand at three billion Euros (Israel pays stipends to yeshivas for each student and families for each child). Considering that nearly 25 percent of first graders are Ultra-Orthodox, this economic burden will greatly increase unless something is done. Even the International Monetary Fund has noted that the cost of subsidizing the Ultra-Orthodox will put a significant drag on Israeli economic growth.

Critics have noted that even during the days of the *shtetl*, most Jews worked, and only the most scholarly spent their lives in Torah study. Today, most of the Ultra-Orthodox in other countries work, and yet about 60 percent of Ultra-Orthodox men study Torah and do not (although recent data show that the percentage of married Ultra-Orthodox men who now work has risen from 31 percent to 38 percent as of 2012).

Israelis, in general, resent the Ultra-Orthodox exemption because they and their children must do military service (risking their lives), pay taxes to support the Ultra-Orthodox, and look askance as many Ultra-Orthodox try to impose their extreme social conservatism on all of Israel, attacking the Women of the Wall, trying to segregate buses by sex and harass Orthodox girls on their way to school, all while continuing to oppose the modern secular state of Israel.

This situation is starting to change. In February 2012, the High Court ruled that the Tal Law was unconstitutional. Israel's Supreme Court agreed this year, issuing a ruling overturning the military exemption of the Ultra-Orthodox and ordering the state to reform the policy.

Jews in America have also become more assertive in opposing the Ultra-Orthodox. Reform and Conservative Jews in particular have denounced some of the more aggressive efforts of the Ultra-Orthodox community to segregate society by sex and their seeming hostility to the state of Israel. In June 2013, Barbra Streisand came to Israel to accept an honorary PhD from Hebrew University. While in Israel, she sharply rebuked the Ultra-Orthodox for their treatment of women, including a reference to the American racial civil rights movement: "It's distressing to read about women in Israel being forced to sit in the back of the bus, or when we hear about 'Women of the Wall' having metal chairs thrown at them when they attempt to peacefully and legally pray." It is difficult to imagine most American Jews supporting the Ultra-Orthodox continuing their exemption from military service and receiving government funding.

For their part, some within the American Ultra-Orthodox movement have also become involved. During the summer of 2013 in Brooklyn, New York, to protest the proposed Knesset law that would draft Haredim into the Israel Defense Forces. The Satmar speakers continually urged the crowd not to show anti-Zionist signs during the rally and tried to focus solely on this bill (one printed sign spotted at the rally stated: "Orthodox Jews Will PROUDLY GO TO JAIL Rather Than Join The Zionist Army"). Yaakov Shapiro, who spoke for the Satmar community, equated the draft law with the destruction of yeshivas and the Jewish people: "Nothing else maintains the continuity of the Jewish people.... Without the yeshivas we are extinct as a people, and that's what they are trying to do." On the other hand, The Rabbinical Council of America, which represents Centrist Orthodox Jews, denounced the protest as being anti-Israel.

The Ultra-Orthodox in Israel maintain that they are the spiritual foundation of the country, and should be valued for that. They have also used their political clout to align with fragile coalitions in exchange for preserving their military exemption. The current government came to power without Ultra-Orthodox party support, but Prime Minister Benjamin Netanyahu is not known for dramatic political gestures, so it is unclear what will happen.

Some wonder if the Ultra-Orthodox can serve, since most have only had a religious education, and have no computer or other modern skills, which makes them ill-suited for military or even alternate civilian service. Fortunately, there are some outlets that may offer a solution. For example, I (along with a JFNA delegation) had the chance to visit a JDC organization in Ashdod, Israel, called Mafteach ("key"), which helps bring Haredi Jews in Israel into the army and get them trained to have the skills to be productive in the workplace. This is a much-needed program that should be expanded.

If a Jew does not want to serve in the army then they can live in the Diaspora; they cannot take state benefits yet opt out of state obligations. Further, if one has to put their children's lives at risk to protect the country, and another family is not willing, one might come to think that the Ultra-Orthodox actually believe that their lives are worth more, God forbid. In the Messianic era, the rabbis teach that Israel will have complete sovereignty and security, but until then, we must support the state in whatever ways we can (advocacy, financially, militarily, and spiritually). We cannot rely merely upon wishes and prayers to protect our nation. Torah has a crucial role to play in spiritually and morally building the country (like it hasn't had in two thousand years) and that Torah inspire courageous action and leadership. One community cannot monopolize that power of Torah; rather it must be made accessible within all of Israel to ensure national and universal transformation.

Requiring ultra-Orthodox service in the army is not only good for Israel economically and socially it's also good for Torah. The Torah was meant to be lived putting Jewish values into practice. Rabbi Yoel Bin-Nun, the former rosh yeshiva of Yeshivat Kibbutz Hadati, wrote:[32]

> In the IDF one learns to live by the Torah in all situations, even in difficult circumstances, and on Shabbat one cannot simply call one's *posek*... In the quota of those exempt from service in the army, if implemented, I would only include those whose religious commitment is weak and who may end up abandoning Torah observance during their service-as they are the ones who will not be asking the questions in Hilkhot Eiruvin. In such a scenario, the quota of exemption would become a sign of shame, and the service in the IDF a symbol of pride for the Torah world (even that which is not Zionist). This is what is correct from a Torah and *halakhic* perspective.

---

[32]   http://morethodoxy.org/2013/07/04/what-threatens-the-world-and-the-rabbinate-by-rav-yoel-bin-nun/

The Ultra-Orthodox community is rapidly growing and their poverty rate is growing too, and in the near future may comprise a quarter of all Israelis. Fortunately, Israel is nowhere near the type of internal religious conflict that exists elsewhere in the Middle East, but a deep, enduring conflict is a strong possibility. If not in the army itself, there may be other ways to serve the nation to ensure the country benefits and the Ultra-Orthodox youth can gain the workplace skills to improve their financial situation and become productive members of society. With national unity and solidarity, the Torah can illuminate the world with its fullest potential and grandeur.

9

To Dust You Shall Return: The Dignity Of Burial

After the horrific stories of burning bodies in crematoria, the thought of any burnt body haunts me.

Jewish law argues that the return of the human body to the earth should neither be slowed (mummification) nor quickened (cremation). Rather it should be a natural process of returning one to the earth that one came from (after cleaning the body, dressing it in modest shrouds, and placing it in a modest box). The human being is created in the image of God and the human body is the vessel that carries the soul in this world; it is not to be desecrated and mutilated.

Today in America, however, we seem to be moving away from the dignity of a burial. For every person who is now buried in America, four are now cremated. Even further, the human body has been turned into a spectator exhibit.

It's true that funerals and burials can be expensive, but they need not be and I have argued against the rising costs. Cremation may be a simpler and cheaper solution, but to honor the deceased we owe them better. Every human being has the right to the dignity of a proper burial and natural return to the earth. Loved ones often desire a physical reminder of their loved ones and a place to where they can direct their love, prayers, and kindness. The Talmud explains that doing kindness for and honoring the deceased is a necessary part of religious life:

> Our Sages taught: *Gemilut chasadim* (physical acts of loving kindness) are greater than *tzedakah* in three ways: Acts of *tzedakah* involve only one's money – *gemilut chasadim* can involve both money or one's personal service. *Tzedakah* can be given only to the poor – gemilut chasadim can be done both for the rich and for the poor. *Tzedakah* can be given only to the living – gemilut chasadim can be done both for the living and the dead (*Sukkah* 49b).

The Torah teaches that man came from the dust of the earth and the rabbis understood this to be an essential ethical point in the existential condition of man:

> God gathered the dust [of the first human] from the four corners of the world—red, black, white and green. Red is the blood, black is the innards and green for the body. Why from the four corners of the earth? So that if one comes from the east to the west and arrives at the end of his life as he near departing from the world, it will not be said to him, "This land is not the dust of your body, it's of mine. Go back to where you were created." Rather, every place that a person walks, from there he was created and from there he will return (*Yalkut Shimoni*, Genesis 1:13).

There are barriers to doing burials today, as they need to be less expensive and parent-child bonds need to be stronger. But for the sake of the sanctity of the body, the honor of the deceased, and the healing and moral journey of the descendants, we should encourage returning bodies modestly to the earth they came from.

10

Breastfeeding Is A Right: Nursers Unite

Laura Trickle, a mother committed to breastfeeding, was called to jury duty and brought her baby even though her request to bring the child was denied. She will now have to face the court herself. Breastfeeding women are exempted from jury duty in twelve states; it ought to be in all states. The rabbis teach that a mother should determine whether or not she should nurse and no one else, not even her husband. As it is taught:

> If she (the mother) says that she wishes to nurse her child and he (the father) says that she shall not nurse it, we listen to her (because) the suffering would be hers. What about where he says that she shall nurse (the child) and she says that she will not nurse it? Whenever (nursing by the mother) is not the practice of her family, of course, we listen to her (*Ketubot* 61a).

The rabbis even appreciated that many women may choose to nurse for an extended period of time:

> A child nurses continuously for twenty-four months. From that age onward (he is to be regarded) as one who sucks an abominable thing: these are the words of Rabbi Eliezer. And Rabbi Joshua says: (He may be breast fed) even for five years continuously (*Niddah* 2:3).

The rabbis even believe that women should be exempt from work when nursing:

> A woman is obligated to care (*tippul*) for her child for the entire twenty-four months. Whether it is her child or whether it was a child given to her to nurse, the woman who is given a child to nurse should not do work (while caring) for him and should not suckle another child with him (Ibid. 2:4).

There are solid scientific data supporting this. Breastfeeding, which is endorsed by many medical organizations such as the American Academy of Pediatrics, is obviously the preferred method of feeding for infants, as a mother's milk is far better suited to provide the proper balance of vitamins and other nutrients than other methods, and also is the best way to provide infants with resistance to harmful bacteria and viruses. The benefits for breastfeeding for the infant are many:

- Infants who are exclusively breastfed for the first six months of life are less likely to be hospitalized or be brought to a healthcare provider for care, as they have less likelihood for respiratory ailments, ear infections, or persistent diarrhea

- Breastfed babies have a reduced incidence of allergies, asthma, and incidence of sudden death infant syndrome (SIDS)

- Children who were breastfed are more likely to gain weight in a more gradual way and have higher IQ scores than children who were not breastfed

In addition, there is ongoing research to determine whether anecdotal evidence concerning whether there is a connection between breastfeeding and reduced risk for obesity, type 2 diabetes, and some types of cancer.

Mothers also benefit from breastfeeding. In addition to the bonding that occurs through the physical contact with infant children and the knowledge that breastfeeding provides the child with the best chance for a healthy life, breastfeeding helps the mother by lowering her risk for breast and ovarian cancer, assists in the lowering of weight following pregnancy, helps restore the uterus to its size before pregnancy, and saves the time and money that would otherwise be devoted to purchasing and preparing infant formula.

In spite of this evidence, mothers who attempt to breastfeed in public continue to be challenged. Consider these examples over the past ten years:

- In 2006, Emily Gillette was taken off an airliner while it was still on the ground for refusing to adequately cover herself while breastfeeding her infant child. The case was only settled for an undisclosed sum in 2012, and there is no guarantee that the airline will not repeat this behavior in the future.

- In April 2007, Jessica Mayo-Swimeley brought her 17-month son Tobin in for brain tumor surgery and then a follow-up procedure. Afterward, she stayed at a Ronald McDonald House in Houston, Texas. When she tried to breastfeed Tobin in a public area, she was told that she could only do it in her private room (in spite of a Texas law permitting breastfeeding in public areas). When she complained, she was advised to seek accommodations elsewhere. Only after the story reached the Internet and as a flood of protests did the Ronald McDonald House back off its earlier behavior.

In 2013, Laura Trickle was charged with contempt of court for reporting for jury duty with her infant son instead of arranging for other childcare arrangements. The notice sent to her read that she had "willfully and contemptuously appeared for jury service with her child and no one to care for the child." She appeared in court to challenge the citation, which entails possible jail time and up to a $500 fine. It is perverse to prevent a mother from engaging in a scientifically proven healthful practice and pay out of her own funds for childcare in order to perform jury service. Breastfeeding is healthful and not a crime. If a mother has left the workface to care for a child, she should be granted a deferral from jury duty (even if she is not nursing). We must come together to promote best health practices, support for new mothers, and stronger parental rights.

11.)

Intimidation, Alienation and Suicide: Creating Nurturing Communities Together

Suicide is prohibited in Torah (Genesis 9:5-6, *Bava Kama* 91b). One remarkable passage shows how far one sage went to preserve his life:

> The Romans found R. Hanina b. Teradion sitting and occupying himself with the Torah, publicly gathering assemblies, and keeping a scroll of the Law in his bosom. Straightaway they took hold of him, wrapped him in the Scroll of the Law, placed bundles of branches round him and set them on fire. They then brought tufts of wool, which they had soaked in water, and placed them over his heart, so that he should not expire quickly.... His students said to him, "... Open then your mouth so that the fire enter into you [and you may die quickly]." He replied, "Let Him who gave me [my soul] take it away, but no one should injure oneself" (*Avodah Zara* 18a).

According to the National Institute of Mental Health, 34,598 Americans died from suicide attempts in 2007. In 2010, it was over 38,000. Since about eleven people attempt suicide for everyone who dies, approximately 380,000 people attempted suicide that year. While it is the tenth-leading cause of death overall, it is seventh overall for men and third overall for those age 15-24 (at this age, about 5-6 times as many young boys and men commit suicide than girls/women). The incidence of suicide also surges among the elderly. We should all be on the lookout for those most likely to commit suicide:

- More than 90 percent of suicides have depression and either one or more mental disorder and/or substance abuse disorder

- Suicides have a high incidence of a family history of mental

185

- disorder, substance abuse, suicide, or violence/sexual abuse

- More than half of men committing suicide use firearms, while 40 percent of women use poison, and younger children use suffocation more

- American Indian and non-Hispanic whites are more than twice as likely to commit suicide as non-Hispanic black and Hispanic people

These factors by themselves do not predispose an individual to suicide, and other factors cannot be seen. For example, chemical changes in the brain, especially decreased levels of the neurotransmitter serotonin, also occur in those who commit suicide. It is imperative that we do not assume that people with risk factors or who were unsuccessful in a suicide attempt will not commit suicide.

Even before the modern age of scientific studies and databases, there was an understanding that those who committed suicide had suffered. Consider this passage that demonstrates the rabbinic sensitivity to this situation:

> It once happened that the son of Gordos of Lod fled from the schoolhouse and his father pointed to his ear (indicating that he would hit him on it) and he became frightened of his father and destroyed himself in a pit. They went and asked Rabbi Tarfon and he said, "We do not withhold any (burial rites) from him." .... It once happened that a young child of B'nei Brak broke a bottle on Shabbat and his father pointed to his ear (threatening to hit him on it) and the child became frightened of his father and destroyed himself in a pit. And they asked Rabbi Akiva (if the boy could have full burial rites) and he said, "We deny him nothing." From this (these two cases) the Sages said, "A person should not threaten a child with boxing of the ears, but should hit him at once or be silent and say nothing" (*Semakhot* 2:4-5).

Today we understand that physical punishment of children is not acceptable, but we see here how sensitive the rabbis were to intimidation and to those who committed suicide out of bullying.

The suicide of 12-year-old Rebecca Sedwick in Florida in September 2013[33] highlighted an alarming new trend: cyberbullying, where groups of teenagers (usually girls) bombard someone with hateful texts and other messages that literally drive the person to suicide. In this case, even the cancellation of her Facebook account and move to another school did not stop the harassment and social isolation. An examination of Facebook and search terms on Sedwick's computer revealed that many of the girls harassing Rebecca literally sent messages hoping she would die, and Rebecca began to search for information regarding the number of pills necessary to die before eventually jumping to her death from a water tower. This case illustrated the need for renewed efforts to deter bullying and keep track of our children's social media content, and also raised calls for parents to be held responsible for their minor children's cyberbullying.

Mental illness can be a form of suffering that is relative and subjective. Consider this rabbinic teaching:

> What is the measure of suffering? Rav Eleazer said: if a man had a garment woven for him to wear and it does not fit him. Rav Zeira (some say Rav Samuel b. Nachmani) demurred to this: more than this has been said. Even if he was to be served hot, and it was served cold; or cold, and it was served hot! And you require so much? Mar the son of Ravina said: even if his shirt got turned inside out. Rava (some say Rav Hisda, some say Rav Isaac, or as was taught in a Baraita) even if he put the hand into his pocket to take out three coins…he fetched only two (*Arakhin* 16b).

No one can judge for another what is truly suffering, or what small irritant will prove to be, as the saying goes, the straw that breaks the camel's back. In the history of *halakhah*, embracing suicide as something other than "hate for God" was the main entry point in

---

[33] http://www.cbsnews.com/news/12-year-olds-suicide-spotlights-cyber-bullying-threat/

to grappling with the reality of mental illness. Initially, one who committed suicide was not to be mourned for; however, there was serious transformation in the *halakhic* process, and real responsibility and empathy was cultivated in many cases for those who suffered with mental illness (*Semakhot* 2:1-3 through *Chatam Sofer* Y.D. 326). The Arukh HaShulchan (Y.D. 345) wrote:

> In regard to suicide we find whatever circumstance we can to remove the person who has apparently committed suicide from the denial of mourning rites. For example, to ascribe the act to fear or suffering or insanity or that the deceased thought that by committing suicide he was avoiding the possibility of transgressing some of the commandments of the Torah. We do this because indeed it is improbable thing that a person would commit such an ugly act with a clear mind. Go and learn from Saul the righteous one who fell on his sword in order to prevent Philistines from tormenting him. And situation similar to his is considered "under duress."

Many today are suffering and we must do all we can to act out against hate, intimidation, and suffering. We must ensure our community is safe and nurturing and never, God forbid, creating alienation or suffering. Consider for example the tragic case of Uriel de Costa. When it tragically leads to suicide, we must mourn the victim and comfort the family.

One of the best things you can do if you believe there is a risk of suicide for yourself or someone else is to call the National Suicide Prevention Lifeline, which is staffed 24 hours a day, every day. The calls are confidential, so you need not worry about repercussions in a personal or work situation. In addition, do not leave a suicidal person alone, but try to get them to a healthcare provider or the emergency department of the nearest hospital, or even call 911 if nothing else can be done. Be sure to check that there are no firearms or prescription medications accessible to the suicidal individual. We do not have to be helpless in the face of someone at risk for suicide.

12

Prescription Drugs, Bill Gates, and Global Health

Imagine you live in a small village in Africa and your child is dying of a treatable disease. It is brought to your attention that the drug used to treat your child's disease costs less than one dollar to produce but you would have to pay more than $1,000 to purchase it (an amount that is impossible for you to pay). Tragically, you watch your child die as you are consumed with grief, confusion, and resentment for global pricing structures.

Of course, pharmaceutical drugs cannot be free. Companies need incentives to conduct research and to increase research and development. Without this incentive, unfortunately, we cannot be assured that the industry would advance as quickly and effectively as we would hope, or come to have relied upon. But there must be some limit here.

A U.S. Senate Committee found that the profit margins for pharmaceutical companies were four times those of other companies. The report also showed that pharmaceutical drug price inflation was six times that of the general rate of inflation (between 1980-1992).[34]

American law has abetted the dramatic increase in prescription drug costs. Medicare Part D, an unfunded mandate passed during the Bush Administration in 2006, offered prescription drugs to Medicare beneficiaries for the first time. Under the law, however, the federal government is forbidden from negotiating drug prices with pharmaceutical companies. As a result, Americans are compelled to pay the highest prices in the world for prescription drugs. While there are measures that would change this policy, it is unlikely to pass the Republican-controlled House or a Senate filibuster. Consider the consequences of America's policies[35] for the consumer:

- The average American spent nearly twice as much for

---

[34] http://writ.news.findlaw.com/student/20040113_kanabe.html

[35] http://www.businessinsider.com/see-how-much-more-americans-pay-for-prescription-drugs-2012-8

prescription medicine in 2009 as in 1999.

- An estimated 48 million Americans were financially unable to afford prescription medicine in 2010.

- For thirty popular prescription drugs, the American consumer pays about twice as much as consumers in the United Kingdom, France, The Netherlands, and Australia.

- About 1 million Americans travel to Canada to purchase prescription (and over-the-counter drugs unavailable in the United States) drugs due to the cost differential; under American law, it is illegal to import such drugs into the United States, ostensibly because the quality of these drugs cannot be confirmed.

- Mexico is experiencing, what they refer to as, medical tourism. Mexican pharmacists estimate that about 70 percent of their business comes from US tourists who cannot, or do not wish to, pay the exorbitant prices of prescription medication.

Sometimes, pharmaceutical companies are allowed to stretch their profits even further, especially for "blockbuster" drugs that bring in billions of dollars annually. Pharmaceutical companies usually have a ten-year proprietary license to market their drugs in the United States, free from competition, on the grounds that it enables pharmaceutical companies to recoup the money they spent conducting research for the drug. After that decade passes, other companies may begin to produce generic (and much cheaper) versions of the same active drug. However, if a large pharmaceutical company can make a deal (or launch a legal proceeding that they know will fail) that delays the production of a generic equivalent, the company can then continue to earn up to billions of extra dollars per year.

There are some fortunate emerging trends. Many pharmaceutical companies have realized that the expense of their proprietary drugs has literally caused people to reject prescriptions for these medications. They have employed various discounts and coupons (co-pay assistance for example) that have made available some new, promising drugs to people for as low as a few dollars a month. Other pharmacies offer free antibiotics and anti-diabetic medications in their generic versions. In addition, the Affordable Care Act authorizes the U.S. Food and Drug Administration (FDA) to allow for the licensing of generic biotech drugs that target specific sites in the body to combat diseases from rheumatoid arthritis to cancers and anemia, among other conditions. These measures are necessary because the drugs were developed after federal law authorized generics for existing drugs in the 1980s, and now a year of treatment with these drugs can amount to $100,000-200,000 annually per patient. Currently, more than half a million people in the world have taken one of these drugs. For example, Humira (adalimumab), a biotech monoclonal (tumor necrosis factor) antibody drug used to treat various autoimmune disorders such as rheumatoid arthritis, can cost over $20,000 per annum (and has earned its manufacturer, Abbott, tens of billions of dollars). A generic equivalent of this antibody drug would greatly help patients who have been prescribed Humira (adalimumab). Without the Affordable Care Act, and without a commitment to allow the FDA to establish a clear path to generics, these drugs will remain outside the reach of most people worldwide, who simply cannot afford to treat their infirmities.

Ramban taught that one is forbidden from profiting like this when it comes to healing (*Torat ha-Adam, Inyan ha-sakanah*, 44-45). In his line of thinking, providing medication for one in need is a fulfillment of the mitzvah *hashavat aveida* (to return a lost object to another) and fulfills *hashavat gufo* (returning one's body to them); the halakhic authorities (Tur, Shulchan Aruch, Aruch HaShulchan) also follow this approach. Rabbi Hayyim David HaLevi, on the other hand, taught that one has the right to a comfortable salary, including those working in the pharmaceutical industry (*Tashlum Sekhar ha-Rofeh ba-Halakhah, Shevilin* 1977).

Another serious problem in the drug industry is the prioritization of research for common diseases and lack of research and development for rare diseases. This is simply explained by profit motives. Aidan Hollis and Thomas Pogge, two professors fro the University of Calgary and Yale University, respectfully,, have estimated that about six billion dollars a year would be needed to sufficiently fund drug company incentives to register products that target diseases that commonly plague the poor. Peter Singer argued for this imperative by suggesting that, "[A]ffluent nations would also benefit from cheaper drugs and from medical research that was focused on reducing disease rather than on [maximizing] profits." [36]

There is reason to be hopeful: new approaches are saving millions of children's lives each year. In 1990, more than 12 million children died before the age of five. Now that figure is down, close to six million. Bill Gates, whose foundation with his wife, Melinda, pioneers the development of the vaccines and medicines saving these lives, tells us that in his lifetime the number will of children dying before they reach the age of five will drop below a million. I hope and pray that we can find a just balance: we must raise the necessary costs to develop ideal, targeted therapy that uses the latest knowledge and technology to optimize pharmacotherapy, but we also need to provide optimum treatment for the sick, regardless of how rare their disease is or what their income level is. It is unequivocally and morally wrong to condemn people to death simply because they cannot afford to pay for medicine.

---

[36] http://www.theguardian.com/commentisfree/2008/sep/16/health.pharmaceuticals

13

Jewish Conversations About Sexuality

Whenever I leave a group of teenagers or young adults where I have led a session on Jewish approaches to sexuality, I am reminded of how few healthy and normal spaces there are to learn and discuss these issues in sophisticated, safe ways.

The conversation tends to be much more open and thought provoking then the young adults anticipated since Judaism holds nuanced approaches to issues regarding sexuality. Every religion places heavy emphasis upon the soul. Judaism is certainly no exception, but the religion also places heavy emphasis upon the value of the human body. Consider this teaching:

> "He who does good to his own living being is a man of piety" (Proverbs, 11:17). Such a one was Hillel the Elder. After taking leave of his disciples, he proceeded to walk along with them. His disciples asked him, "Master, where are you going?" He answered, "To perform a mitzvah." "What mitzvah?" "To bathe in the bathhouse." "But is this a mitzvah?" "It is indeed! Just as they take the icons of kings and set them up in theaters and circuses, and someone is appointed to look after them, and he scrubs and washes them down, and he receives a salary for the work. And what's more, he is esteemed as one of the notables of the empire. All the more so am I required to scrub and wash myself – I, who have been created in God's image and likeness, as is written, 'In the image of God He made man!' [Genesis. 9:6]" (*Leviticus Rabbah* 34:3).

Rabbi Abraham Isaac HaCohen Kook went further, arguing for the religious value of exercise and of strengthening the body:

> We need a healthy body. We have dealt much in
> soulfulness; we forgot the holiness of the body. We
> neglected physical health and strength; we forgot
> that we have holy flesh no less than holy spirit...
> Our return (*teshuva*) will succeed only if it will be–
> with all its splendid spirituality–also a physical
> return, which produces healthy blood, healthy
> flesh, mighty, solid bodies, a fiery spirit radiating
> over powerful muscles.... The exercise the Jewish
> youths in the Land of Israel engage in to strengthen
> their bodies, in order to be powerful children of the
> nation, enhances the spiritual prowess of the
> exalted righteous, who engage in mystical
> unifications of divine names, to increase the
> accentuation of divine light in the world. And
> neither revelation of light can stand without the
> other... (*Orot HaTechiya*, 33)

Sex is a normal human activity and the Torah seeks to elevate this human encounter to make it sacred. It is to be learned and discussed as naturally as learning Torah. A comical story illustrating this point:

> Kahana once went in and hid under his
> Rabbi's bed. He heard him chatting and
> playing and joking and "taking care of his
> needs." He said to him: One would think that
> Papa's mouth had never tasted this dish before!
> The Rabbi said to him, "Kahana! Are you in
> here?! Get out! This is not appropriate!"
> Kahana replied: This too is Torah, and I must
> learn! (*Brachot* 62a):

This Talmudic episode (while taken to an obvious extreme) demonstrates the importance of parents and teachers talking with their children and students about sex and sexuality: "This too is Torah!" Of course, we do not condone the wanton licentiousness of certain ancient pagan civilizations, which encouraged abusive sexual relations based on class and social status. Nevertheless, there are contemporary signs that we have not learned the lessons of Torah, and sex is often used as a symbol of abuse and oppression. For example, it is estimated that there are nearly 748,000 sex offenders[37] in the United States, ranging from pedophiles to those who assault their significant others. In addition, it is difficult to determine how many women are raped in the United States annually, as the majority of incidents are not reported. Estimates range from 300,000 (reported) to about 1.3 million (based on surveys indicating that 1 in 5 women have been raped). Even with these alarming figures, twelve other nations have rape statistics that are worse.

While certainly less physically abusive, adultery is also an improper use of sex. A survey conducted by the National Science Foundation several years ago concluded that, while the percentage of adult infidelity tends to be about 10 percent, the adultery rate has been rising among people older than 60 (28 percent for men, 15 percent for women) and among couples age 35 and younger (20 percent for men, 15 percent for women. Perhaps all those ads for drugs that correct dysfunction have had an unintended consequence, and the increasingly heterogeneous workplace, with long hours and many business trips, has created temptations beyond what existed in the past.

Our society has tried various approaches to introduce sex to children in a responsible way. The Centers for Disease Control and Prevention (CDC) conducted research on teenage heterosexual activity. While virtually all teenagers have been exposed to some form of sex education, far more have been taught about how to say no to sex (81 percent boys, 87 percent girls) than have been taught about birth control methods (62 percent boys, 70 percent girls), figures that reflect the values prevalent during President George W. Bush's tenure as president. However, the CDC concluded that the most effective way to achieve delayed sexual activity and use of birth control was related to parental communication with their teenage children.

Indeed, programs that only deal with abstinence and avoid any discussion of birth control or avoidance of sexually transmitted infection (STI) backfire. Several academic studies have concluded

---

[37] http://news.yahoo.com/number-registered-sex-offenders-increasing-213100455.html

that abstinence only programs do not reduce but may increase the level of STIs and teen pregnancy, and often spread false ideas due to a religious bias that runs counter to scientific fact. According to CDC data from 2006-2008, nearly 40 percent of adolescent girls age 15-17 have engaged in sexual activities with the opposite sex, while among boys of the same age about 48 percent have engaged in these sexual activities. The preservation of ignorance therefore is worse than exposing children to knowledge that they already may be experimenting with their sexual proclivities.

There is such a demand for open conversations about the body, sexuality, and holiness today and I hope educators will see these opportunities to help guide conversations toward more reflective and intentional choices The spiritual and emotional value of sex is not lost by talking and learning about it appropriately.

14

Expert Witnesses: Jewish Legal Requirements For Testimony

Truth is one of the highest religious values. The Torah requires that we not only refrain from lying, but that we also actively seek to perpetuate truth. Consider this Talmudic teaching:

> The rabbis teach that God hates "he who possesses evidence concerning his neighbor and does not testify for him; and he who sees something indecent in his neighbor and testifies against him alone" (*Pesachim* 113b).

In accordance with Judaic values regarding the truth, the rabbis were very concerned about the motivation of expert witnesses: "The testimony of one who receives pay to testify is invalid" (*Bechorot* 29a). The testimony can, however, become valid if the witness returns the money (*Choshen Mishpat* 34:18). Giving testimony is in itself a mitzvah, so the rabbis frowned upon compensation; but the rabbis' more pragmatic concern was that a witness might come to lie if he or she was being paid. The rabbis did allow for one to be compensated, however, for his or her time away from work (*schar batala*).

According to a 2012 survey analyzing expert witness fees in a variety of fields, expert witness fees have reached new highs. Some of the highest paid (per hour) expert witnesses included physicians ($429), psychiatry ($414), computer/Internet/technology specialists ($414), business/financial fields ($352), and engineering/science specialists ($263). On average, across the fields, an expert witness spends approximately 47 hours on a given assignment. Further, experts with 10 or more years of litigation experience received, on average, 15 percent more per hour. Thus, tech specialists earned an average of $46,196 per assignment, and business experts earned an average of $30,644, well above the yearly income of millions of Americans. The rabbinical concern regarding the influence of money in court testimony seems even more poignant today, when experts are regularly being paid tens of thousands of dollars for their testimony that favors the prosecution or defense.

The legal practice in the Unites States of allowing the parties in a conflict to present testimony from paid expert witnesses, who have been chosen presumably because of their favorable opinion, is unique. In most countries, expert witnesses are chosen by judges and are meant to be neutral, objective, and independent of partisan influence. The famous attorney Melvin Belli once said: "If I got myself an impartial witness I'd think I was wasting my money." While humorous, this is particularly insightful into the problems the adversarial system of expert testimony presents. Another attorney explains: "One's biased for the defense. The other's biased for the state. I think it's who's signing their paycheck." So judges and jurors are generally left with conflicting expert testimony that basically cancels the other out. Samuel R. Gross, a law professor at the University of Michigan, states bluntly: "The contempt of lawyers and judges for experts is famous. They regularly describe expert witnesses as prostitutes."

In fact, there have been numerous incidents of expert witnesses being charged with perjury. Consider these appalling cases that tarnish the concept of an impartial expert witness:

- A California man claimed, with success, to be a computer forensics expert and testified as such in numerous court cases before being discovered as a fraud. The man plead guilty to charges of perjury and was sentenced to nearly two years in prison. His lawyer briefly acknowledged the financial incentives that led to his client's illegal behavior.

- In Florida, a man claimed on his website that he was a "professor of medicine" and was available for criminal defense work at a rate of $300/hr. He testified in a child abuse case before his credentials were determined to be invalid and he was charged with perjury.

In 2013, a doctor in Georgia was found to have bolstered his credentials in order to be selected as an expert for a trial where he would be paid a professional fee

Even more troubling in these cases is that the expert witness' perjury calls into doubt the ultimate verdict in the case and in some instances may deprive victims of justice or cause innocent men and women to be wrongfully imprisoned.

The S'ma (33:1) makes an important point, arguing that we are concerned with expert witnesses because we are not dealing with simple testimony but judgment, which "…depends on logic and thought…changes due to friendship and enmity, even without evil intention." It is evident that the large sums of money that expert witnesses are being paid brings a possible incentive for immoral, unethical, and illegal behavior. Logic and thought, the S'ma states, should be the basis of any testimony and the eventual verdict; however, lying, false bolstering of credentials, pandering, and perjury are unduly influencing the administration of our legal system.

Perhaps, Rashba's crucial distinction that a witness should not be paid when they have already witnessed the case would make a difference in ensuring the integrity of testimony (*Bechorot* 3:1). Rashba continued to states that if the witness is being asked to go out and observe something that they have yet to observe then this work may be compensated. Still, the later Polish authority, the Netivot Hamishpat (34:10) argued that one can only be paid if they're paid by both parties to the contention, because if he or she was paid solely by a single party the witness would feel an obligation to the paying party.

In surveys conducted by the Federal Judicial Center of lawyers and judges, the biggest cited problem regarding expert testimony was that experts abandon objectivity and become advocates for the side that hires them. One solution found in Jewish law is to have three appraisers give judgment in some cases rather than just having one (*Choshen Mishpat*, 103). This helps mitigate unique or biased opinions inherent in all judgments and value determinations. Hiring three expert witnesses is very expensive, however so Jewish courts often use just one witness, but have both sides determine the acceptability of the expert so as to prevent either side from exacting a partisan influence on the expert and to ensure the expert's objectivity.

An alternative approach would be to use the experts to discipline themselves. One possible proposed solution is for expert groups (medical societies for example) to establish a code of conduct for expert witnesses, including the ability to revoke the license of a witness who makes unsubstantiated claims or misleading statements. Thus, the financial incentive of testifying would be balanced by the threat of losing one's license if the code was violated. Dr. Aaron S. Kesselheim of Brigham and Women's Hospital in Boston made this proposal in 2007: "An expert should review the entire case history before providing an opinion in court—and base opinions on peer-reviewed evidence whenever possible." Just think how much more reliable expert witnesses would be if each area of expertise had these codes. We should look to the wise counsel provided to us to avoid future scandals.

There is great value in testimony and expert witnesses. Sadly, many challenges have been shown to securing accurate expertise due to the influence of financial incentives. Each expert should hold him/herself to the highest standard of truth and we should call for reforms to ensure that expertise is engaged with greater balance and without conditions that often lead to bias.

15.)

Shabbos Dinah: Preventing Rape and Domestic Violence

In the Torah portion *Vayishlach*, Dinah, daughter of Jacob, is raped. In regarding such a tragedy, the Torah reminds us just how vulnerable women are. Sadly, this Torah portion is still as pertinent today as it was in antiquity with regards to rape, domestic abuse, and sex trafficking, horrible crimes against humanity that plague modern society.

The Rabbis were unequivocal about respecting women and concerning their dignity:

> Our Rabbis taught: One who loves his
> wife like his own body and one who
> respects her more than his own body and
> one who directs his sons and daughters
> to a straight path and one who carries
> them close to their time [of maturity],
> about him it is written "And you shall
> know that peace is upon your tent"
> (*Yevamot* 62b).

However, today, worldwide attitudes toward rape are often shameful and shocking. A recent United Nations (U.N.) survey of 10,000 men[38] in Bangladesh, Cambodia, China, Indonesia, Sri Lanka and Papua New Guinea found that close to one-quarter of the men admitted to having raped a woman, with half committing a rape as a teenager, and the vast majority (72 to 97 percent) facing no legal punishment for their crime. The U.N. noted that perpetrators overwhelmingly expressed a singular rationale for why they raped women: "the most common motivation that men cited for rape was related to sexual entitlement – a belief that men have a right to sex with women regardless of consent."

Rape statistics reported by the U.N. are self-reported by each participating nation-state. Thus, while the United States reported 85,593 rapes in 2010 (compared with a Justice Department estimate of 300,000 and a CDC estimate of about 1.3 million rapes

---

[38] http://www.npr.org/blogs/parallels/2013/09/10/220983619/rape-widespread-across-asia-pacific-u-n-survey-says

annually), India's report of 22,172 rapes that year (about 1.8 rapes per 100,000 people, about one-fifteenth of the lowest U.S. estimated rate) is highly suspect. Indeed, the reported statistics might actually indicate that there is still a social stigma attached to reporting rape in many areas of the world, and that the low numbers reveal more about the lack of prosecution of rapists than the prevalence of the act itself.

It is an absolute imperative that we condemn rape, and ensure immediate punishment for the offender. The rabbis shunned even those who considered abuse:

> Reish Lakish said: He who raises his
> hand to his friend, even if he doesn't hit
> him, he is called an evil person, as it
> says, [Moshe] said to the bad person,
> "Why are you going to hit your
> friend?" (Exodus 2:13) (*Sanhedrin* 58b)

One nation with a troubling recent history of violence against women is India. In India, however, the acceptance of violence against women and rape may be undergoing a positive societal transformation. In 1972, a teenaged Indian woman named Mathura made history when she accused two policemen of having raped her while she was being held in a police station. At that time, the names of rapists were not revealed, and it was assumed that any woman who was in police custody was presumed to have given consent to sexual activity. Indeed, many wondered why someone who had been sexually active, and whose occupation (drying cow manure to be sold as fuel) marked her as an untouchable (the English word pariah comes from the southern Indian Tamil word for this low caste) would dare make such an accusation. The court acquitted the policemen and accused Mathura of lying, and a series of appeals affirmed the outrageous ruling in 1978. However, this spurred some Indian jurists and feminists such as Seema Sakhare to decades of efforts to change Indian attitudes toward the abuse of women, including rape. Eventually, the laws that were in place that protected assailants and police officers were repealed.

In December 2012,[39] a 23-year-old woman from New Dehli and her male friend were attacked on a bus by the driver and five other male passengers. The man was severely beaten, while the woman was gang raped so violently that, in spite of having most of her damaged intestines removed, she succumbed to her injuries. However, unlike the 1972 case of Mathura, there was widespread condemnation of the brutal gang rape, and crowds cheered when the rapists were sentenced to death.

The condemnation of rape must be accompanied by other changes in attitude. India is still home to 40 percent of all child brides, and it is estimated that during the current decade, some 18.5 million Indian girls younger than age fifteen will be married. This disturbing custom is evidence that we must work to diligently educate and change social norms. We must ensure that education results in social change and that women are treated with respect and dignity, without exception. The rabbis suggested that parents must only "allow" their daughter to marry a learned, civilized, and respectful man:

> We learn that Rabbi Meir would say:
> "Anyone who marries his daughter to an *am ha'aretz* [A non-observant Jew from a lower socioeconomic background, usually a farmer]—it is as if he has bound her and put her before a lion. Just like a lion attacks and eats without shame [in doing so], so too an *am ha'aretz* hits and rapes [his wife] and has no shame [in doing so]" (*Pesachim* 49b).

The rabbis were very concerned that only controlled men be granted access to marriage for the physical and emotional protection of their daughters. The Rama, a great legal authority, ruled that "a man who regularly gets angry and expels his wife, we coerce him to divorce.... it is not the way of Jews to hit their wives, for that is the way of idolaters" (*Laws of Divorce, Even Ha'ezer* 154:3). But it was not only physical abuse, but also verbal and emotional abuse the rabbis feared and denounced:

---

[39] http://www.cnn.com/interactive/2013/11/world/india-rape/index.html?mobileSource=blogs.cnn.com&hpt=hp_c2

> Rav Chanana son of Rav Idi said: "What does
> it mean when it says [in Leviticus 25] 'A person
> shall not oppress a member of his nation'?"
> The people who are with you in Torah and
> mitzvot you should not oppress. Rav said: "A
> man should always be wary of
> verbally/emotionally abusing his wife, for
> when her tears are found, verbal and
> emotional abuse is near" (*Bava Metzia* 59a).

The rabbis' codification of Jewish law even went so far as to allow violence to protect wives:

> He who says "I will not feed or support [my
> wife]"-- we hit him until he feeds [her]. If the
> court cannot coerce him to do so, like when he
> cannot support her [financially] and he doesn't
> want to get a job to feed her, and she wants
> him to do so, we coerce him to divorce her and
> pay back for the marriage contract
> immediately. We also do this for someone who
> won't sleep with his wife (*Shulchan Arukh, Even
> Ha'ezer, Laws of Divorce*, 154:3).

When we re-read *Vayishlach* and observe the current worldview towards women, we must not compromise with those who abuse or who condone the abuse of women. As the Beit Yosef ruled:

> I saw in the response of our Rabbi Simcha that
> [regarding] one who hits his wife...we are stricter
> with him than one who hits his friend. For
> regarding his friend, he is not obligated to honor
> him. However, he is regarded to honor his wife
> more than his body (*Yebamot* end of 62b)... If the
> husband cannot honor the peace agreement and
> continues to hit her and embarrass her, we agree to
> take the matter to the non-Jewish courts to force a
> divorce or to do what the Jews say to him (*Gittin*
> 88b) (*Beit Yosef, Even Ha'ezer 154:3*).

It is our ethical and moral obligation to take action, whether through education, lobbying our elected officials, or supporting just organizations to ensure that the atrocities of rape, domestic violence, and sex trafficking are adequately addressed worldwide. We should be inspired to action by the story of Dinah. Let us stand in solidarity with women the world over who have suffered terrible abuse. Let's fight for change and the hope that no more women will have to experience the plight of Dinah and so many like her.

16.)

Covering The Blood Before Us

In the Torah portion of *Acharei-Mot*, we learn the obligation of *kisui ha'dam*, to cover the blood produced from slaughtering (Leviticus 17:13).

Commentators take a number of different approaches to explain the reason for this mitzvah. Rambam argues that this ritual is to distance Jewish practice from pagan blood rituals. He suggests that pagans would collect the blood after slaughter and eat the animal's meat while sitting around the blood; for Rambam, we pour out and cover the blood to distance ourselves from these pagan practices of using the blood to connect with spirits.

> ...they imagined that in this manner the spirits would come to partake of the blood which was their food, whilst the idolaters were eating the flesh; that love, brotherhood, and friendship with the spirits were established, because they dined with the latter at one place and at the same time (*Guide for the Perplexed* 3:46).

Rabbi Shimshon Rafael Hirsch took a very different approach. He suggested that we cover the blood in order to distance ourselves from the animalistic essence of human beings. Animals kill other animals without thought, but, as humans, we must be more elevated. According to Rav Hirsch, we do not consume the blood to demonstrate that we are not animals and to prevent the life force of the animal (the blood) from entering into our life force. The *Sefer Ha'Chinuch* (187) suggests that we cover the blood in order to refine our character. He suggests that if one were to become accustomed to merely slaughtering animals and immediately consuming them while their blood still lies before us on the ground, we might become insensitive and even violent. The Torah requires us to cover the blood, according to the *Sefer HaChinuch*, in order to cultivate compassionate virtue. Each of these approaches acknowledges that there is something very sensitive about killing animals and how it affects people. There seems to be a traditional discomfort with the way other societies have handled this recklessly.

Some may see these rules as the basic *kashrut* manner of food preservation, since it was evident even in ancient times that bloody meat spoiled quickly, whereas meat drained of blood and salted could be preserved. Other cultures follow parallel principles, such as the Muslim *halal* rule of draining blood, and the old European then American custom (from colonial times) of smoking and salting meat. However, the Jewish sages obviously had more in mind than a meat inspection code. Similarly, blood-borne diseases, such as rabies, malaria, hepatitis B, and HIV, lead modern health care workers to be very careful, but this knowledge (and even HIV) is a modern development; as recently as the mid-nineteenth century the predominant belief was that foul odors (miasma theory) caused disease more than blood.

There must be another reason. One clue is the continuing human revulsion toward blood. Scientists estimate that about 15 percent of people feel weak or even faint at the sight of blood. It even has a scientific name, blood-injury phobia.

One reason, perhaps, for this phobia is that humans have always been cognizant that blood meant injury and very often death (even during the American Civil War, wounds to arms and legs often resulted in amputation, and wounds to the torso were almost always fatal). They could also see that animal blood had the same appearance as human blood, and modern science has confirmed this similarity. Humans and most vertebrates share many components, including red blood cells (erythrocytes), white blood cells (leukocytes, such as lymphocytes that are necessary for the immune system), and platelets (which allow for blood clotting to stop bleeding). Thus, most animals have the same red blood cell antigens that result in blood types such as O, A, or B, as well as the Rhesus antigen. Human blood is also more than 80 percent water (the plasma that contains the white and red blood cells and platelets is almost all water), further confirming the similarity with animal blood. Thus, humans perceive a connection between any kind of animal blood and death.

I would suggest that the primary reason the Torah is telling us to cover the blood is because we feel shame. In fact the Talmud teaches that this mitzvah is where the very concept of *bizui mitzvah*, shaming the Torah, is derived from (*Shabbat* 22a). We look at the blood of the animal pouring off the knife, dripping down our hands, and filling a pool upon the earth, and we feel profound embarrassment because we realize what we've done. That blood looks identical to our own, and we realize our own mortality and the fragility of our existence. All we can do in that moment is rush to cover it up.

This is yet another attempt from the Torah to move us toward vegetarianism. The Torah did everything possible, short of prohibiting the consumption of meat, to make it very difficult to eat meat and to distance ourselves from death.

17

The Tears of Immigrants Reach The Heavens

I was in a meeting in early 2014 with two-dozen rabbis when I received an email that six immigrants started a hunger strike ("*huelga de hambre*" in Spanish) because their loved ones were detained. I rushed immediately to downtown Phoenix, where these humble individuals were camped out in front of the ICE (Immigration and Customs Enforcement) Unit of the Department of Homeland Security.

I went to be with these people. I went to hear their stories. The hunger strikers were gentle, kind and modest. They were also tired and hungry, since this was the third day of their hunger strike. José's son has been held in detention for a year at the Eloy detention center near Phoenix in Arizona, while Hermina's husband, daughter and sister-in-law have at one time all been detained or deported. In all, they estimate that about 45,000 human beings are currently being held in various ICE detention facilities in preparation for deportation, which will separate them from their families for years, possibly forever. Besides circulating a petition advocating for the discharge of their loved ones from custody, their last hope is to join with their detained relatives and community members in a hunger strike.

The ICE deportations have proceeded at an alarming rate. The number of the "total removals" ("Immigrant Fugitives," "Repeat Immigration Violators," "Border Removals" and "Other Removable Aliens") by ICE for the following fiscal years has ranged from 175,000-255,000 a year. Many of these people are held in ICE detention facilities throughout the country (for example, twelve in Texas, five in Arizona, eight in California, five in Florida, six in New Jersey), a network that would probably shock most Americans.

Tragically, these hunger strikers have been being humiliated, as anti-immigrant forces have tormented them by showing up routinely to come and eat lunch in front of them. Others have thrown burritos at them, occasionally with hate speech messages written on them.

In the face of such hatred, these individuals remain camped out day in and day out, starving and exhausted, in the hope that their loved ones will return to them. I told them they were my heroes, as they modeled the merciful virtues of God, and we prayed together. A few cried while I led a prayer of hope for them. Afterward, I asked why they had cried, and I was told that after three days I was the first clergy person to visit them.

The Jewish tradition teaches that at special moments in life the gates of heavens are open. I felt standing among these vulnerable, powerless immigrants crying for their daughters, husbands and sisters that the gates of heaven were open to their prayers. As a Jew, my ancestors have been eternal immigrants from Abraham to Ellis Island. They were my heroes as are the modern immigrants striving to survive and thrive in a challenging world. May the day come soon when our society sees the immigrants among us not as scoundrels but as heroes who are willing to make courageous treks from familiar homes to support their families and contribute to society in new, dangerous and uncertain environments. Let the Merciful One, and our fellow citizens, hear our prayers for compassion and justice.

18

Muhammad Ali to Yuri Foreman: Does Jewish Law Allow Boxing?

Sports should emphasize athletic talent, respectful competition, and fun, not the involvement of cruelty and violence. In fact the Jewish tradition teaches that sports should not involve cruelty. Consider for example the position of Rabbi Yechezkel Landau, the Noda B'Yehuda, where he rules that it is forbidden to hunt for sport because of the cruelty involved (*Yoreh Deah* 10). Further, the Rambam taught that it is forbidden to injure another in a contentious manner (*Hilkhot Chovel u'mazik* 5:1). If boxing posed only a minimal risk to participants, Jewish law might allow our participation (like hockey, contact football, and wrestling), but boxing poses a moderate to very high risk of injury to the participants. Self-defense is, of course, permitted (*Kitzur Shulchan Aruch* 184:1), but not entering violent situations or sport in the pursuit of fame or money.

Boxing originated at least as early as the time of the ancient Greeks and Romans. There are documented boxing matches in Europe as early as the seventeenth century CE. The first attempt to provide some limits to the sport's cruelty came from the 9th Marquess of Queensbury, John Sholto Douglas, whose twelve rules of boxing mandated the use of boxing gloves, a match consisting of 3-minute rounds with 1 minute of rest between each round, and rules governing what constituted a knockdown, in which the other boxer was to return to his corner and not continue the fight until the other fighter got up; these are the rules still used in regulated boxing today. Daniel Mendoza was perhaps the first Jewish boxer, and was champion of England from 1792-1795 in spite of his lightweight. He was widely credited with bringing strategy and defense into a sport that had previously been associated with brute violence and muscles. The sport entered the Olympics in 1904, and has been there ever since. Boxing has been defended as an avenue for immigrants to get out of poverty (although the percentage of those making a sufficient living has always been very small), as Irish, Italian, and later black and Hispanic fighters have been able to achieve great fame and fortune. While not as numerous, there have been a number of Jews who made it out of the ghetto through boxing. Consider some of the more notable Jewish pugilists:

- Barney Ross (Barnet Rasofsky) turned to boxing from his early training as a Talmudic scholar after his father was murdered in Chicago in 1924 and several of his siblings were placed in an orphanage. He eventually became a champion lightweight and welterweight fighter, and was elected to the Boxing Hall of Fame

- Benny Leonard (Benjamin Leiner) was a long-term lightweight champion. Although he was the son of Orthodox Jews in New York, Leonard learned to fight in the streets of New York, frequently in brawls with Italian and Irish children.

- Ruby (Reuven) Goldstein grew up in the Henry Street Settlement on New York City's Lower East Side. His nickname was the "Jewel of the Ghetto," and although he never had a title, he was an accomplished boxer and later referee. Although he was an esteemed referee, his career was marred by what many viewed as his failure to stop the 1962 fight in which Emile Griffith killed Benny Paret on live television.

Today, several Jewish boxers have emerged from the immigrant communities that fled the former Soviet Union. Dimitriy Salita, who was born in the Ukraine but whose family moved to Brooklyn when he was nine, became an observant Orthodox Jew. As a leading welterweight boxer, Salita still refuses to fight on the Sabbath or on Jewish holidays. In November 2013, Salita lost a sold out boxing match on points that was touted as a battle of Brooklyn's best boxers. Salita, only in his early thirties, is weighing his career options after his defeat. He also moonlights as a promoter, a potential post-boxing career opportunity. In contrast, Yuri Foreman, who was born in Belarus and has lived in Israel and the United States, has had more recent success. He has been a World light middleweight champion, and convincingly knocked out his Mexican opponent in the first round of his November 2013 match.

While a few individuals greatly benefit from boxing, the majority of its participants risk severe permanent injury from this deadly sport. Some of the sports most famous and charismatic boxers have tragically evidenced the toll that this brutal sport exacts on the body. Muhammad Ali, with his ever clever witty banter with opponents and the media was the delight of the sporting world for years; however, "The Greatest" was diagnosed with Parkinson's disease at the age of 42, and even before that his speech had slurred and the quick wit had substantially diminished. Mayo Clinic physicians concluded that Ali had suffered damage to his brain stem as a result of boxing, and the resultant disruption in dopamine production likely accelerated the development of Parkinson's symptoms. While some within the boxing world have claimed that Ali suffered the brain damage because he did not retire from the sport early enough, it should be noted that Ali was remarkably gifted at avoiding punches during his career (his face remained unchanged throughout his career), and it cannot be denied that Ali has suffered a remarkably swift decline in his physical abilities since his retirement in 1981.

Sugar Ray Leonard, a former Olympic gold medal winner and middleweight boxing champion, was one of the most popular boxers of his day, but then he suffered a retinal detachment that jeopardized his sight, caused from enduring blows to the head and eyes. This condition requires immediate surgery to prevent blindness, which Leonard underwent in 1982. While a healthy recovery is likely, a return to boxing (as Leonard did five years after his detached retina) can expose the boxer to further eye damage. Less than two years after his first eye surgery Sugar Ray had to have minor eye surgery, again, to fix a loose retina.

While these high-profile cases have garnered the most attention, cumulative brain injuries do the most damage to boxers. The American Association of Neurological Surgeons estimates that 9 of 10 boxers suffer some type of brain injury. For more than 20 years, scientists have known about the pathology of chronic traumatic encephalopathy (CTE), which was previously known by such terms as dementia pugilistica, boxer's dementia, and "punch drunk" syndrome. As the former names imply, the condition is strongly connected with boxing. The brains of boxers with CTE exhibit many torn nerve fibers and neurons filled with deposits of proteins, including amyloid, that is most commonly associated with Alzheimer disease. The result is that these former boxers have increasingly severe memory problems, slow movement, and alarming personality changes such as alcoholism, substance abuse, explosive tempers, and outbursts of violence (sometimes self-inflicted). This is best illustrated in the career of heavyweight champion Joe Louis, the "Brown Bomber," who squandered the vast amounts of money he earned in the ring, suffered from paranoia, was addicted to cocaine, and was already wheelchair-bound for several years before his death at the age of 66 in 1981. Emile Griffith (mentioned earlier), who saw boxing as a way out of a childhood in a detention facility in the Virgin Islands, later wound up with dementia and spent the later years of his life in a nursing home.

The process leading to damage is directly traced to punching. In addition to the obvious physical damage (cuts, swelling, etc.), punches to the head and neck cause the cerebral cortex to rotate around the midbrain and spinal cord. Ironically, boxing gloves, which are seen as minimizing damage, actually accelerate this cerebral cortex rotation, as it increases the force of the punch. Although hemorrhaging may occur, the more likely and insidious result is that the punch causes small tears in the blood vessels in the brain. Eventually, this damage to the frontal cortex adversely affects impulse control, contributing to the harmful personality changes seen in former boxers. Thus, unlike many other sports in which equipment or rules changes can alleviate much of the risk of brain damage, boxing is unique, as Professor John Hardy, head of the Department of Molecular Neuroscience and Chair of the Molecular Biology of Neurological Disease at the University College London Institute of Neurology, and a leading Alzheimer disease researcher, wrote in New Scientist: "No other sport has the express goal of causing injury to the brain." Indeed, as noted earlier, the use of boxing gloves appears to exacerbate the harmful effects to the brain, so there is no conceivable reform that would lessen injuries in boxing.

Some Jewish authorities have argued that one may not harm another even if they give their consent (*Shulachan Aruch Harav hilchot*

214

Nizkai Haguf 4. 885) even though we know that one may waive liabilities to damages in advance (*Bava Kama* 93a). Even if one were to argue that boxing is technically permitted, since both have given consent to engaging in an activity that will lead to mutual damages, we should consider the words of Rabbi Aaron Lichtenstein:

> Which of us has not, at times, been made painfully aware of the ethical paucity of his legal resources who has not found that the fulfillment of explicit *halakhic* duty could fall well short of exhausting clearly felt moral responsibility?

We have a moral responsibility to promote peace and welfare. Boxing does not offer a realistic possibility for rescuing people from poverty, and inevitably destroys even those who are able to succeed for a time, such as boxing legends Muhammad Ali and Sugar Ray Leonard. Boxing promotes violence and a type of competition that requires and even endorses painful measures, and should not be condoned. I do not believe that Jewish law allows anyone to participate, as a fighter or spectator, in the barbaric activity of boxing.

Child Marriage: A Jewish Response

Child Marriage (usually defined as marriage before the age 15 for girls) is a major and pervasive problem in the world. In the developing world, more than 10 percent of girls are forcibly married by age 15, and the United Nations estimates that 25 to 50 percent of girls in these areas give birth to their first child before they reach the age of 18. The highest prevalence of child marriage occurs in sub-Saharan Africa (where current estimates suggest that child marriage will double by 2030). The leading cause of death for girls aged 15 to 19 is related to pregnancy and childbirth, and those younger than 15 years old have an especially high mortality rate. According to the International Center for Research on Women, girls younger than 15 (who have undeveloped bodies) are five times more likely than women in their 20s to die in childbirth. These adverse health effects extend to their children as well. According to UNICEF, the children of mothers younger than 18 are 60 percent more likely to die during their first year of life. India, which has a lower prevalence of child marriage, nevertheless has the largest single number of child brides in spite of official laws that forbid marriage before age 18.

A 2014 Council on Foreign Relations report noted that about 40 percent[40] of the 70 million child brides worldwide are in India, and about 14,000 Indian girls from age 8 to 15 are married each day. The report noted many disadvantages for these child brides:

- Child marriage prevents girls from finishing school, which further diminishes their ability to earn an income and gain power within the family.

- They suffer twice the beatings of other brides, are three times more likely to be raped (8 of 10 child brides surveyed reported that their first sexual experience was forced).

---

[40] http://www.indiawest.com/news/17354-child-marriage-stagnating-india-s-economic-growth-report.html

- They are more likely to acquire a sexually transmitted disease, and have the highest rate among married women for maternal death.

It's true that in the times of the Bible and Talmud that child marriages were permitted. An attempt at marriage initiated by a male minor is inconsequential (*Kiddushin* 50b) and does not even require a divorce (*Yevamot* 112b). The Talmud, however, taught that a father has the ability to betroth his daughter at only three years and one day old (*Sanhedrin* 55b, *Kiddushin* 41). She can later protest (me'un) and get out of the marriage (Even Ha'Ezer 155). Yet, we know that, according to many, these betrothals are forbidden because a bride needs to be able to decide whom she wants to marry (and a child cannot know that). The Tosafot commentators gave us economic context to the position in the medieval time:

> Now we are accustomed to marry off our daughters even when they are minors. This is so, because every day the exile becomes stronger. Thus, if a person is able to provide his daughter with a dowry, perhaps at some later time he will be unable to do so, and his daughter will remain a spinster forever.

Indeed, there are many sources that emphasized the earlier a woman is married, the better the situation is for all involved due to finances, reproduction, and culture; others challenge this belief. The *Shulchan Aruch* forbids marrying minors (*Even Ha'ezer* 37:8), but the Rema quotes the previously mentioned Tosafot (that in exile, early marriages are crucial). However, the Remah teaches that a *ba'al nefesh* (a spiritual and ethical person) will not be sexually involved with minors (*Yoreh Deah*, 193:1). In a similar vein, the Jerusalem Talmud recommended 18 as the proper age for marriage and marital relations. Perhaps Rambam was most adamant that children not be married:

> Even though the father has the right to betroth
> his daughter when she is a minor or when she is
> a maiden [i.e., ages 12 to 12.5] to whomever he
> wishes, it is not fitting that he should do so.
> Rather, the Sages commanded that one should
> not betroth his daughter when she is a minor
> until she matures and says, I want so-and-so. It
> is likewise not fit that a man should betroth a
> minor girl, nor should he betroth a woman until
> he sees her and she is fit in his eyes, lest she not
> find favor in his eyes, and he will divorce her or
> lie with her even though he hates her.

Jewish law has generally allowed for great flexibility depending on the needs of the time. Today, it is clear that only adult marriages are appropriate even if some Jewish legal authorities technically permitted child marriage in the past and only under certain circumstances. There is a very long, complex, and rich discourse about marriage in Jewish law that is far beyond the scope that will be presented here.

In the industrialized western world, child marriage is rare. In Israel during the 1950s, the National Rabbinical Conference forbade men to marry women under the age of 16. In the United States, nearly all states allow men and women to marry without parental consent only at age 18.[41] From about age 16 until 18, parental (or guardian) consent is usually required, with pregnancy often being a deciding factor in permitting marriage. Many states will not allow children younger than age 15 to marry, although some states (California, Delaware, Mississippi) have no specified age limit, North Carolina is 14, in New Hampshire, brides can be 13 and grooms can be 14, and, shockingly, in Massachusetts, brides are permitted to be 12 and 14 for grooms. Nevertheless, these early marriages are extremely, extremely rare. The Pew Research Center reported that the average age for a first marriage for Americans is 26.9 for women and 29.8 for men. In industrialized northern Europe, the average age at first marriage is even older. On the other

---

[41] http://www.usmarriagelaws.com/search/united_states/teen_marriage_laws/

hand, in developing countries the age of first marriage is much younger, such as in Afghanistan, where the average is 20.2 years. Generally, as statistics show, the poorer a society is, the more prevalence of child marriage is much higher.

In 2010, then Secretary of State Hilary Clinton launched a campaign to eliminate child marriage by 2030, noting that unless this was accomplished, other health and economic progress could not take place. In Kenya, for example, if all the girls who were married had instead been educated through secondary school, it would add approximately the equivalent of $3.4 billion annually to the nation's income, a staggering amount in such a poor nation. The amount of economic, social, and health progress that could be made with that kind of financial resources is unfathomable.

Eliminating child marriage will take a good deal of effort, as girls are often bartered as brides to pay off debts. This is exacerbated in times of economic hardship, such as drought or civil war, which is why in many areas the incidence is predicted to increase. In addition, many poor people have misconceptions concerning child marriage, including the idea that girls will be better off married, that they will have less of a chance of being raped if they are married, and are encouraged to marry their girls early because, if the girl is raped, she will not be acceptable as a bride. Clearly, there is an uphill battle ahead, and it will take the creation of a more just world society with better economic equality and less violence to adequately address this terrible problem.

20

Ending Violence Against Women and Girls Worldwide

When I was studying to be a rabbi, I spent several years doing volunteer service work in India, Thailand, El Salvador, Ghana, and many other countries. During that time, I heard many wrenching stories from women who had been the victims of violence. They told me they felt powerless, vulnerable, and scared. I pledged on each encounter that I would commit my life to giving voice to their cries. I prayed for an end to this epidemic and sought ways to take action to fulfill the Biblical mandate to pursue justice. Today, each and every one of us has an opportunity to do something tangible to help, and I urge you to join me.

The statistics are staggering and devastating: An estimated one out of every three women worldwide will be physically, sexually or otherwise abused during her lifetime. Every year, 10 million girls under the age of 18 enter into early and forced marriages, making them more vulnerable to violence. Six thousand girls a day (more than 2 million a year) undergo genital cutting. In every corner of the globe, girls, women, and LGBT people suffer violent domestic abuse, rape, and hate crimes. A world that allows such atrocities to take place on a regular basis, and in which all people are not treated with infinite human dignity, is deeply flawed. But thankfully, there is something that each and every one of us can do to repair it.

The United States has taken some important steps to create change here at home. Twenty years ago, Congress passed the Violence Against Women Act of 1994 (VAWA), which extended important protections to women and girls in the United States. It has been reauthorized and extended three times since then, under President George W. Bush and President Barack Obama. Each bipartisan effort affirmed the American commitment to end gender-based violence in our country. Last year, Senator John McCain was among those who supported this legislation, and we must now urge him to act again—this time on behalf of women and girls overseas.

The new bill is called the International Violence Against Women Act (IVAWA), and if it passes it will guarantee that the U.S. foreign aid program will account for and prioritize the rights of women and girls in its work around the world.

I am proud to be advocating for this legislation as a supporter of American Jewish World Service's "We Believe" campaign, dedicated to ensuring that women, girls and LGBT people around the globe can live free from violence and fear and that all girls have the freedom to determine their own futures. Back in late 2013, the Senate was expected to introduce a bill that could save women's lives around the world, and we needed to tell Arizona's senators that we wanted them to ensure its passage. This bill needed bipartisan support, and John McCain's vote could have made the difference. We are aware of the atrocities taking place and we must act to ensure that preventing violence against women and girls remains a top U.S. diplomatic priority. Each and every person is created with infinite dignity and the absolute right to live a life free from abuse. We must turn this promise from dream to reality. We all pray for an end to this devastating worldwide problem; but we now have an opportunity to go beyond prayer, to action.

21

The Religious Right To Discriminate?

There are many benefits to living in Arizona, but one of them is certainly not 2014 bill that proposed to allow discrimination on the basis of religious freedom. SB-1062, had it passed, would have allowed businesses to reject service to any customer based on the owners' religious beliefs. The bill included: "'Exercise of religion' means the practice or observance of religion, including the ability to act or refusal to act in a manner substantially motivated by a religious belief whether or not the exercise is compulsory or central to a larger system of religious belief." Many considered this legislation a strategy to legalize discrimination against LGBT individuals. Senate Democratic Leader Anna Tovar stated:

> SB 1062 permits discrimination under the guise of religious freedom. With the express consent of Republicans in this Legislature, many Arizonans will find themselves members of a separate and unequal class under this law because of their sexual orientation. This bill may also open the door to discriminate based on race, familial status, religion, sex, national origin, age or disability.

Thankfully there was great pressure put upon Arizona Governor Jan Brewer, who has gained notoriety for her extreme comments and policies regarding undocumented immigrants; she vetoed the bill. She vetoed a similar bill last year, largely because it would have undoubtedly hurt the state financially through boycotts and rerouting of conferences and conventions to other states – a message that has not been lost on the state's business community. Even Jeff Flake, one of Arizona's Senators and a staunch conservative, urged the governor to veto the bill.

This development may be seen as the latest in a series of extreme reactions that began with the election of President Barack Obama, with opposition to virtually any legislation or policy moves taken by the administration, regardless of whether they were ideas promoted by either the Democratic or Republican party. Then last year, the Supreme Court overturned federal opposition to gay marriage, and the federal government subsequently recognized gay marriages in terms of government benefits. Since then, lawsuits have been filed in about three-quarters of the thirty-three states that currently ban gay marriage. The ban has already been overturned in Utah, Oklahoma and Virginia, and more are bound to follow in rapid succession. So far, Utah and Oklahoma have appealed the rulings overturning the marriage ban.

Not surprisingly, these rapid changes to the status quo have been followed by reactionary legislative action. Republicans in Arizona, Hawaii, Idaho, Kansas, Mississippi, Ohio, Oklahoma, Oregon, South Dakota and Tennessee have introduced legislation that either directly or indirectly would allow businesses to discriminate against the LGBT community. Among the most aggressive is South Dakota, whose law proposes:

> ...No person or entity may bring suit against a business for refusing to serve a person or couple based on sexual orientation. The Legislature finds that businesses are private and that their views on sexual orientation are protected to the same extent as the views of private citizens.

Certainly, no private business must be compelled to employ a person based on sexual orientation. The Legislature finds that any federal recognition of any specific sexual orientation as a protected class does not apply in South Dakota and may not be enforced within the geographical boundaries of South Dakota.

Unfortunately such oppressive and hateful responses to minority progress is nothing new, in fact we have seen similar events in the past. In the 1920s, for example, the United States became a majority urban nation, women had the right to vote, and jazz and opposition to Prohibition flourished in the cities. In the countryside, however, Americans turned to Nativism, with unprecedented support for the Ku Klux Klan (which now combined hatred of

223

Catholics and Jews with its traditional hatred of blacks), Christian fundamentalism (the banning of evolution in the schools) and immigration restriction. When people do not comprehend change, they often become fearful, and engage in extreme oppositional behaviors and political actions.

The United States is not alone in extreme anti-gay measures. Russia passed a notorious anti-gay agenda in 2013, and the President of Uganda signed a law in February 2014 that provides severe prison sentences for anyone who is gay. Incredibly, the justification for many of these laws (along with religion) is that the LGBT community exists only in the West and is unduly influencing the rest of the world. Shockingly many assert that true non-Western societies do not have gay people, thus justifying severe punishments for LGBT people. One of the more notorious examples of this belief system was the absurd statement from the bellicose former President of Iran, Mahmoud Ahmadinejad, who told an American audience at Columbia University in 2007 that, "In Iran, we don't have homosexuals, like in your country." Similarly, Ugandan President Yoweri Museveni, upon signing his country's anti-gay legislation stated, "No study has shown you can be homosexual by nature." These kinds of ignorant and terrible statements reflect the level of bigotry and discrimination that the global LGBT community has been enduring for countless years. These kinds of attitudes and political actions have no place in civil society and must be stopped, especially here in the United States.

Fortunately, many religious leaders have boldly objected to the spurious use of religion to justify bigotry and discrimination. At the core of religion is a celebration of human dignity, uniqueness and diversity. Each person in his and her own way is created in the image of the Divine. Rabbi Jonathan Sacks wrote:

> Until we make theological space for the other, people will continue to hate in the name of the God of love, practice cruelty in the name of the God of compassion, wage war in the name of the God of peace, and murder in the name of the God of life. That is the greatest theological challenge of the 21st century, (*Future Tense*, 83).

We must encourage our leaders to refrain from using religion as a device to enforce discrimination and oppression on other human beings. Let us begin here, at home, and rally to tell our political leaders that legislation, like SB-1062 in Arizona, should never pass, for the so-called free exercise of religious freedom or any other reason. As Americans we all have the right to be treated equally under the law and legalizing discrimination under the guise of respecting religious freedom is an abomination to our Constitution and to religion. I urge all my fellow Arizonans, and residents of states proposing similar legislation, to stand with the LGBT community and mightily oppose discrimination.

Tzedakah, Economy, and Jewish
Business Ethics

1.)

Lessons on *Tzedakah* from the Sanzer Rav

Sometimes we are more concerned with not being duped than we are with ensuring that we achieve the right goal. Perhaps it's okay to be naively taken advantage of a little bit if it helps ensure that we do not harden our hearts.

The Sanzer Rav, a Hassidic leader in Galicia (on the border of modern Poland and Ukraine) in the nineteenth century, was reputedly so committed to helping those in penury that he would not rest each day until every last penny he owned was distributed to those in need. During Sukkot, he would not only give all his money to the poor, but would try to give extra money so that the poor did not have to spend time worrying about the bills after the holiday. As he sat in his bare *sukkah*, he stated that while others decorated their sukkah with expensive ornaments, his *sukkah* was decorated with *tzedakah*. One man suggested to him that every beggar might not be honest and the Sanzer Rav rebuked him, saying, "Do you know the difference between you and me? I'm willing to give to a thousand poor people, even if 999 are dishonest, just to help the one who really needs the help. You are willing to turn down 999 valid requests just to protect yourself from the one who is taking advantage of you."

We need to teach the value of *tzedakah* to our children from a very young age. One parent recently shared an inspiring story with me about their child. Every night before bed the kids put one of their coins into their *pushka* (*tzedakah* box). One time, their young boy woke up screaming in the middle of the night as if he was having a terrible nightmare. He then told his parents, after being calmed down, that he could not remember whether or not he had given his *tzedakah* before sleeping and he was terrified that he may have shirked his responsibility and missed his opportunity to do the right thing.

The Sanzer Rav was so serious about not shaming an individual who may be in need that he put a great challenge upon his own son. A struggling individual came to the Rav for assistance in buying a *tallis* for his future son-in-law. Just as the Rav was about to buy the new *tallis* for him, the Rav's son interjected – "How can you tell this lie? I saw you just yesterday buying a *tallis!*" The poor man quickly ran away in deep humiliation. The Rav was startled and reprimanded his son, teaching that the man may have needed something else for the wedding (like a wedding dress) which he was embarrassed to request so he asked for this. (He always tried to give people the benefit of the doubt.) The son, realizing what he had done, ran to the poor man to ask for his forgiveness. The man went back to the Rav and asked whether he should forgive his son or not. The Rav said that he should forgive him, but only on the condition that he committed to paying for the entire wedding.

We must teach our children the great significance of honoring the dignity of those who approach us with their needs and of doing all we can to maximize the impact of our *tzedakah*. We also must account for different personalities to ensure that all people can maximize their potential in giving. Consider this study cited in *Chip and Dan Heath's Switch: How to Change Things When Change Is Hard*, looking at why some college students donated to a canned-food drive and others did not. The researchers divided students into two groups: the students most likely to donate ("saints"), and those least likely to contribute ("jerks"). Then they tried to see whether the approach might affect the likelihood that even some "jerks" might contribute. Some "saints" and "jerks" randomly received a general advertising letter asking for donations for the food drive coming up the following week. Others received a more detailed letter with a specific request, a specific location, and a suggestion on when they should bring it. Students who were given the ambiguous letter did not donate much: Only 8 percent of "the "saints" gave and none of "the "jerks" gave. However, when given a letter with specific instructions, not only did 42 percent of the "saints" donate but also a whopping 25 percent of the "jerks." Changing the situation and helping others to lead to big results! As the authors of Switch explain "If you're hungry and need a can of food, you're three times better-off relying on a jerk with a map than on a budding young saint without one."

We must recall the lessons of the Sanzer Rav and *Switch*, devoting ourselves to giving and educating for giving. Only by being the change we want to see in the world will we see it.

The Food Aid Bill: We Will Progress Step by Step

Late in 2013, there was a great opportunity on Capitol Hill to pass a comprehensive, updated Farm Bill, which by a strange arrangement governs foreign food aid as well as the domestic Supplemental Nutrition Assistance Program (SNAP, also known as food stamps). Thus far, there has been a frustrating series of reversals at all attempts to update and improve the bill.

American farm policy combines several outdated premises. First, it assumes that nothing has changed at home since the 1930s, when the Agricultural Adjustment Administration paid subsidies to farmers in order to ensure an adequate food supply. In spite of big business' takeover of agriculture, the government continues its subsidies to the industry.

Second, foreign food policy is governed by Cold War ideology, as if nothing has changed abroad, assuming that a future war against Russia or China would require the maintenance of many cargo ships and mariners. In 1954, legislation was passed that a majority of foreign food aid had to be shipped from the United States on ships registered in the United States. Even though there has not been a single instance when the United States has needed to call on these ships for military or wartime use, this grossly wasteful, misguided, and gratuitous policy remains in place. On top of the millions of dollars spent on these vessels, it is estimated that foreign companies own more than 40 percent of them. It is interesting to note that the Danish company Maersk is one of the leading opponents of changing the Farm Bill, which indicates how "American" these ships are. If the rules were changed, a few hundred maritime jobs might not be guaranteed, but the annual cost savings in shipping alone would be $100 million.

So far, attempts to reform any of the outdated policies have been met with defeat, from both sides of the political aisle. In a measure supported by the conservative Heritage Foundation, House members Ed Royce (R-CA) and Karen Bass (D-CA) introduced an amendment to the Farm Bill that would end "monetization," a practice whereby the government donates food to charities that then sell the food with the intention of using this money for activities that encourage development. Conservatives maintain that the monetization program has spent millions more than was necessary to give the aid. Further, the amendment would also the requirement that all food must be grown in the United States and shipped on American ships, so that cheaper alternatives can be used. This amendment has not been adopted.

The Senate version of the Farm Bill, the only version to pass, and various House versions maintain farm subsidies such as one for the sugar industry, which also is protected by limited imports on sugar: farmers still receive more than $15 billion a year in subsidies; unfortunately, the one area that there appears to be a consensus is the cutting of SNAP benefits. The Senate version would cut benefits by $3.9 billion over life of the bill, 10 years. For its part, the latest House version contained cuts of $20.5 billion over the same period. At a rate of $2 billion cuts per year, the version in the House would cut two million people from food stamps. The House defeated an amendment by Jim McGovern (D-MA) to restore all SNAP funds by cutting agricultural insurance (for example, on sugar), but it was defeated by a vote of 234-188, with Republicans almost exclusively opposed. Representative McGovern admonished the House: "The price of a farm bill should not be making more people hungry in America." On June 20, the House also defeated the draconian Republican bill, although some Republicans complained that the cuts were not enough. There is a possibility that the next bill will actually cut more from SNAP.

Why is SNAP being cut when, according to the *Wall Street Journal*, the number of people on food stamps has increased 70 percent since 2008? The answer combines profound misunderstanding and perverse economics. Republicans, in considering the large increase of food stamp recipients while the economy is theoretically improving, have concluded that it is too easy to get food stamps, with some on the floor of Congress speaking to the camera and claiming falsely that people use their food stamp cards to bail themselves out of jail and other absurd stories. Thusly, the key to stopping the increase in food stamps is just to cut the budget.

The reality is far removed from the political rhetoric. According to the Department of Agriculture, a single person younger than sixty can have no more than $2,000 in a bank account and have a gross yearly income no greater than $14,532 in order to qualify for food stamps. The reasons that the number of people on food stamps has increased include that the poverty rate has risen and that the long-term unemployed have exhausted their savings and have been forced to use any available resource to survive. How is it that Congress, which gives the oil industry $7 billion a year in subsidies, has to cut more than $2 billion for food stamps that feed struggling Americans, 45 percent of whom (sadly) are children?[42]

Judaism demands that we oppose such efforts to give money to special interests while punishing the poor. Avraham, son of Rambam, taught:

> Proper generosity does not entail
> spending money indiscriminately, in the
> ways that the common people
> appreciate; namely, that you would
> bestow much food and give gifts to
> whoever comes your way. Rather,
> proper generosity is the sharing of God's
> gifts with the needy and deserving (*The
> Guide to Serving God* 5:3).

Why are there so many efforts to impose means tests, drug tests, and other obstacles to eligibility for food stamps while the financial giants of this country were bailed out with a no-strings-attached $700 billion bailout in 2008? In a message that Congress needs to hear, the prophet Amos made starkly clear how God views our neglect and abuse of the poor of the world:

---

[42] http://online.wsj.com/news/articles/SB10001424127887323699704578328601204933288?mg=ren
o64-
wsj&url=http%3A%2F%2Fonline.wsj.com%2Farticle%2FSB100014241278873236997045783286012
04933288.html%22%20%5Ct%20%22_hplink

Thus said God: For three transgressions of
Israel, [even] for four, I will not revoke [my
wrath]. Because they have sold for silver those
whose cause was just, and the needy for a pair of
sandals. Ah, you who trample the heads of the
poor into the dust of the ground, and make the
humble walk a twisted course! Father and son go
to the same girl, and thereby profane My holy
name. They recline by every altar on garments
taken in pledge, and drink in the House of their
God wine bought with fines they imposed (Amos
2:6-8).

These have been sad days in the United States Congress.
There will be many other opportunities for victims but for now at
least we must mourn the millions who could have been saved instead
have perished. We may have lost this for now, but there was also
progress. Over two hundred members of Congress are now on
record as being in favor of reform before who were not. The
Modernizing Foreign Assistance Network wrote: "Today and the last
several days reminded me why I moved to DC in the first place. A
great policy debate and while we didn't win we have A LOT to work
with. I for one can't wait for the next battle." Stephanie Mercier, a
Senate Agriculture Committee staffer for over twenty years, said,
"The status quo folks on food aid are the defensive for the first time-
let's keep pushing them."

While a House version and a final Farm Bill have yet to be
considered, we do not have much reason for optimism as AJWS
continues to lead the way for the Jewish community to have a voice.
May we feel strengthened to press our elected representatives to act
in the interests of the American people and of our best values.

3.)

Debt Crisis: National and International

Since the economic crash of 2008, millions of Americans have suffered as they drown in debt.

The national economic picture has been grim during this Great Recession, which was largely brought on by deregulation of the financial sector, an increased desire for quick returns and easy availability of credit that turned much of the economy into a virtual casino. A few basic statistics make the extent of the damage clear:

- As of 2011, there were 8.2 million foreclosure starts, quadruple the pre-recession rate.

- Federal Reserve statistics reveal that Americans lost $15.6 trillion during this recession. As of March 2013, the average American household had only regained 45 percent of its losses, while two-thirds of all new wealth has gone to the very wealthy, thanks to huge gains in stock prices during the past several years.

- There have been approximately 7 million bankruptcies during this period, with a rise of more than 31 percent from 2007 to 2008 and 32 percent from 2008 to 2009.

- In July, the interest rate for seven million people with student loans doubled, from 3.4 percent to 6.8 percent, which will lead to a further swelling of the existing $1 trillion of student debt.

- The total federal debt is estimated to be about $17 trillion, and several of the federal budgets during these last few years featured trillion dollar deficits.

In the Torah portion of *Ki Tavo*, Moses taught the people of Israel about the terrible curses that would befall them if they strayed from God's path of righteousness and justice. One of them is the curse of intractable debt: "He will lend to you, but you will not lend to him. He will be at the head, while you will be at the tail" (Deuteronomy 28.44). The concomitant blessing if the people remain upright is eternal freedom from debt: "You will lend to many nations, but you will not [need to] borrow" (Deuteronomy 28.12).

The continuing plight of the developing nations, countries in the Global South, amply demonstrates the devastating effects of decades of heavy debt. According to a 2005 report, since the 1970s, approximately sixty of the poorest nations have paid $550 billion on their international debt of $540 billion, and yet due to interest on the principle, they still owed an astonishing $523 billion. At that point, developing nations paid $13 in debt payments for each dollar they received in new grants.

While much has been made of the decision by representatives of the major industrial nations, the World Bank and the International Monetary Fund to forgive the debt of many African nations (and, to cite the obvious, these nations had already paid more than the amount they originally borrowed), it appears they did this because there was little chance of their recouping the debt anyway. Many nations in Latin America and Asia did not have their debt forgiven. As a result, a 2012 World Bank report noted that poor nations owe $4 trillion, which translates to $1.5 billion in debt payments daily. There can be no thought of social-welfare programs in these countries as long as their crushing debt payments (and therefore, their inability to borrow more) remain.

There is more to this story than irresponsible borrowing, although rampant corruption and gratuitous military spending has obviously contributed to the problem. We must remember that the nations of Europe (and in some cases, the United States) colonized many of these lands and exploited their resources. Many nations were developed for their cash crops, a single commodity that would be sold by the colonial power for its own gain. Thus, roads, railroads and other infrastructure were all built solely to get the cash crop to the coast (with a few landlocked exceptions, such as modern-day Zimbabwe).

When these nations won independence, they had an economy and infrastructure centered solely on a single commodity, and with the inevitable collapse of the market the nation would be thrown into catastrophe, forcing it to borrow. In addition, the new nations had to pay just to undo what the colonial powers had done to their countries, adding to the burden. Finally, international lenders exact a heavy price on developing nations, from long-term interest costs to restraints on the social programs that the nations can undertake. This is the worst example of the pitfalls of borrowing and unethical lending.

This destructive model illustrates a point made by Friedrich Nietzsche, in *On the Genealogy of Morals*, where he points out the etymological link between debt and guilt (from the German word "*schulden*"). Debt demoralizes the people of whole regions, reinforcing the idea that the West is only out to exploit the developing world.

Systems of borrowing and lending, of course, are not all bad. In fact, the Talmud teaches that it is better to make a loan than give charity (*Shabbat* 63a). Rashi explains that this is because the poor individual is not embarrassed in the same way when receiving a loan as when he receives charity. Maimonides states, as law, that giving someone a job (the means to support himself or herself) is the highest form of *tzedakah*. It is only when one is trapped in an unforgiving abyss of debt where we see a problem. When the potential for socioeconomic mobility is destroyed and the rich dominate the poor, the system is broken. Responsible lending and payment can yield positive results. For example, the federal deficit for fiscal year 2013 is expected to be $642 billion, a proportion less than half as large as in the fiscal year 2009 budget, at the height of the recession. Bankruptcies, while still high, dropped by 11.5 percent in 2011 and 13.4 percent in 2012. Foreclosures have dropped from a monthly average of more than 90,000 for most of 2010 to a projected 500,000 total in 2013. According to many economists, these results could be greatly improved if the government borrowed money (at the lowest interest rates in history, and thus having little impact on the debt), stimulated the economy by funding infrastructure repair and other necessary projects, and then collecting tax, Social Security, Medicare and other payments instead of paying out unemployment benefits and other relief expenses.

In developing nations, there are some glimmers of hope. For example, the microfinance movement, which provides small loans to dozens of countries, frequently shows success and has compiled repayment (at low interest rates) of close to 100 percent. As citizens of the world, we can participate in these small-scale operations, and we can urge governments to pursue an ethical debt structure, in which responsible projects (e.g., those that do not destroy the environment and are used to improve the lives of people) are promoted, which will enable these nations to structurally improve and thus be able to repay debts. These solutions can be accomplished if only we work for them.

Excessive mortgage debt, student loan debt, medical debt and more have placed untenable burdens upon millions of the working and struggling. As we learn from our Torah portion, a cursed society is one in which factions are trapped in merciless power dynamics as debtors. The Jewish community must be at the forefront of working toward more just solutions to ensure that the most vulnerable are not trapped under unforgiving debt, making social mobility impossible. This is what our tradition demands of us.

4.)

Work-Life Balance: Valuing Time Off for All in the Workplace

A 2011 survey found that over 60 percent of childless women between the ages of 33 and 47 believed that their colleagues with children were given more schedule flexibility with employers. It is a positive development that the workplace tends to acknowledge the importance of parenting, but we must also be sure that the life choices and circumstances of other employees are not devalued. Kat Stoeffel in New York magazine questioned whether "children are the only extra-professional pursuit moral enough to justify working a flexible 40-hour week."

Further, as Tara Siegel Bernard of the *New York Times* suggested, it seems that men may "be penalized more severely than women, because they're viewed as feminine, deviating from their traditional role of fully committed breadwinners." One study found that men who take paternity leave are less likely to be promoted or receive raises. Do we not need to help raise families, maintain their health, volunteer, and becoming more educated as well?

It may surprise Americans to find out how work-oriented this society is compared with the rest of the world. A survey of the richest twenty-one nations revealed that the United States is the only one whose government does not guarantee that all workers receive a single paid vacation day or holiday. European nations routinely guarantee at least twenty days of vacation, and many have 30-35 days of combined paid vacation and holidays. Even Japan, considered the hardest-working nation in the world, guarantees its workers ten paid vacation days annually, although surveys indicate workers actually take less paid time off than they are entitled to. The United Kingdom, guarantees its workers twenty-eight paid vacation days annually. On July 4th, some American workers may wonder about the wisdom of freedom that guarantees no paid days off. On top of this, nearly all Americans who are entitled to vacation days lose whatever vacations time they have not used by December 31st. Even so, in 2011, Americans took an average of 14 days' vacation, but in 2012 they averaged twelve days of allotted vacation, and only took ten of those days.

In addition, the United States is the only developed nation that does not require its employers to give paid sick days to its employees. As a result, about 40 million American workers have to either work sick or risk being fired, a system that leads to the possible spread of illness. This puts American workers below workers in dictatorships such as Zimbabwe and monarchies such as Saudi Arabia.

One result of these norms is that Americans tend to take shorter vacations, and less frequently. Employers should note that a well-rested and well-balanced employee is likely to be more effective on the job. Further, we owe it to all to create a society that only sees work as a part of life and not as the dominant goal in life. All should have a vocation and an avocation. We have seen the physical as well as spiritual dangers of the "supersized" lifestyle. *Quality* of life should be more valued than *quantity* in life.

Famously, the Chofetz Chaim was known to only work as long as necessary to earn the money needed for his family to meet his needs. When he earned enough to support the family, he would close the shop until the next time funds were low. Part of the choice today is on legislators to regulate the workweeks, part is on employers to create healthy policy and norms, and part is on employees who must make hard choices on how to spend their time and energies. Together we can achieve work-life balance and work-life integration. Employers should offer incentives to employers to continue their education, to maintain their health, and to spend more time with their families. The choices are not easy, as we all want to be professionally and financially stable, but we also cannot sacrifice our families, health, happiness, and other major life commitments. As a society, we should make the choice less difficult for individuals through lobbying employers and the government to guarantee a reduction in the conflict between work and life. We must demand a lot of our minds, bodies, and souls. To achieve our life goals, we must work hard in and out of the office. We must also rest fully (not in mindlessness, but in mindfulness) to ensure that we are able to give our absolute best.

5.)

The Rabbis on Materialism, Greed, and the Desire for Wealth

The Jewish tradition includes a varied and complex set of perspectives on the pursuit and disbursement of money, and the fulfillment, or sublimation, of desire. Still, we can discern a balanced view that teaches us to strive to elevate our mundane existence through our spiritual values and ideals, rather than to quench all physical desire.

Rabbi Bahya ibn Pakuda, the eleventh century philosopher, illustrated the complexity of Jewish thought on this subject. He propounded the value of asceticism:

> The [material] world rules them,
> stopping up their ears and closing their
> eyes. There is not one among them
> who occupies himself with anything but
> his own pleasure—wherever he can
> attain it and the opportunity presents
> itself. [Pleasure] becomes his law and
> religion, driving him away from God
> (*Chovot HaLevavot*, "On Deprivation,"
> 9:2).

On the other hand, ibn Pakuda also acknowledges that we all cannot live a completely ascetic existence, so he offers a middle path (similar to Rambam), which some may find easier to attain:

> The first [way to partake of the permitted] is
> partaking [only] of food that is not consumed for
> pleasure, without which one could not live or
> continue to exist. The second is partaking of
> permitted food in a [more] liberal fashion,
> aiming for moderation in pleasure without
> extravagance or profligacy... The same applies
> to dress, living accommodations, and other
> needs. The third is overindulging in permitted
> pleasures purely for the sake of luxury. This
> leads one to forbidden pleasures and keeps him
> from performing the duties he owes God (Ibid,
> 9:5)

241

Ibn Pakuda provides an alternative path for those whose constitution cannot tolerate extreme abnegation, but the ascetic position is weighted far more positively in his philosophy. Nonetheless, different individuals with varying needs tolerate different levels of abstinence. Maimonides also promoted asceticism at times and looked down upon pleasures of the body in comparison to noble developments of the mind and soul. Of course, ibn Pakuda and Maimonides lived and wrote nearly a thousand years ago, when resources were more scarce and the average mortality was much lower; the ascetic path would have been a more realistic lifestyle at that time. Today, most people live past the age of seventy, and those approaching retirement must contend with the prospect of supporting themselves, possibly for decades, without an income, which necessitates accumulating wealth during the active working years. Modern needs, including the high expense of health care, would not have been relevant to people in previous centuries (sadly, even in the modern world, replete with resources made available, there are still swaths of subsistent people left to starve).

Wisely, Judaism has primarily never been an ascetic religion and has tended to embrace the belief that humans need resources to survive and thrive. Voices in the tradition forbid certain pleasures but also encourage many others; many human pleasures are understood as means to attain a greater end.

The Rabbis recognized that, on a number of levels, self-interest and physical pleasure must be present for the practical world to function:

> The *Anshei Kenesset ha-Gedolah* [Men of the Great Assembly] said: since it is now a time of Divine favor, let us pray for the [evil] inclination [to be subdued before us]. They prayed and it was delivered into their hands. [Then the evil inclination] said to them: See that if you kill [me] the world will become desolate. They imprisoned it for three days. [Over those three days] they sought a freshly laid egg throughout Israel and it was not to be found (*Yoma* 69b).

Without the desire for pleasure and self-gain, there would be no reproduction in the world, which would lead to the end of Jewish continuity, as well as human existence. The Midrash teaches that without self-interest commerce ceases (*Bereshit Rabbah* 9:7). There would be no productivity without some level of societal jealousy, competition, and greed, all traits the rabbis assumed were needed for one to excel in the competitive business marketplace. Another teaching demonstrates the power of the profit motive.

> Some of the rabbis were skeptical (or perhaps realistic) of human motives and felt that strong religious commitment and wealth could not be compatible. "Men do not do anything except to achieve profit or to avoid loss.... Rabbi Yehoshua ben Levi said: The Men of the Great Assembly observed twenty-four fasts so that those who write (Torah) scrolls, *tefillin*, and *mezuzot* would not become wealthy, for if they became wealthy they would not write" (*Pesachim* 50b).

We can see this principle illustrated in the pharmaceutical industry, in which business and health care interests intersect. For example, orphan drugs are medications that treat rare diseases (those that affect 200,000 or fewer Americans) and would not be developed without government incentives because they are not lucrative enough. Indeed, before legislation assisting orphan drugs was passed in 1983, there were fewer than forty orphan drugs (those specifically developed to treat rare conditions); as of 2010, more than 350 orphan drugs had been approved, covering approximately two hundred rare diseases. In the open market the profit motive may have hindered the greater good, but by giving incentives towards research and development, the government utilized the profit motive and channeled it towards the greater good by offering government subsidies to facilitate the development of orphan drugs. Quite frequently, we see how inherent responses to human selfishness require some degree of moral and pragmatic compromise.

Similarly, throughout America we find hospitals that feature a new wing or department endowed by wealthy businessmen, and many of our charitable organizations and artistic and cultural organizations owe their survival to contributions from wealthy corporations and citizens. Of course, these contributions are tax-deductible, which enables the wealthy and corporations to pay less in taxes. While many decry the current inequity in tax policy, others worry that a new tax code that eliminated such tax deductions might lead to the destruction of symphony orchestras and museums, deter the creation of new medical facilities and dry up funds for charities. Alternatively, we must develop a more robust public trust in the welfare system, which would eliminate the need to cater to the profit-motive in private interests.

Yehuda ha-Levi, the twelfth century Spanish poet-philosopher, described the value of wealth quite positively:

> Nor is the decreasing of wealth an act of piety if such wealth happens to have been gained in a lawful way and its further acquisition does not prevent him from occupying himself with Torah and righteous deeds, especially for one who has family and dependents and whose desire is to spend his money for the sake of God...For you are, as it were, enjoying the Lord's hospitality, being invited to His table, and should thank Him for His bounty, both inwardly and outwardly (*Kuzari*, II: 45-50).

This balance is precarious. In order to thrive, capitalism needs continuous expansion, which means constantly increasing consumption. Mass marketing techniques, perfected in the second half of the last century, have succeeded in convincing millions of people that the latest fad or gadget will solve all their problems and give them lasting happiness. However, \as many have discovered that, after filling their attics and closets with these "treasures" so assiduously marketed to them, a life consumed with gain and consumption merely for one's own personal pleasure leads down a dark and scary emotional and spiritual path. Capitalistic mass consumption may be justified as the right to enjoy God's world; it may also be understood as an abuse of creation and an interference with God's majesty. Philosopher Lewis Hyde explains this phenomenon of insatiability well:

> The desire to consume is a kind of lust... But
> consumer goods merely bait this lust, they do not
> satisfy it. The consumer of commodities is invited
> to a meal without passion, a consumption that
> leads to neither satiation nor fire. He is a stranger
> seduced into feeding on the drippings of someone
> else's capital without benefit of its inner
> nourishment. A paradox of gift exchange: when
> the gift is used, it is not used up. Quite the
> opposite, in fact: the gift that is not used will be
> lost, while the one that is passed along remains
> abundant. (*The Gift*, 8, 26)

Hyde explains how the philosophical benefit of giving gifts outweighs that of pure consumption. Rabbi Abraham Isaac ha-Kohen Kook, was so concerned about the spiritual and moral pollution of personal gain over collective gain that he came out against capitalism and private property altogether.

> Without determining the economic system
> envisaged by the Torah, it is evident that a
> consistent application of the Torah's socio-
> economic norms is incompatible with the tenets of
> Capitalism. The Torah's statutory insistence in
> "thou shall do that which is right and good"
> harbors such severe limitations upon private
> property as to render it virtually untenable and
> unprofitable (*Vision and Realization*, p. 194)

Modern economic trends tend to justify Rav Kook's revulsion; our society is clearly doing a poor job in caring for its most vulnerable. From 1983-2004, the top 1 percent of Americans took in 42 percent of the new wealth generated, versus 6 percent of new wealth going to the lowest 80 percent of Americans. By 2010, in terms of non-home financial wealth, the top 1 percent of Americans possessed 42 percent of the total while the bottom 80 percent owned less than 5 percent of this wealth. When wealth distribution is balanced we can work toward more healthy dynamics of consumerism.

Even if we were to restore a more equitable distribution of

wealth and created new jobs and wealth, ethical production and consumption is not just what or how much we buy or make. It's also about what we do with those things. The rabbis of the Talmud evocatively explored this issue:

> In times to come, the Holy One, blessed be He, will take a scroll of the Law in His embrace and proclaim: "Let him who has occupied himself herewith, come and take his reward."…the Kingdom of Edom (Rome) will enter first before Him…the Holy One, blessed be He will then say to them: 'Wherewith have you occupied yourselves?' They will reply…."we have established many marketplaces, we have erected many baths, we have accumulated much gold and silver, and all this we did only for the sake of…Torah." The Holy One, blessed be He, will say in reply: "You foolish ones among the peoples, all that you have done, you have only done to satisfy your own desires. You have established marketplaces to place prostitutes in them, baths to revel in them, [as to the accumulation of] silver and gold that is Mine (*Avodah Zarah* 2b).

Is American wealth today used more for pleasure and individual gain or for bolstering our cherished values? How can we shift economic activity to further our collective moral pursuits? Centuries later, Rambam sought to articulate the correct priorities and their consequences:

> One should not aim first at accumulating wealth and then devoting time to the study of the Torah. Rather, one should see one's study as permanent and dominant and one's economic endeavors as marginal and temporary. This study is not meant, however, to be a means to economic or personal profit… Torah study, which is not accompanied by economic activity, is liable to end in sin, and those engaged in this form of study will end up by robbing their fellow men. (*Hilkhot Talmud Torah* 3:7,10)

We must first and foremost, Rambam says, concentrate on the spiritual moral pursuits and not be overly consumed with wealth. I would add that we might also, on the societal level, de-incentivize the acquisition of mass wealth and mass production where harmful. While we must be responsible and meet our societal and familial financial obligations we dare not fall into greed. The desire to disregard the true purpose of life is not a modern problem. Abarbanel, a fifteenth century Portuguese Jewish philosopher, explains that it originated in the beginning of time:

> The sin of this generation (the builders of the Tower of Babel) is similar to that of Adam, Cain, and his sons. The latter were not satisfied with the munificent bounty bestowed on them by a generous Deity and the material plenty available through natural means. Instead of using their status of being created in God's image for the perfection of their spiritual aspects, they devoted themselves to the perfection of crafts, animal husbandry, and agriculture. All of these were attempts to improve and exploit the natural order of things, which the Deity, in His wisdom, provided as sufficient for the needs of mankind. To this 'sin' the builders of the tower of Babel added that of urbanization and political organization. They created a kingdom ruled by Nimrod which supplanted their previous egalitarian society and built cities which destroyed their rural environment. In addition the greed and aggression following the introduction of a class system of ruled and ruling, they pitted men again each other by their rules of private property. It is this absolute view of private property which led men to declare, 'What is mine is mine and what is yours is yours.' By traveling from the east, the builders of the Tower of Babel separated themselves from God by their desire for business and artificial goods, (Commentary on Genesis, Chapter 18).

Abarbanel reminds us that political and economic realities we often view as inevitable are not a necessary component of the human condition. Rather many societal structures were often chosen very early on in human existence based upon selfish and evil motives and not on the welfare of the world. Each generation has a new task before itself to combat the refreshed desire for self-worship, the immersion in self-pleasure, and the neglect of supporting the vulnerable while attaining as much property for oneself.

The prophets teach us that the paradigmatic wicked society is one that collectively neglects its poor. "Behold, this was the iniquity of your sister Sodom: pride, fullness of bread, and careless ease was in her and in her daughters; neither did she strengthen the hand of the poor and needy" (Isaiah 16:49). Further, the rabbis teach that one who embraces private ownership at the expense of the poor living by a principle of "Mine is mine, and yours is yours" is like the paradigmatic evil Sodomite (*Ethics of the Fathers* 5:10). A model of capitalism that allows for significant wealth accumulation but does not also enforce levels of wealth redistribution is not a model Judaism can promote. Economic equality and care for the poor are Jewish values to be defended, and Jews should be on the front line advocating for ethical taxation and leading on other issues that help to achieve economic equality.

There are many ways to commit financial wrongs, not only through indiscrete stealing. In the eighteenth century, Rabbi Moshe Chayim Luzzato, the Ramchal, explained that the Torah asks much more of us than simply not to steal:

> Most people are not outright thieves, taking their neighbors' property and putting it in their own premises. However, in their business dealings most of them get a taste of stealing whenever they permit themselves to make an unfair profit at the expense of someone else. (*Mesillat Yesharim*, Chapter 21)

This lesson has fascinating and highly demanding implications for how we think and act with regard to our spending and even our philanthropy. Almost all of us take more from the world than the amount we give back. What if we were to radically reverse this trend? What if we could subversively create a new generation that was willing to stand up and reject these norms by challenging the power structures and market forces at place, refusing to embrace a marketplace devoid of care for the poor, curbing the desire for comfort and security, achieving wealth redistribution, and demonstrating a much higher commitment to giving.

Today, rabbis this how we are able to best invest our personal funds into something that is of crucial significance to the community. In a new study by Jewish Jumpstart, a philanthropic research and design lab based in Los Angeles, on Impact Investing, upwards of 90 percent of rabbis surveyed agreed that the Jewish community should align its investments with Jewish values, that social and environmental values must be considered along with financial gain, and that there is a moral obligation to avoid investing in companies that cause societal harm; 58 percent – more than half - argued that one should be prepared to have lower financial gains in order to align investing with Jewish values. These rabbis believe that investors must avoid states that sponsor terrorism and permit or abet in child labor, predatory lending, mass pollution, animal testing, worker's rights violations, as well as trafficking in tobacco, gambling, adult entertainment, non-military firearms, etc. On the positive front, the rabbis counseled prioritizing support for Israel, education, alternative energies, diverse workplaces, etc., in investing.

Investment to slow climate change is important, and represents the upward struggle for ethical investment. According to United Nations data, investment for renewable energy hit $257 billion in 2011. Nevertheless, renewable energy (excluding hydroelectric power) was still only about 6 percent of energy generated in 2011, and China has now surpassed the United States in renewable energy investment, while many American tax incentives for these investments have expired. Fossil fuels continue to be subsidized worldwide at a rate six times higher than renewable energy. Clearly, there is a need to greatly increase this type of investment.

Overall, sustainable and responsible investing has grown significantly from $639 billion in 1995 to $3.744 trillion in 2012. We have a long way to go to continue to move the community from traditional investments to socially responsible investing to policy-determining investments, to create a permanent investment philosophy where values are prioritized over profits.

In his work *Or L'Yisrael*, Rabbi Yisrael Salanter, the founder of the *mussar* ethical and spiritual development movement, taught that one must first do *kibbush ha'yetzer* (conquest of desire) and only then can one engage in *tikkun ha'yetzer* (repair of desire). Again, the goal is not to destroy desire altogether but rather to have control over it and to repair it toward the noblest purposes. In the end, the goal is not to look for satisfaction and life fulfillment through physical desire but to elevate one's existence in pursuit of the grand noble ideals of our tradition. Rabbi Joseph B. Soloveitchik articulated this well:

> With the birth of the norm, man becomes
> aware of his singularly human existence which
> expresses itself in the dichotomous experience
> of being unfree, restricted, imperfect, and
> unredeemed, and, at the same time, being
> potentially powerful, great and exalted,
> uniquely endowed, capable of rising far above
> his environment in response to the divine
> moral challenge. (*Lonely Man of Faith*, 59)

We have severe limitations as humans, but also immense potential for noble pursuits. Rabbi Soloveitchik further taught an important point about emotions relevant to our understanding of human desire:

> The worth of a particular emotion must not
> be measured by some intrinsic quality it
> possesses, but rather by the relevance and
> significance of its correlate object. There are
> neither bad nor good emotions; instead there
> are bad or good emotional objective
> references. (*A Theory of Emotions*, 182)

Feeling desire and natural as long as it is a desire for morally justifiable things. It is the job of government to regulate industries. It is our job to regulate our hearts. One of the classic rabbinic teachings is that *rachmana liba ba'ei*, that the Compassionate One, i.e. God, desires heart and not just deed, intention and result (Rashi's commentary on *Sanhedrin* 106b). Jews are asked first and foremost to be aware of this conflict and engage it in their lives; pursue justice, the Torah implores – what we find at the end of the pursuit may end up being less important.

Today, many aspects of economic systems, day-to-day commerce, and human greed go unchecked. The Torah requires that we balance freedom with regulation and human desire with human limitation. This must be achieved on many levels: personal, communal, societal, national, and global. The Jewish people, inspired by the wisdom of our tradition, should be at the forefront of modeling this, both at work and home. We should advocate for change at the office and in legislation. We must leave society stronger and more equitable for our children. As the great sage Honi taught (*Ta'anit* 23a): "I myself found fully grown carob trees in the world; as my forebears planted for me, so am I planting for my children." Today, we must go even further. In many ways, we have found a carob-less world and we must plant.

6

Discrimination In The Workplace: How Do You Judge?

The Torah teaches that God does not show favoritism (Deuteronomy 10:17). God does not discriminate, and we are asked to emulate that example. This command is made explicit (Deuteronomy 16:19): People are to be treated equally. When it comes to procedural justice, all (even the poor) are to be treated equally: "You shall not favor the poor and you shall not honor the great" (Leviticus 19:15). However, when it comes to social justice (dealing with legislative matters rather than judicial matters), the vulnerable must be given extra support.

The Torah makes it particularly clear that people are to be treated equally in the workplace as well. The foreign worker who worked in an Israelite community (*ger toshav*) was granted all of the same rights as the Israelite worker: "One law and one manner shall be for you and the stranger that lives with you" (Numbers 15:14-16). Unfortunately, this value has not been emphasized enough today on the legislative, corporate, or grassroots levels. This is particularly distressing since access to equal employment opportunities is such an integral aspect of securing financial stability, opportunities for education, social mobility, crime, drug and alcohol abuse, and a litany of other opportunities and issues that affect quality of life and social justice.

Seeking redress for discrimination is a long, arduous process, and opposition may come from the government as well as from management. Title VII of the Civil Rights Act of 1964 was the first effort undertaken by Congress to address discrimination by employers on the basis of race, color, religion, sex, or national origin. The measure ensured that employers could not make discriminatory decisions about hiring, firing, advancement, demotion, or wages without facing possible prosecution. In 1971 the Supreme Court, in *Griggs v. Duke Power Co.*, held that when an employment practice has a disparate impact on minorities, that is the practice is "fair in form, but discriminatory in operation," the practice violates Title VII. However, in the late 1980s the Supreme Court issued a series of decisions (*Wards Cove* and *Patterson*) that undercut victims of employment discrimination and their rights for filing complaints and opportunity for redress. Congress quickly acted to counter the Court's rulings and enacted the Civil Rights Act of 1991, which reestablished the broad scope of Title VII protections. It is this sort of broad congressional action that we must demand to further guarantee that the vulnerable are protected in the workplace today.

Lilly Ledbetter worked as a supervisor in a Goodyear plant in Alabama for nearly 20 years. When she found out that she had been paid far less than her male counterparts, she sued, and a jury awarded her in back pay and $3.3 million in damages. However, in 2007 the Supreme Court nullified the award on the grounds that Ms. Ledbetter had filed suit too late. The Supreme Court reasoned that Title VII of the Civil Rights Act of 1964 requires employees to file a complaint within 180 days (six months) "after the alleged unlawful employment practice occurred." The Court calculated the 180 days to have begun running from the day Ms. Ledbetter had received her last discriminatory paycheck or raise denial, not the date she discovered that she had been discriminated against. Incredibly, the ruling encouraged businesses to cover up discriminatory pay for six months, and then they would be beyond legal redress. Undeterred, Ms. Ledbetter lobbied Congress, and in 2009 Congress passed the Lilly Ledbetter Fair Pay Act, which President Barack Obama made the first bill he signed into law as President of the United States. Today, in large part due to this Act, women, and other victims of discrimination, have far more rights in challenging discriminatory pay, and employers no longer have immunity from prosecution.

In another crushing blow to employment equality safeguards, the Supreme Court, in *University of Texas Southwestern Medical Center v. Nassar*, undercut employment anti-discrimination efforts. In this case Dr. Naiel Nassar, an Egyptian-born Muslim, claimed he suffered racial and religious persecution and harassment from hospital superiors and after complaining of discrimination was retaliated against with promotion denials, threats of loss of salary support, and threats of job loss. A federal jury found for Dr. Nassar and ordered UT Southwestern Medical Center to pay him more than $3.6 million. However, the Supreme Court reasoned that the provision in Title VII of the Civil Rights Act of 1964, which protects employees from retaliation when they assert their rights, to require complaining employees to show that there was no other reason for which they could have been demoted, fired, etc., other than retaliation. The requirement to show "but-for causation" stands in direct contradiction to the purpose of the law. As Justice Ruth Bader Ginsburg explained in her spirited dissent, "employees can be protected by civil rights laws only if they feel free to approach officials with their grievances." This decision now allows employers to retaliate against employees and avoid liability if they can think of a single reason to justify the punishment. Justice Ginsburg concluded that Congress should pass a Civil Rights Restoration Act to overturn destructive and far-reaching rulings like this one.   Furthermore, the Supreme Court has continued to weaken the ability of women (indeed, anyone else) to sue corporations. In two separate decisions in 2011, the Court virtually dismantled the ability of workers to file class-action suits against large corporations (in one case, Wal-Mart). In short, the Court resurrected the more than a century old and discredited legal doctrine of "freedom of contract," which presupposes that a worker with no financial resources is on an equal plane with a billion-dollar corporation in bargaining ability. Today, women must again look to Congress to bypass judicial obstruction. The Paycheck Fairness Act would correct many of the deficiencies of the original Equal Pay Act of 1963 and expand the scope of the Fair Labor Standards Act. However, Congress too has yet to stand for equality in the workplace. The Paycheck Fairness Act has been introduced twice in Congress since 2009 and both times the legislation has failed to become law. This legislation is essential in ensuring that women no longer earn 77 cents for every dollar that their male counterpart receives, a median income disparity of over $11,000 a year, according to the US Census Bureau.

Immigrant workers also face serious discrimination, based on race and immigration status, in the workplace. A case that exemplifies some of these issues is the case of *Morales v. Terra Universal, Inc.* Terra Universal, a laboratory manufacturing company, employed both citizens and non-citizens at their factory and utilized a two-tier system which set rules regarding hours, wages, and working conditions for their employees. Non-citizen employees were paid less than half of what their citizen counterparts were paid, were required to work non-paid overtime hours to make up for sick days, were required to work up to fourteen hours a day on weekends or holidays without overtime pay, and were subject to abuse and reduced hours if they complained about working conditions. Sadly, these types of stories are all too common and many end with tragedy as many undocumented workers are deported and their families are torn apart. Last year alone ICE stated that they deported over 410,000 immigrants but would not provide details as to the number of workplace raids. However, if the infamous Postville Raid, where nearly 400 immigrant workers were arrested and deported, is any indication it is safe to assume a large number of the deported were workers trying to provide for their families. In fact during President Obama's first term a record number of deportations took place. The United States Congress needs to address these issues with comprehensive immigration reform to ensure that immigrant workers are protected and treated with dignity and equality.

The other type of serious discrimination found in the workplace today is against those in the gay community. As of this writing, there is no comprehensive federal law that protects gay or lesbian individuals from discrimination from their employer. Currently, 29 states allow people to be dismissed from their jobs sole based on sexual orientation and in 33 states no laws exist that prohibit employment discrimination based on gender identification. The Employment Non-Discrimination Act is a proposed solution to prohibit this discrimination and "level the playing field." A recent poll showed that 73 percent of Americans support ENDA. Further, 88 percent of Fortune 500 companies already have policies prohibiting any type of discrimination against gay and lesbian employees. Fity faith groups recently came out in favor of this legislation. It is time to ensure that all people have the right to work at a job where they are entitled to equal pay and treatment. There is a long road ahead before the inequities with regards to sexual orientation are rectified. Even if one does not agree with a person's choice of lifestyle or outlook, this does not mean that discrimination is the proper way to behave. All people have the same basic right to dignity. This is the command of Torah and our obligation as moral citizens of the world.

7

False Advertising, Jewish Morality, and the Tobacco Industry

Advertising and marketing are everywhere we look: on billboards and blimps, on television and film, in our newspapers and magazines, on the food boxes we eat from, even on the clothes we wear. This is a far cry from our society fifty years ago – have you ever seen an old film or television show with product placement? These advertisements often increase and shift our desire and even tell us how we might feel and act. Consumer behavioral shifts based not on personal needs, economic considerations, or ethical concerns, but on the power of myopic gimmicks and social branding.

For better or worse, the United States has become the advertising capital of the world. Total advertising expenditures in the US reached nearly $140 billion in 2012, more than a quarter of world advertising expenditures. These can range from the sponsorship of valuable cultural activities or messages urging a more healthful living style to deceptive ads from businesses that endlessly claim to be going out of business and holding one final sale.

One example of an industry full of deceptive advertising is big tobacco, which promotes one of the most addictive and life-threatening substances known to humanity; from top to bottom, it issues false propaganda. For example, in 1994, executives of seven tobacco companies testified before Congress and lied by saying that smoking tobacco was not addictive. Significantly, however, when pressed, the executives added that they hoped that their children would not become smokers.

In the past, tobacco advertisers have proven extraordinarily resilient and successful in promoting their products. While tobacco ads have been banned from radio and television for more than a generation, they have discovered other ways to advertise. They have learned to increase their messaging through sponsoring sports and social events where people cannot avoid exposure to their logos. In addition, cigarette companies target specific populations using various tactics:

Adolescents are targeted with ads that make smoking

appealing. Numerous studies have concluded that tobacco advertising plays a key role in turning adolescents from occasional to addicted smokers, and are especially successful in hooking those who believe that they will not become addicted. Virtually every schoolteacher can confirm that students congregate in bathrooms to show their defiance of authority by smoking.

- Women are targeted with special brands that show very thin, fashionable women, encouraging the idea that smoking is a way to reduce weight.

- Latino Americans are targeted by cigarette brands with Spanish names such as Rio and Dorado.

- Studies have shown that African Americans are exposed to several hundred more cigarette ads than white people each year.

Fortunately, society can take steps against such harmful advertisements and promotions, and we can resist false messages. We no longer have to contend with smoke-filled restaurants and theaters, or feel obligated to have ashtrays in our home ready for anyone who chooses to come in and smoke at will. Also, the percentage of American smokers has declined from about 42 percent in 1965 to 19 percent in 2011. In addition, the federal government passed legislation in 2009 that empowered the FDA to regulate tobacco products and gave states the right to restrict cigarette advertising and promotion through means such as restricting the time and place where these activities could occur. Thus far, twenty states now restrict or prohibit places where free tobacco samples can be distributed. Still, today nearly 44 million Americans smoke tobacco, and in 2011 cigarette companies spent $8.37 billion on advertising and promotional activities in the United States. Advertising has the power to persuade, and to deceive. As religious Jews, one pertinent question about advertising and its relationship to deception and promoting harmful decisions and habits is, what is *halakha's* view of this?

In *The Impact of Jewish Values on Marketing and Business Practices"* Hershey Friedman, a professor at Brooklyn College, argues that while Jewish law may not explicitly forbid the influencing of consumers, it clearly violates the spirit of the law. (Specifically, it is *geneivat data*, deception, which is a Biblical prohibition).

The Talmud gives an example of how business must not include any deception, towards Jews or non-Jews: "A person should not sell shoes made of the leather of an animal that died of natural causes (which is inherently weaker) under the pretense that it was made from the leather of an animal that was slaughtered (*Chullin* 94a); the Shulchan Aruch sees this as *halakhah* (CM 228:6).

Businesses need to compete, and advertising is the norm in commercial life. It is not an option to stop advertising. Further, Jewish law does embrace the notion that a reasonable person's expectation can be assumed. One Talmudic passage gives an example:

> Mar Zutra was once going from Sikara to Mahoza, while Rava and R. Safra were going to Sikara; and they met on the way. Believing that they had come to meet him, he said, "Why did you take the trouble to come so far to meet me?" R. Safra replied, "We did not know that you were coming; had we known, we would have done more than this." Rava said to him, "Why did you say that to him? Now you have upset him." He replied, "But we would be deceiving him otherwise." "No, he would be deceiving himself" (*Chullin* 94b).

Rav Safra argues that one may not gain from the false perception of another. Rather, one must proactively correct that misunderstanding to ensure an unfair moral debt is not created. Rava, on the other hand, believes there is responsibility from the other not to be self-deceived. Aaron Levine, author of *Case Studies in Jewish Business Ethics*, explains that one must not only avoid wrong but also proactively assure consumers of the truth. "The seller's disclosure obligation consists not only of a duty not to mislead in an affirmative manner but also of a requirement to disabuse the customer of his reasonable misperception about the product."

We see from these sources that Jewish law demands that we be extremely cautious in protecting and promoting the truth. We should take note of and observe these principles in our daily interactions with our fellows on the street, in the *beit midrash*, in workplace, and in the voting booth and when we talk about creating regulations for advertising.

8

A Five-Dollar Renoir: The Responsibility Of The Buyer

Does a buyer have any obligation to inform a seller of a true product value?

This question appeared in the "Ethicist" column of the *New York Times Magazine* by Chuck Klosterman:

> Is it ethical to buy something at a yard sale or a flea market at the seller's asking price if you know the value of the item to be significantly higher than what is being asked? Let's say, for example, someone is selling an old comic book worth thousands of dollars but asks for only a quarter because he or she does not know the true value. Is it incumbent on the seller to do his or her research? If the seller does not, is it fair game?

Value is complicated and sometimes subjective. We need not reveal how much we personally value an item we want to buy, nor does a buyer need to reveal how much she values a particular item. In particular, antiques and rare items are especially complicated to put an objective, or wholly accurate, value on.

The Torah teaches the prohibition of *ona'ah*, taking advantage of another in business (Leviticus 25:14). An owner may not overcharge for an item and a buyer may not underpay. The Talmud considers *ona'ah* to be like theft. Generally, *ona'ah* mandates that an owner may not charge more than 1/6th of the market price for an item and the buyer may not pay less than 1/6th of the going rate.

Further, there is a *halakhic* concept that an acquisition is not valid if crucial information was not known at the time that would have persuaded the buyer or seller not to make the deal (*mekach taut*). Knowing something is a rare valuable antique when the buyer does not know is not merely a case of *ona'ah* (under-pricing) but is a case of *mekach taut* (a faulty deal) since there is a level of deception involved. This principle is meaningfully illustrated in the story of Simon ben Shatah:

> Simon ben Shatah was occupied with preparing flax.
> His disciples said to him, "Rabbi, desist. We will buy
> you an ass, and you will not have to work so hard."
> They went and bought an ass from an Arab, and a pearl
> was found on it, whereupon they came to him and said:
> "From now on you need not work anymore." "Why?
> He asked. They said, "We bought you an ass from an
> Arab, and a pearl was found on it." He said to them,
> "Does its owner know of that?" They answered, "No."
> He said to them. "Go and give the pearl back to him."
> "But, "they argued, "did not Rabbi Huna, in the name
> of Rav, say all the world agrees that if you find
> something that belongs to a heathen, you make keep
> it?" Their teacher said, "Do you think that Simon ben
> Shatah is a barbarian? He would prefer to hear the
> Arab say, 'Blessed be the God of the Jews,' than possess
> all the riches of the world…It is written, "Thou shall not
> oppress thy neighbor." Now your neighbor is as your
> brother, and your brother is as your neighbor. Hence
> you learn that to rob a gentile is robber," (*Bava Metzia*
> 34a).

Garage and rummage sales frequently raise questions about false perceptions. In one case covered by the media, a woman bought a box of miscellaneous items at a flea market. Among the items, she liked a painting because it had a nice frame. Rather than discard the painting, she put it in a garbage bag and took it to an auction house, which told her that she had actually purchased an authentic Renoir painting worth $75,000. Since neither the buyer nor the seller knew that the painting was genuine, this was clearly not deliberate deception. On the other hand, if the purchaser had been an art dealer and known of its value, or if the seller had pretended that a known forgery was a masterpiece, then that would have been another matter.

In the United States the legal doctrines of *caveat emptor* ("let the buyer beware") and *caveat venditor* ("let the seller beware") generally apply to the exchange of goods, and or real property, between buyers and sellers. The case of *Laidlaw v. Organ* is the paradigmatic and most cited, decision regarding the principles of warranty, non-disclosure, misrepresentation, and/or mistake. The decision holds that when two parties are dealing at arms length and both have equal access to information that pertains to the bargained-for exchange there is no duty to disclose, for either party. However, if a party intentionally deceives another the contract is subject to rescission; the deception can either be fraudulent misrepresentation or material misrepresentation, and both forms make the contract entered into void.

There are exceptions to the general – no duty to disclose – rule. Courts will hold parties that are in fiduciary and/or confidential relationships to higher standards due to their unique status. Fiduciary relationships, such as the relationship between business partners or attorneys and their clients, are based on one person's ascendancy over another through the placement of trust and confidence, or the assumption of a position of influence. For these types of relationships to function successfully they require a high degree of candor between participants and therefore both parties are held to rigorous standards. Confidential relationships, such as the relationship between brother and sister, husband and wife, doctors and patients, clergyman and parishioner, are not so much the product of a legal status as they are the result of unusual trust or confidence reposed in fact. Parties with these sorts of relationships aren't held to the same rigorous standards as those in fiduciary relationships but, legally, one party cannot take advantage of the other or deal on unequal terms.

A particularly evil case occurred in the then British colony of Pennsylvania in 1763, when a British commander endorsed the idea of selling blankets from a smallpox hospital to the unsuspecting local Native Americans, in the hope that the Native Americans would contract smallpox and die. While the specific events and outcome remain controversial among historians, it seems clear that the sellers were not only distorting the value of the blankets, they were literally trying to kill the buyers. While such despicable and brutal acts of deception may seem so evil that it is hard for us to actually comprehend the act's perpetration, similarly malevolent practices are taking place today.

The current economic crisis that our nation is slowly recovering from was largely set off by predatory subprime lending by major American investment banks. Banks would attract subprime borrowers with advertisements offering loans with no down payments and their no-savings requirements, then provide borrowers with adjustable rate mortgage (ARM) loans for the full purchase price of the home which have a fixed, below market, interest rate for the first 2-3 years but then are adjusted every six months to a much higher rate for the duration of the thirty-year loan. These banks made loans to borrowers on terms that the borrowers would be unable to pay, which the banks knew. In determining what the borrower could afford, through the standard debt-income ratio, the banks would only consider the introductory interest rate and not what the ratio would ultimately be when the interest rate skyrocketed after the 2-3 year introductory period. These investment banks preyed on millions of families who sought their share of the American Dream, who wanted to raise their children in a home, who sought safer neighborhoods and better schools, all the while knowing that once that introductory interest rate went up after 2-3 years, and if the market didn't increase allowing for re-financing, that these families would have their homes foreclosed and lose everything.

Overall, there needs to be some order in the marketplace in order to equally protect buyers and sellers. Indeed, the motivation behind many investments, or purchases at garage sales, is the hope, on both sides of the bargain, that there will be financial gain and there is nothing inherently wrong with this. The issue, very simply, is one of fairness. We must be cognizant of Torah and the prohibition of *ona'ah*, as well as American legal precedent regarding misrepresentation and non-disclosure. However, the maxims of *caveat emptor* and *caveat venditor* stand for principles of being prudent, cautious, and informed buyers and sellers; therefore, we must be responsible and diligent in our business undertakings while remaining ethical and socially conscious.

9.)

Should I Claim All My Rights?

The origin of human rights has long been debated. There are those that argue human rights come from directly from God. Others believe governments grant human rights. Some argue that they have emerged as a collective social acceptance. In 1775, Alexander Hamilton wrote:

> The sacred rights of mankind are not to be rummaged for among old parchments or musty records. They are written, as with a sunbeam, in the whole volume of human nature, by the hand of the divinity itself, and can never be erased (*The Farmer Refuted*).

Further, consider the words of Rabbi Ahron Soloveichik in "Logic of the Heart, Logic of the Mind:"

> This key concept of *k'vod habriyos*, the dignity of all human beings, constitutes the basis of human rights. The maxim of "Man was endowed by his Creator with certain inalienable rights" was not an innovation of the founders of the American republic. These men were impressed with the doctrine of human rights which flows naturally from the concept of "the dignity of man" and the "image of God in which He created Man," as they knew from their Biblical background. The concept of *k'vod habriyos* is the basis of all civilized jurisprudence, as well of all the laws of justice in the Torah. Civil law and the *mishpatim* (rational laws) of the Torah, on the whole, bear a remarkable correspondence for the simple reason that every law in modern jurisprudence is based exclusively upon the doctrine of human rights which the nations of the world adopted from the Scriptures. For example, it is a crime to commit homicide, to commit assault and battery, or to trespass upon another's property, because every human being has a fundamental right to be secure in person and property against any attack, assault or molestation. Everyone has such a right since everyone was created in the image of God and consequently deserves to be treated with dignity and respect (*Civil Rights and the Dignity of Man*, 61-68).

John Locke, the famed philosopher of the Enlightenment, wrote, in his *Second Treatise on Government* (1690) that prior to the establishment of governments there existed a "state of nature" in which individuals lived in complete freedom and served their own interests. In this state each individual possessed "natural rights," including the right to life, liberty, and property. Locke explained that individuals formed social groups and governments to secure and enforce these natural rights more effectively. Locke's thinking regarding natural rights was indelibly influential during the Enlightenment and was famously adopted by the Founding Fathers of the United States. This can be seen in the language of the Declaration of Independence, where Jefferson clearly copied much of the core rights from Locke, and the Constitution, particularly in the first ten amendments known as the Bill of Rights. The idea of natural rights became more commonly accepted over time and was extrapolated to the idea of universal human rights. One can see the similarities in philosophy in the definition of human rights adopted by the United Nations High Office of the High Commissioner for Human Rights, "...rights inherent to all human beings, whatever our nationality, place of residence, sex, national or ethnic origin, color, religion, language, or any other status. We are all equally entitled to our human rights without discrimination."

Locke, Jefferson and others developed the theory of modern human rights in answer to the previously dominant doctrine of Absolutism, which espoused the Divine Right of Kings, that royalty was literally endowed by God to rule over people, and thus that rebellion was blasphemy as well as treason. While this seems archaic, it should be noted that it lasted until 1917 in Russia, when the czar was finally deposed by violent revolution. This line of thought, which advocated total rule by a single ruler for stability, was subject to extreme abuses. During the feudal period, for example, the lord ruled over his serfs and estates with the approval of the local church. If anyone on the manor felt wronged, the only recourse was to appeal to the local court, which was presided over by the lord himself. Often, this meant that the criminal was the judge, with predictable results.

While natural rights espoused by Locke and others worked for the upper and elite classes, the workers of the early Industrial Revolution were left on their own volition without assistance. They fought long and hard to match the extraordinary political power of wealthy business owners, in an effort to earn the right to unionize and earn a living wage and decent working conditions. Karl Marx and other economists and philosophers began to enunciate these ideas in the mid-nineteenth century, but in America it was not until the Great Depression that these notions were achieved; New Deal legislation established the rights of workers to organize, have a minimum wage, and have decent working conditions. The Universal Declaration of Human Rights, passed by the United Nations as a worldwide model of human dignity, has many Articles that embody the ideals of Locke and the Bill of Rights. However, beginning with Article 23, there are a series of economic rights that embody the newer twentieth century economic rights:

- Everyone has the right to work, to free choice of employment, to just and favorable conditions of work and to protection against unemployment.

- Everyone, without any discrimination, has the right to equal pay for equal work.

- Everyone who works has the right to just and favorable remuneration ensuring for himself and his family an existence worthy of human dignity, and supplemented, if necessary, by other means of social protection.

- Everyone has the right to form and to join trade unions for the protection of his interests.

Regardless of the origin or definition, rights are to be protected and honored. It is up to each individual, and no one else, if they wish to accept and claim their full rights or not. The rabbis teach that God loves one "who does not insist on his (full) rights" (*Pesachim* 113b). While this may seem counterintuitive or even illogical, there is deep wisdom in the teaching.

Although one may have a right to privacy, being transparent is virtuous. One may have a right to ownership, but sharing is righteous. We all have obligations that we must fulfill. But we all have rights that we need not always assert. In relationships of intimacy, we are less interested in fairness (completely even sharing) and more interested in love (giving).

John Rawls, a philosopher from Harvard University, argued that society must embrace the liberty principle (that all people have equal claims on basic liberties) and the difference principle (that economic and social inequalities must be addressed by giving the greatest benefits to the most disadvantaged). Even though we all have equal rights in society (liberty principle), those with more power and privilege should sacrifice some equality to be merciful to those struggling (difference principle). Everyone has a "right" to the money they earn on their own. But the founders of the American government (and every government) have decided that each individual should give up a portion of their rights to their own property for the welfare of the collective. We see this in Article 23 of The Universal Declaration of Human Rights, cited above.

The Giving Pledge is an effort that has attracted widespread media attention and critical acclaim. The Pledge is a group of billionaires who have pledged to donate at least half of their wealth to philanthropic causes. The campaign began with Warren Buffett, who committed to donating 99 percent of his wealth to charitable organizations, a significant amount to the Bill and Melinda Gates Foundation, during his lifetime and at death, to Bill and Melinda Gates. As of 2013, more than 113 billionaires have signed the Giving Pledge. This incredible amount of money is now being used for global health programs such as The Global Fund to Fight AIDS, Tuberculosis, and Malaria, polio eradication, children vaccination programs, micro-financing for women entrepreneurs in Latin America, agricultural development, water sanitation, sex education, construction of schools, libraries, and hospitals, and other incredible work. This is just a single example of individuals deciding to cede a portion of their property rights to the advancement and betterment of our world.

The rabbis taught that God has the "right" to destroy the world (since humanity has not been as virtuous as expected), yet the Divine suspends what is fair and deserved to act with mercy. It is this model that we must emulate. We must defend the rights of the vulnerable. Yet in a society where steadfast and antagonistic claims of right are part of everyday life, let us reflect, cooperate, and act with mercy and love, just as God does with us.

10.)

The Lure of Lost Money

In late 2013, an Orthodox Jew made headlines when he returned close to $100,000 he found in a desk that he had purchased. The values that this man exemplified run very deep in Jewish tradition:

> Shimon ben Shetach once purchased a donkey. The original owner had neglected to check the saddlebag before he made the sale, and inadvertently left diamonds in the bag. When they discovered the treasure, Shimon ben Shetach's students were exuberant, for now, they were certain, their teacher would be able to teach Torah without the constant financial worries that had been plaguing him. Shimon ben Shetach did not join in their excitement though. "Do you think I am a barbarian?" he exclaimed, "I bought a donkey, not diamonds!" He promptly returned the diamonds. When the owner received them he cried out, "Blessed is the God of Shimon ben Shetach!" tradition (*Jerusalem Talmud, Bava Metzia* 2:5).

The mitzvah of returning lost objects, *hashavat aveidah*, is at the core of our tradition and contributes to our definition as a people.

What is uncanny about the recent story is how closely it parallels that of the Jerusalem Talmud. Noach Muroff, High School Rebbi at Yeshiva of New Haven, bought a used desk online for less than $200. When the desk arrived, it did not fit through his door. When Noach and his wife took the desk apart, they discovered a bag with $98,000 in cash hidden inside. Without hesitation, they decided to contact and present the stunned original owner with the money, which most likely was part of an unknown inheritance. In return, they received the following thank you note: "I do not think there are too many people in this world that would have done what you did by calling me. I do like to believe that there are still good people left in this crazy world we live in. You certainly are one of them."

Sometimes, however, returning lost money does not result in a happy heartwarming story. A homeless man, James Brady of Hackensack, New Jersey, found $850 and turned it in to the police.

When no one claimed the money within a six-month period, the money was returned to him as a reward. Things seemed to be looking up for Brady, who had recently been able to find housing and was honored by the City Council for his honesty. However, he then found out that because he had failed to report the money as income, he had been cut off from Medicaid and general assistance, a troubling indicator of how quick and callous governments can be in cutting off aid to the poor. Perhaps the many people who expressed a desire to contribute money to make up for Mr. Brady's lost benefits will be able to positively impact the situation.

While instances of people returning lost money often receive media attention, it is difficult to assess how many others decide to quietly keep what they find. As such, experiments are usually done on a small scale and cannot generally be regarded as scientifically rigorous. Nevertheless, some studies warrant examination. In a recent test,[43] *Reader's Digest* reporters placed twelve wallets with the equivalent of $50 cash and some coupons, and identification with a phone number, on the ground in sixteen cities throughout the world. Helsinki, Finland, turned out to be the most honest (11 of 12 wallets returned). New York City fared better than some might expect (8 of 12 returned), while the Iberian Peninsula fared the worst, with Madrid (2 of 12 returned) and Lisbon (1 of 12 returned, and by a tourist) placing at the bottom. Overall, only about 47 percent of the wallets were returned, as most of the people (gender, age, and other factors appeared to be unimportant) pocketed the wallet and the money. Of those who returned the wallets, all reported having been raised with a strong belief that lost items should be returned.

Finding lost money or items can be viewed as a test. Are we willing to betray the mitzvah of *hashavat aveidah* for $50, $500, or $50,000? For those raised with a strong sense of morality, it is a test that can, and should, be passed. We should not look for media attention or a handsome reward; our reward is performing a mitzvah and the knowledge that we have, at least for one or maybe a few people, restored belief in the goodness of people. This knowledge, alone, is priceless.

---

[43] http://www.rd.com/slideshows/most-honest-cities-lost-wallet-test

What If You Found A Diamond? The Mitzvah Of Returning Lost Objects

Leaving aside religious conviction, local laws, and even secular morality for a moment, consider this question: What would you do if you were homeless and stumbled across a very valuable object that could help you eat and get back on your feet?

A diamond engagement ring was accidentally thrown into homeless Billy Ray Harris' cup but when he saw Sarah Darling again, he made sure to get the ring back to her. Once this good deed hit the headlines, over seven thousand donors have pledged over $150,000 to support Harris. Harris' response is most telling: "I like it, but I don't think I deserve it… What has the world come to when a person returns something that doesn't belong to him, and all this happens?" What Harris considered the obvious right thing to do, and his motivation to carry that out in the face of a lucrative (and probably much-needed) payoff may not be everyone's inclination, but it should be.

Jewish law is unequivocal about the obligation to return lost items (Deuteronomy 22). The Torah prohibits ignoring property that clearly was lost and keeping a lost object, and commands returning such an item. *Halakhah* says that these laws only apply to objects that have a *siman* (a distinguishing feature that only an owner would be able to identify). A typical $1 bill on a sidewalk, for example, has no distinguishing feature indicating that it has a particular owner. This limitation only applies, of course, if there is no other way to identify who the owner is. The rabbis teach that it is *midat hasidut* (pious and good) to work to return a lost object even when it has no clear unique feature to it. How does our modern society fare on this subject?

Some data on lost items is encouraging. Worldwide, in 2009 airlines lost 300,000 bags of luggage, more than half during flight transfers. About 97 percent of these bags were eventually returned to their owners, but about 80,000 bags were eventually given away, offered for sale, or destroyed. In another largely encouraging example, in 2012, the ASPCA published the results of a poll of cat and dog owners. Of those reported as lost, 93 percent of dogs and

75 percent of cats were returned to their owners. Of dogs found, only 15 percent were identified by microchip or identification tags and 6 percent were found in shelters, so most were returned by the good will of strangers.

Sadly, there are also many examples of people who were tempted to take what did not belong to them or to hide items that came to them through unethical means. For example, as of October 2012, about 400 TSA employees have been fired for stealing items from airline passenger luggage.

The art world, even in the best of times, is filled with fraud, as many art works have "disappeared" from museums and never reappeared, most likely because an unscrupulous art collector has hidden it away in their private quarters. One of the most notorious examples of modern art theft occurred during the Nazi era, when thousands of art objects were stolen from Jewish citizens and museums throughout Europe. In the succeeding decades, many of these objects were returned to the original owners or their descendants, but progress has been slow. In 1998, the United States joined more than forty other nations in signing the Washington Principles on Nazi-Confiscated Art, which was supposed to set up principles that would help descendants of former owners recover art objects stolen by the Nazis. However, the Holocaust Art Restitution Project and other organizations have accused many American museums of deliberately being uncooperative or delaying the transfer of these art objects to their rightful owners. If the accusations are true, the museums would be violating the Jewish commandment not to keep a stolen object and not to hide the stolen object in order to retain possession.

While much of the documentation on many objects stolen during Nazi rule is murky, there is no contesting the facts of the most famous case of stolen art. The "Elgin Marbles," statues taken from the Parthenon in Athens by the British ambassador in the early nineteenth century and still on display at the British Museum in London, have drawn controversy for some time. The Greek government has requested their return for about thirty years, but the British are adamant that the Parthenon statues belong to the world and that they have the best ability to display them, an argument that betrays a continuing colonial attitude. The UNESCO convention in 1970 established rules (mostly voluntary) restricting the ability of one nation to expropriate property from another country without legal authority, but these rules only cover transactions after 1970.

These types of rules, and people regularly and without fanfare carrying them out, are both a mitzvah in the Jewish sense and a norm that builds trust within and across societies. When one has lost something, it can be very disorienting. If a lost item is returned, it rebuilds ones sense of trust in one's fellow person. Daily, we see inspiring examples of those who go out of their way to return valuables, while we also see depressing examples of people who claim to be refined, yet behave in a deceitful manner to prevent people from recovering lost goods. Jewish law can teach us much in promoting and achieving a just society, and universal morality and shifting social norms will create needed change. Whatever the source, looking out for our fellows and the worldly possessions that contribute to who we are, the integrity that comes with acquiring something honestly, will ensure deeper societal trust making the world a better place to live.

12.)

The Triumph of Art and the Triumph of Souls

Near the end of 2013, authorities in Germany found a huge cache of artwork that was originally plundered by the Nazis. These paintings and drawings, with their enduring beauty, have survived. It's an inspiring story, similar to the Jewish people. Just as these masterful works of art have emerged from unknown places, so too the stories of our ancestors continue to emerge from out of the darkness. It's a story of a tenacious victory over the Nazis and their attempts to steal the art and then, in spite, to hide this art from the public. In essence, the very fact that these unfairly gained (indeed, stolen) works are now out in the public consciousness means that their power to elucidate beauty and meaning have been restored to all.

> Who knows whether these pictures were preserved out of greed or fear or love? What matters in the long run is only that they made it. Artists tend to produce art as a vain bulwark against time, a gamble on posterity; and for many of the artists whom Hitler loathed, art was an explicit attempt to prevent him from getting the last word.

The story began as a customs investigation in 2010[44] that led to a raid of the Munich apartment of 76-year-old Cornelius Gurlitt on February 28, 2012, which uncovered 1,405 art treasures that Gurlitt's father Hildebrand, a noted art dealer who dealt with the Nazis, had eventually possessed. Many of the works seized came from Jewish owners, and include art from the sixteenth century to the twentieth, from works by traditional masters as well as at least one previously unknown Marc Chagall masterpiece.

It is estimated that the Nazis seized 700,000 art works from Jews. Hermann Goering was especially active in accumulating the stolen items. However, what makes this recent finding significant is that many of these works represented what the Nazis termed

---

[44] http://www.haaretz.com/jewish-world/jewish-world-news/.premium-1.556471

273

"degenerate art" (*Entartete Kunst*), which comprised not only anything by a Jewish artist, but also virtually anything that was non-representational, such as Cubism, Dada, Surrealism, and even Impressionism; Chagall, Pablo Picasso, and Otto Dix (who had served as a soldier in the German army in World War I, and still was ostracized) are several of these artists whose works were found among the hoard.

The history of these works is extraordinary. In July 1937, Hitler inaugurated the House of German Art (*Haus der deutschen Kunst*), while on the next day in a nearby space the *Entartete Kunst* exhibit was launched in a deliberately haphazard manner, with nearly 600 works crowded on walls and hung irregularly with wire or even burlap, and with derogatory statements on the wall to hammer home the approved message that this was the art of inferior peoples. Interestingly, only a handful of the more than one hundred artists whose works were condemned were Jewish, and ironically the painter who had the most condemned works in the exhibit was Emil Nolde, a man sympathetic to Nazi ideology.

Unexpectedly, the *Entartete Kunst* exhibit proved to be more popular than the Nazis had expected, traveling to twelve other cities and viewed by millions of people by 1941, many times more than ventured to see the approved German art in Munich. Similarly, a room devoted to denouncing the Jewish composer Kurt Weill and his *Threepenny Opera* (*Die Dreigroschenoper*) in the 1938 "Degenerate Music" (*Entartete Musik*) exhibit in Düsseldorf had to be closed because so many people crowded in every day to listen to the music.

History has vindicated this judgment. The prized Nazi aesthetic consisted of horrid caricatures of classical art. Instead of the symmetry of the columns of the Parthenon or the dome of the Pantheon, Hitler demanded huge, unwieldy buildings and exaggerated sculptures; the *Haus der deutschen Kunst* was (and is) an extremely ugly building, and the original art, consisting of nude men with ludicrously huge muscles among other things, has rightly been forgotten. On the other hand, the *Entartete Kunst* has formed the core of modern art museums throughout the world. Indeed, the recently recovered works have initially been valued at about 1 billion Euros.

As indicated earlier, the newly discovered art works include a previously unknown masterpiece by Chagall, who spent his early years in a Russian shtetl before settling in France (and barely escaping to the United States during World War II). Today, his paintings and other works are present in museums throughout the world, as well as in other notable locations, such as:

- New York City's Lincoln Center, where his murals, *The Triumph of Music* and *The Sources of Music*, adorn the front of the Metropolitan Opera and are the first thing that the visitor sees upon coming to the square.

- The United Nations, where his stained glass window for peace is visible in the public lobby.

- Zürich, Switzerland, where he designed a series of five stained glass windows and a rosette window for the Fraumünster church.

- Ein Kerem, Jerusalem, where he presented a magnificent series of stained glass windows to the Abbell Synagogue at the Hadassah University Medical Center. As Chagall noted: "All the time I was working, I felt my mother and father looking over my shoulder; and behind them were Jews, millions of other vanished Jews—of yesterday and a thousand years ago."

The cost to humanity during this period – in lives and culture – continues to defy rational explanation. The recovery of some of the lost art of this period offers a slight recompense, as culture has a restorative quality. Rambam stated:

> If one is afflicted with melancholy, he should cure it by listening to songs and various kinds of the melodies, by walking in gardens and fine buildings, by sitting before beautiful forms, and by things like this, which delight the soul and make the disturbance of melancholy disappear from it. In all this he should aim at making his body healthy, the goal of his body's health being that he attain knowledge. (Introduction to his Commentary on *Avot*, Chapter)

The stolen Nazi loot affects Holocaust survivors and their heirs stolen Nazi loot affects Holocaust survivors and their heirs: the rightful owners.[45] There has been tremendous stubbornness on the part of governments and related institutions who feel recalcitrant in returning artwork or objects that are not rightfully theirs, either through a callous attitude of the past or just that they feel that they are too far removed from the events to have had any illicit dealings with those who stole the art in the first place. We are encouraged that the American government has taken the position that the Washington Principles of 1998 should be enforced, so that stolen art recovered from any source should be returned to the rightful owners.

There are databases of many thousands of works that remain officially lost (only a fraction were returned to their rightful owners). While some are confident that all the works will be returned to their rightful owners outside Germany, others wonder why it took the German government to publicly acknowledge the existence of this hoard. Fortunately, there is a team of art experts who are examining the works, and have promised to publish the list, which will help the rightful owners lay claim to these works and perhaps once again share them with the world.

As people continue to seek lost art treasures and (we hope) seek to trace the obscure paths to their rightful owners, let us treasure the value of art in human life. As Rabbi Avraham Heschel said in a 1972 television interview: "… above all, remember that the meaning of life is to build a life as if it were a work of art. You're not a machine. And you are young. Start working on this great work of art called your own existence."

---

[45] http://www.theguardian.com/commentisfree/2013/nov/05/stolen-nazi-art-holocaust-munich

Falling Fruit: Curbing Food Waste And Feeding the Hungry

Having lived in California and Arizona, I've seen luscious fruits hanging from trees all around during the spring season. Unfortunately, a lot of the fruit that these trees produce ripen fall to the ground and go to waste. One organization, Falling Fruit, has been trying to address the problem of this wasted opportunity to help those in need.

The Jewish tradition emphasizes quite adamantly that the earth is not our own and that we ought not waste its bounty. The hunger pandemic is not a crisis of sufficiency (there is enough food in the world to feed everyone) but of distribution (food must be allocated to other regions). Falling Fruit, as an organization has truly taken the Jewish tradition and awareness of world hunger to heart and is working to actualize the Biblical mandate to surrender field crops to the local poor. This inspiring group is reacting to fallen fruit, something most people pay little attention to, and is taking initiative to address hunger while deeply cherishing God's creation.

Today, there are new open-source Internet maps showing fruit trees available for free harvesting in urban environments all over the globe. We should consider taking advantage of these resources to enjoy local produce and do our part to stymie waste. Any effort to reduce food wastefulness should be encouraged. A 2012 report from the National Resources Defense Council[46] estimated that about 40 percent of food in America (about $165 billion or 240 pounds of food per person annually) is discarded. While the U.S. Department of Agriculture does not keep many statistics on the wasting of fruits and vegetables, it estimates that supermarkets waste $15 billion in unsold produce every year. Households and food services lose a great deal as well: American households on average throw out about 25 percent of the food brought home. Of all food losses from retail, households, and food services, fruits and vegetables comprise 30 percent while 22 percent

---

[46] http://www.nrdc.org/food/files/wasted-food-ip.pdf

come from fresh fruit and vegetables, and an additional 8 percent from processed produce.

A 2011 survey of the United States, Canada, Australia, and New Zealand, the food product with the highest percentage of loss to be fruits and vegetables (52), greater even than seafood (50), and far greater than grains (38) or meats (22). Tracing the greatest loss of fruits and vegetables from harvest to consumption, it is estimated that 20 percent is lost in production, 12 percent in distribution and retail sale, and 28 percent through consumer behavior.

Paradoxically, it is estimated that about six billion pounds of produce is either not harvested or not sold, partly due to a shortage of labor and partly due to the public's demand for produce that looks good, meaning that fruits and vegetables that do not have the right color or shape, for example, may not even be harvested. A producer of citrus, pitted fruit, and grapes estimated that anywhere from a fifth to half of his produce was edible but could not be sold to distributors due to its appearance. While sending this produce to processors would seem a logical alternative, it is not often possible as the transportation costs might be too costly to make it a worthwhile venture, and processors may have already made contracts with other farms and not need more produce. Therefore, perfectly edible produce is simply discarded or goes to waste over time.

Furthermore, uneaten food creates environmental problems and hazards. The water and energy used to produce this food is squandered, and about a sixth of the critical landfill space is occupied by uneaten foodstuff. In addition, it is estimated that 23 percent of all methane (a much more dangerous greenhouse gas than carbon dioxide) generated comes from uneaten food. A United Kingdom survey concluded that uneaten food in landfills, if removed, would be as beneficial to lowering greenhouse gases as ridding the nation of one-fifth of its cars.

Even a slight reduction in waste could literally result in the ability to feed tens of millions of hungry people; the environmental damage should also be a strong incentive to conserve food. Yet, per capita, Americans waste ten times as much food as people in Southeast Asia; this amount of food waste is 50 percent more than it was forty years ago. In contrast, the European Union has embarked on a concerted and diligent mission to reduce food waste. In a similar vein, the United Kingdom has had remarkable success in food waste reduction waste and has cut their waste by 18 percent in the past five years.

Falling Fruit exemplifies a positive step in the campaign to drastically reduce the staggering amount of wasted food. While most of us cannot drive out to farms and efficiently pick fresh and local produce, we can take advantage of what is accessible in our own neighborhoods and backyards. In addition, the public can be educated further in the efficient use of foodstuffs. For example, if an apple is not perfectly symmetrical or not uniformly red, it is still perfectly edible. Another example of positive strides can be seen in some supermarket chains that no longer stack their produce bins as high as the Himalayas to get people to buy. Still, we must do more and encourage food services to not discard anything that does not look like a magazine cover. One way to increase consumption of cosmetically substandard produce is to employ farmer's markets or to use food banks, where irregular sizes and shapes are not barriers to consumption.

The Biblical prohibition against being wasteful is actually learned from fruit trees (Deuteronomy 20:19). It is the paradigmatic example for our responsibility to take care of the earth and feed the hungry. Jewish law has taught that feeding the hungry trumps other needs of those suffering in poverty:

> If someone comes and says, "feed me," you don't check him to see if he is an imposter, but you feed him right away. If there is a naked person who comes and says, "Give me clothing," you check him to see if he is an imposter. And if you know him, you give him clothing right away, *(Shulchan Aruch, Yoreh Deah, Laws of Tzedakah* 251:10).

Certain requests may warrant transparency, but that is not so with food. The rabbis teach we must immediately feed those who are hungry. In addition to meeting the needs of the hungry, the reduction of waste in fruit and other food items must be achieved. Skeptics might consider that only a generation ago Americans had no idea what recycling was, and yet today we take it for granted. We can succeed in this endeavor – it is our ethical and moral obligation to do so.

Moral Education

Violence In Sports: Promoting Character Development In Youth Athletics

I grew up as a hardcore competitive athlete. I learned to cultivate perseverance to run the extra mile at full speed, teamwork to pass the ball, and a disciplined work ethic to challenge myself to the next level. But it was not always pretty. I can recall bloody backyard football games, injuries in varsity basketball, and elbow checks in cross country meets. Growing up as a committed competitive athlete had its thrills, but it was not easy or painless.

Sports and regular activity are great for physical and mental health, learning leadership lessons, and engendering teamwork, but many modern sports are also dangerous and prone to conflict. It is not rare for boxers to deeply injure each other, hockey players to fight, or a baseball batter to charge the mound leading to a full team vs. team brawl. There are also fights that happen among fans and spectators, such as the English "hooligans" or numerous South American melees and car burnings that mar soccer matches. Sports are becoming increasingly violent and have even led to death. We would think we have advanced as a civilization from the years of the Nika riots, in which tens of thousands were killed, but in 2013, a 17-year-old soccer player in Salt Lake City punched and killed his recreation-league referee.

Professional sports have become much more of a big business in the past few decades, with ticket and merchandise costs skyrocketing revenue and salaries. Unfortunately, in the competitive quest for individual and team success, unsportsmanlike practices are more pervasive. In hockey, many teams have a player called an "enforcer," whose main job is to physically punish the opposing team; for example, if any of his teammates are flattened by an opposing player's check, the enforcer will retaliate with an equally brutal hit, and he will never shy away from a fight. In football, where every play features hard hits from players weighing 250 or (sometimes many) more pounds, the consequences have been more serious. Over a three-year period,[47] the New Orleans Saints football team players and an assistant coach awarded bounties each time an opposing player was injured, including $1,500 for each player knocked unconscious and $1,000 for each player who had to be carried off on a stretcher. Players who participated in this program earned $50,000 during the team's 2009 championship season. While the story made headlines, insiders conceded that many other teams had bounties, although they were not as lucrative as the Saints'.

A rise in injuries and attempts to reform the sport occur periodically. At the turn of the twentieth century, American football was a very dangerous sport. One newspaper estimated that eighteen students died and 159 were seriously injured in 1904, mostly in prep schools. At that time, the players often did not wear protection for their heads, had little padding, and formed mass formations that were closer to rugby than to modern football. Oddly, President Theodore Roosevelt, who was not known for avoiding "manly" activities, understood that something had to change, and over the next several years he successfully encouraged colleges to band together and change the rules to minimize casualties. In this century, an explosion of concussions and a trend of debilitating brain trauma is forcing professional football to act again. In March 2013, faced with litigation from about four thousand former players who had suffered concussions, the NFL adopted a new rule in which players (in a zone outside the area where the teams line up) would be forbidden from lowering their head and crashing into opposing players with their helmets. While players and fans expressed opposition, it is believed that this will lower the number of concussions and serious injuries.

In other sports, violence is openly discouraged. In baseball, for example, it was common for pitchers to deliberately throw at opposing batters' heads (who had nothing for protection but a cloth cap), and retaliation was the norm. Today, a pitcher can be warned or ejected, fined, and suspended for doing this, and the managers also face discipline. While the "bean ball" still exists, it is less frequent, and now batters at all levels and of all ages wear protective

---

[47] http://espn.go.com/nfl/story/_/id/7638603/new-orleans-saints-defense-had-bounty-program-nfl-says%2522%20%255Ct%20%2522_hplink

helmets at all times. Today, children face more risk of injury from overuse or improperly throwing a ball when pitching, which has vastly increased the need for elbow ligament surgery, than from being hit by a pitch.

Sports are a great way to establish a life-long pattern of exercise, which should be an hour a day for children. The U.S. Government guidelines for physical activity note that people who exercise regularly live longer, healthier lives, are less likely to be depressed, gain weight, develop hypertension, type 2 diabetes, heart disease, certain cancers, and osteoporosis, and help maintain cognitive function and balance, which is increasingly important as we age. If we do not exercise when we are young, we may not be able to engage in the amount or strenuousness of exercise needed as we age.

Sports are a great vehicle for teaching kids collaboration, healthy competition, health, and discipline. However, too often sports teams emphasize or allow for the wrong character traits to develop (aggressiveness, unhealthy competition, bullying, violence, etc.). Parents and other adults should ensure that when sports are played, the rules are enforced with impartiality and that everyone (including the parents) behaves in a sportsmanlike way. If we do this, we can all have a lifetime benefit.

2.)

The *Aish Kodesh*: Inflated Success and Positive Reinforcement

Many child development books today encourage using only positive language with children. Instead of speaking with discouraging, critical, or punitive language, one should frame the direction in the positive. While there is clearly some benefit to this approach, when done incorrectly it may also further a next generation of inflated egos. There is already no lack of unearned "validation" in our culture. Chip and Dan Heath, the authors of *Switch* explain:

> We've all heard the studies showing that the vast majority of us consider ourselves above-average drivers. In the psychology literature, this belief is known as a *positive illusion.* Our brains are positive illusion factories: Only 2 percent of high school seniors believe their leadership skills are below average. A full 25 percent of people believe they're in the top 1 percent in their ability to get along with others. Ninety-four percent of college professors report doing above-avenge work. People think they're at lower risk than their peers for heart attacks, cancer, and even food-related illnesses such as salmonella. Most deliciously self-deceptive of all, people say they are more likely than their peers to provide accurate self-assessments.

But researchers have found that domestic workers seem to be outside of this phenomenon, at least relating to their health and success. Prior to a 2007 study conducted by Harvard University's Alia J. Crum and Ellen J. Langer, 67 percent of domestic workers did not recognize that their work has any exercise value, and more than a third did not think that they exercised at all. The researchers wanted to measure whether telling the domestic workers that they were exercise superstars would have any effect on their self-perception irrespective of any change in activity. They were told that their work is sufficient to receive the full benefits of exercise. They were told that, on average, they would burn one hundred calories for a half hour of vacuuming, forty calories for changing linens for fifteen minutes, etc. In another group, the domestic workers were not encouraged or told that their work was a form of exercise. A month later, the domestic workers who were told of the exercise benefit from their work lost an average of about two pounds, showing improvement in blood pressure and body fat. In addition, at least 79 percent of the informed group now believed that they were exercising regularly, even though their activity had not increased.

While many seem to have a very inflated sense of personal success, many others (often the less privileged) have a more deflated sense of confidence, and reinforcement can make all the difference. When we educate our children, we should not give blanket praise detached from achievement, nor should we be exclusively critical or married only to results-based assessment and validation; rather, we must engage each child according to their respective sense of self-esteem. Thus, creativity, imagination, and inquisitiveness should be encouraged in students; however, those who make basic errors (for example, two plus two equals nine) or write consistently inadequate essays should not be given encouragement, as they will begin to think that their work is fine, and that no further work is needed. Then, when they get pushed through to a higher grade, they will be further behind and may not be able to catch up to the expected level.

Rabbi Kalonymus Kalman Shapira (known as the Aish Kodesh and as the Piasetzener Rebbe, he was murdered in the Holocaust) wrote a remarkable book on education where he begs that we educate our children differently:

> Someone who is trying to educate through [merely] command and habituation need not pay attention to the way... [his child] thinks ... An educator, however, who wishes to uncover the soul of the child that lies hidden and concealed.... must therefore teach according to his [student's] nature, mind, character and other unique qualities... What he commands and instructs one child should be different from what he commands and instructs the next child, whose nature, will, mind, and personality are completely different from the first. And this is what King Solomon is hinting to us, "Educate each child according to his own path" (Prov. 22:6) (*Chovat Ha Talmidim*, 5).

With the proper support, we can all achieve anything. We must help each other to learn our respective potentials. By staying both realistic and positive we can begin to see the positive in what we are already doing and achieve more than we can ever imagine.

3.)

The Value Of Humor: Religious Learning And The Limits Of Purim *Shpiels*

In the Talmud, the Rabbis taught that humor is valuable in Torah study, as it warms people's hearts and brings joy into the learning. For example, before starting to lecture or teach, Rabbah "would tell a joke. The rabbis would laugh. Then he would sit down and in a state of awe would begin the day's lesson" (*Shabbat* 30b); religious education and humor go together nicely.

Humor also presents a challenge to the educator, as it serves as a distraction and lead to frivolity, and the Rabbis were sensitive to this, too. One episode in the Talmud shares how one rabbi tried to conquer his delight in humor.

> On the day that Rabbi laughed, punishment would come upon the world. So he said to Bar Kappara [who was a humorist]: "Do not make me laugh, and I will give you forty measures of wheat." He replied, "But let the Master see that I may take whatever measure I desire." So he took a large basket, pitched it over, placed it on his head, went [to Rabbi] and said to him, "Fill me the forty measures of wheat which I may demand from you." Thereupon Rabbi burst into laughter, and said to him, "Did I not warn you not to jest?" He replied, "I wish but to take the wheat which I may [justly] demand" (*Nedarim* 50a).

Societies from the pagan era to the present have had certain times of the year set aside for when the usual societal discipline was relaxed or completely done away with (think of ancient spring festivals and present-day Mardi Gras in New Orleans or Carnival in Rio). For the Jewish people, Purim is a time when we drink wine (a lot of wine…and other drinks), and the usual discipline is often thrown off. The custom of the Purim *shpiel*, the whimsical play put on by yeshiva students and community members, is the most prominent example of this practice.

The history of the Purim *shpiel* merits examination. In the fifteenth century, Ashkenazi families created humorous plays based on parody rhymes of the Book of Esther. Eventually, these grew into public performances, often of a bawdy nature. By the following century, it was customary for Purim *shpiels* to be staged performances in the home, and wealthy families brought in performing companies to stage elaborate productions. By the eighteenth century, the *shpiel* branched out to include other Biblical episodes, and grew to include musical instruments and longer narratives. At times, the content was deemed offensive; for example, the leaders of the Jewish community in Hamburg banned all Purim *shpiels* in 1728. Today, the Purim *shpiel* varies from congregation to congregation. It tends to be light-hearted, festive, and replete with silly costumes and play-acting.

Fortunately, the humor that is on display in Purim *shpiels* and other religious contexts is not only therapeutic, but it can help us learn as well. Studies have shown that humor helps people retain learning. Studies over the past fifteen years have yielded interesting data on the positive role of humor in learning:[48]

- Students in a statistics course retained more knowledge when the lectures included humorous material that related to the course material.

- Students were more likely to log into an introductory psychology course when they had a professor who made self-deprecating jokes and included cartoons and other topical material in lectures.

- A 1999 study demonstrated that students perceived instructors who injected humor in the classroom as being more intelligent and concerned with students than instructors who did not.

Laughter, which reduces stress hormones such as cortisol, can even be used to lighten the atmosphere in a classroom during a test, and can improve students' performances on

---

[48] http://www.apa.org/monitor/jun06/learning.aspx

those tests.

While concerned educators will rightly point out that humor should not take over in a class setting, because students will consider everything to be a joke and there will be little learning, these studies show that humor is nevertheless helpful in many situations. Rav Ovadia Yosef expresses his concerns on this subject in a responsum:

> I have seen in writing that the Gaon, Rabbi Shimon Sofer, died from the anguish he suffered in the wake of the insults hurled at him by the Rav Purim. May the good Lord atone for this. God forbid, then, that this custom should continue, and especially not in the holy *yeshivot*, which must serve as an example of love, honor and awe of Torah. It is a mitzvah to forcefully object and absolutely abolish this evil custom, the word *minhag* (custom) being a transmutation of the word Gehinnom (*Yechave Da'at V*, no. 50).

Of course, frivolity, mockery, insensitivity, and *lashon hara* (hurtful speech) are not the goals, nor are they acceptable outcomes, of humor in religious life or in education. I recall Purim *shpiels* that went overboard in roasting educators at the yeshiva. Clearly, some of those rabbis felt hurt by what some of the students considered holiday jokes. Some who witnessed this banned Purim *shpiels*.

Recently, a public figure went beyond even the extended limits of the *shpiel*. New York State Assemblyman Dov Hikind was eventually forced to apologize in February 2013 for dressing in blackface during a Purim celebration. The Anti-Defamation League issued a statement saying that Mr. Hikind had shown "terrible judgment" in his choice of costume, which showed insensitivity to the long-standing history of racial bigotry in the United States and was particularly reprehensible in a public figure that was a strong opponent of anti-Semitism.

Rav Avraham Yitzchak Kook taught that joy does not involve evading evil and the challenges of life, for this would not be true joy; rather, there must be a constant desire to integrate life and join with a greater spiritual force, and this can arouse true joy (*Ein*

Ayah Berakhot, no. 61). Humor can be used to bring in new life perspectives and elevate one emotionally, creating the potential for new spiritual heights. May we learn to bring joy into all that we do and may it be the type of joy that elevates us and those around us to higher purpose.

4

Hitting Children For Obedience? Parenting With Compassion

Now, it's true that Rambam thought we should hit children (and women) to instill fear in them (*Talmud Torah* 2:2). Of course, eight hundred years have passed and it was a different time, but even so, his ruling was clear that this hitting should not be out of anger, with sticks or straps, but instead it should come from an educational motivation and with at most a small strap. The *Shulchan Aruch* also rules this way (*Y.D.* 245:10), and the Vilna Gaon seemed to take this approach as well (*Ulim Litrufa*).

To Rambam's credit, he rules that any aggressive acts that are intended to cause harm or embarrass another are forbidden (*Hovel uMazik* 5:1), and his approach throughout is that, rather than experiencing real anger in the moment, one should merely fake anger for the sake of the student's character development (*Deot* 2:3).

Rebbe Nachman saw things differently and made clear that we should never hit children. More recently, Rav Shlomo Wolbe argued that any type of hitting would create a long-term strained relationship between parent and child, so it should be avoided. An important halakhic approach to follow is that one may not hit a young child since it is a violation of *Lifnei Iver* (causing another to err), because hitting the child will likely cause them to hit a parent or teacher back, and thus the child will have committed a sin (*Moed Katan* 17a, *Kiddushin* 30a).

A 2004 study of abusive parents found that 73 percent had assaulted their kids – hitting or punching them with their fists – and 20 percent had engaged in even more violent assaults, resulting in broken bones or severe lacerations. These parents tended to blame their behavior on their "bad" or "stubborn" kids: "They'll say, 'I had to discipline my child this way because he's so rotten and he won't listen,'" researcher Beverly Funderburk said, and they believed that violence was the only way to get their kids to obey.

Other scientific studies support the position taken by Rebbe Nachman and Rav Shlomo Wolbe. Catherine A. Taylor of Tulane University studied urban mothers' use of corporal punishment on their children. She found that a quarter of mothers who spanked their three-year-old child more than twice in the previous month reported that their children were more aggressive by their next interview two years later, independent of any other factor. These results confirm what the findings of numerous previous studies, namely that corporal punishment of children is far more likely to result in greater aggression as the child ages. It is no wonder that the American Academy of Pediatrics continues to oppose corporal punishment for children.

Today, we understand that the best approach in education is through positive reinforcement and showing love, not the "hickory stick" that dominated until the mid-twentieth century. It is never appropriate to use any physical aggression as punishment upon a child and abuse must be reported to the authorities. Of course, there must be rule and structure, but that should not be enforced through physical punishment. We learn best through encouragement, not fear. We must encourage our youth and offer constant positive reinforcement to help them to actualize their potentials and flourish in life.

5

It's Hard to Be a Kid Today

A 2013 American Psychological Association survey[49] noted that American teenagers are now experiencing stress levels equal to those of adults, and for the first time, during the school year American youth experienced more daily stress than adults. These levels of stress are very unhealthy for children. More studies are also revealing the transgenerational effects of stress and their correlation with illness. Even more troubling for a child growing up in economic adversity is that when poverty is coupled with stress[50], there can be significant impact on the brain development and understanding.

We must make sure that our children are growing up in safe and healthy environments:

- Consider the cruelty of two Utah elementary school cafeteria workers who snatched away the lunch trays from forty children whose parents were behind on making meal payments. The school workers then threw the students' meals in the trash humiliating them in front of their peers and leaving them hungry.

- Consider the levels of child abuse: Annually, about 3 million reports of child abuse (involving six million children) are made; in 2010, 1,537 children died of abuse and neglect.

- On average, there was a school shooting every two weeks in 2013. However, in some areas many shootings occur off school grounds and do not figure into these statistics. In 2010, nearly 700 Chicago school children were shot, sixty-six fatally, often in multiple shootings, as when 10 were murdered and 37 wounded by firearms in a single three-day period. Nationally, in 2008-2009 (a 2-year period), 5,740

---

[49] http://www.apa.org/news/press/releases/2014/02/teen-stress.aspx

[50] http://www.sciencedaily.com/releases/2013/10/131021211450.htm

Americans younger than 18 were killed and 34,387 were injured by firearms, a higher casualty rate than American soldiers deployed in Iraq and Afghanistan.

- Bullying: While statistics are difficult to verify, the Department of Justice estimates that one-fourth of adolescents will be bullied, while other studies estimate that as many as three-fourths will be bullied at least once.

- Social-media pressures: Students are often pressured to engage in risky behavior and abuse alcohol and drugs. For example, a National Institute on Drug Abuse-funded study found that in a simulated driving experiment, students were more than twice as likely to engage in risky driving when their friends observed them than when they were alone.

It's hard to be a kid today. Bracketing the extreme cases, schoolwork has often gotten more challenging and demanding. While extracurricular activities have always played a significant role in children's lives, social media now consumes two hours or more of time daily,[51] which can further add to the stress of a full school day.

Another factor to consider is that an astounding 30 percent of American families are single parent (85 percent of those homes are led by single mothers). In homes with two parents, when fathers provide just basic childcare, children are found to have higher levels of educational and economic achievement and lower rates of delinquency. These children are also found to be more empathetic and socially competent. Growing up with one parent is not only extremely challenging for the particular parent, but can take a serious toll upon that child.

Some theological and psychological teachings have stressed the malevolent nature of children. However, Voltaire, the famous French philosopher, saw children differently: "Gather together all the children of the universe; you will see in them nothing but innocence, gentleness, and fear; had they been born evil,

---

[51] http://www.aacap.org/AACAP/Families_and_Youth/Facts_for_Families/Facts_for_Families_Pages/Children_and_Social_Networking_100.aspx

malevolent, cruel, they would give some sign of it...." This approach should be embraced where we view children as delicate and innocent (albeit not fully in control yet) who need to be deeply nurtured. Let us make our children the priority and work to ensure that they are growing up in healthy, nurturing, and safe environments.

6

The Case for Intellectual Judaism: Adults Cannot Rely on Their Third Grade Jewish Education

Piety left the center stage of Jewish life with the destruction of the Temple, when we moved from a religion based in priestly rite to the academic, detailed, and all-encompassing structure of rabbinic Judaism. The paradigm shift not only moved our community from a religion centered on animal sacrifices to a religion of prayer and study, it was also the transition from piousness to an intellectual, legalistic religion. Judaism came and proclaimed to the world, "Ideas matter!"

Rabbi Shneur Zalman of Liadi, the author of the *Tanya* and founder of the Hasidic Chabad movement, taught that we have the spiritual power to bring ideas into existence. In the Baal Ha'Tanya's view, we bring ideas into existence and they have great power once in this world. We are not merely concerned with simple meditations about peace; rather, complex ideas matter in the world:

> Whenever my master [Rabbi Dovber of Mezeritch], conceived an original [Torah] thought, he would voice it aloud, although those present could not understand him. He would speak as if to himself. By articulating the idea, he would draw it into this world. Once the idea was present in this world, it could occur to another person – even one at the other end of the world – who was laboring in the study of Torah and the service of God... Had it not been drawn into this world, even if the other were to toil mightily, he would not arrive at this idea – for it would still be in heaven (*Ma'amarei Admor Hazaken Haketzarim*, 474).

Some have lamented the so-called "decline of the Rabbi-Intellectual." As rabbinical programs have become more focused on pastoral counseling, homiletics, social action, and management, intellectual pursuits have often fallen by the wayside.

In modern times, Jews have a disproportionate number of secular intellectual accomplishments in modern times; for example, that Jews have won 18 percent of Nobel prizes despite only accounting for four-tenths of a percent of world population. This success has not come because Jews are inherently smarter than everyone else; it only shows that the community is very intellectually engaged. Yet, why does that intellectual curiosity not always bridge over into the Jewish learning and discourse?

On college campuses, we see more young Jews interested in engaging lucrative careers as law, medicine, and commerce (all admittedly respectable) and a decline in pursuits of philosophy, literature, and the humanities. For example, among Yeshiva University graduates in 2011, Accounting and General Finance majors were nearly three times as numerous as Hebrew Language and Literature majors. However, it should be noted that, unlike national trends where business degrees were paramount and accounted for nearly one-fourth of total degrees issued in the United States, Yeshiva graduates were most likely to have majored in Psychology or Biology than the business fields. This seeming paradox in Jewish intellectualism extends to the Ultra-Orthodox: whereas Maimonides was also deeply engaged in philosophy, science, and other intellectual pursuits, the culture most engaged with Torah study today rejects altogether the value of secular study.   What is the value of an intellectual Judaism anyway? Why not just work hard, make money, donate, and spend the rest of our time in leisure with family and friends? Why should one be committed to lectures, books, classes, journals, and asking hard questions?

General trends in America may provide a warning to those who think this way. *Reading at Risk*, a 2002 Census Bureau survey of U.S. adults, reached this conclusion: "…literary reading in America is not only declining among all groups, but the rate of decline has accelerated, especially among the young." Among the reasons given is that while reading a book requires concentrated attention, Americans have increasingly turned to activities that "foster shorter attention spans and accelerated gratification." Furthermore, it portended ill for the future, as those who did not read were also less likely to be involved in political or cultural activities. Among the findings of the report, comparing results in 2002 versus 1982, were:

- The share of Americans who read literature declined from nearly 57 percent to less than 47 percent, the first time in history that fewer than half of all Americans read books

- The number of those reading books of any kind declined by 4.3 percent

- Literary reading has declined at all education levels, including a drop of more than 15 percent in those who had completed college and graduate school, and 20 percent among those who had attended college

- In 2002, 43 percent of literary readers performed volunteer and charity work, versus 17 percent of non-literary readers

- This survey took place before the arrival of Facebook, text messaging, and Twitter

Many have expressed the hope that eBooks would improve the situation. However, a December 2011 Pew Internet poll of adults recorded that more than half of U.S. adults reported having read five or fewer books (including eBooks) over the past year.

What are the consequences of this decline in reading and intellectualism? One result is that in an era of pundits on the airwaves, intellectuals and credentialed experts have lost influence. A century ago, Louis Brandeis developed a "Brandeis Brief" for court cases, incorporating sociological, demographic, economic, and legal data to form a compelling legal argument. During the New Deal, President Franklin D. Roosevelt employed a "Brains Trust" of Columbia University professors who worked on legislation that would promote economic growth. However, today many bloggers, talk show radio hosts, and cable news guests are more performer than intellectual. As a result, alarming numbers of Americans retain long discredited conspiracy theories and other illogical fantasies such as:

- A CBS poll released in April 2011 revealed that 25 percent of Americans (and 45 percent of Republicans) believed that President Barack Obama was not born in America, and only

57 percent believed correctly that he was born in America. This poll was taken nearly three years after the charge had been conclusively proven false.

- Polling among registered voters in the spring of 2013 revealed that 13 percent (obviously Christian) believed that President Obama was the Antichrist and another 13 percent were "unsure."

- Several YouTube videos claim the mass shootings at a Newtown, CT, elementary school was a hoax staged by the government in an effort to take guns away from Americans. Recently, a father of a girl slain by gun violence was shouted down by a group of conspiracy theorists that screamed "propaganda" as he tried to mention the name of his daughter at a rally sponsored by Mayors Against Illegal Guns.

These deep-seated, erroneous beliefs have contributed to the complete paralysis of the federal government today. When you see your opponent as the devil, you are not going to engage in respectful behavior or move toward compromise. This is why climate change, the environment, poverty, and other critical issues remain ignored.

Fortunately, we can act constructively by encouraging intellectual activities. Judaism teaches that *Rachmana liba ba'ei* – the Compassionate One, i.e. God, desires the heart. For the heart to be pure it must be honest and critical; to dismiss big and important questions and concerns is to jeopardize one's spiritual health. When we live a life committed to ideas, we declare that we will not close our eyes to reality.

Jewish social justice depends upon a community that is attendant to the human condition, aware of contemporary social systems, well learned in Jewish texts, and critical in merging different systems of ideas. Maimonides goes so far as to argue that if we do not remove our own ignorance then we're at great risk of perpetuating evil in the world:

These great evils that come about between the
human individuals who inflict them upon one
another because of purposes, desires, opinions
and beliefs, are all of them likewise consequent
upon privation. For all of them derive from
ignorance, I mean from a privation of knowledge.
Just as a blind man, because of absence of sight,
does not cease stumbling, being wounded, and
also wounding others, because he has nobody to
guide him on his way, the various sects of men—
every individual according to the extent of his
ignorance—does to himself and to others great
evils from which individuals of the species suffer.
If there were knowledge, whose relation to the
human form is like that of the faculty of sight to
the eye, they would refrain from doing any harm
to themselves and to others (*Guide for the Perplexed*,
3:11).

Many Jews go on to get advanced secular degrees but remain
eight-year-olds in their Jewish knowledge. How can someone take
Judaism (or any religion) seriously if she has a child's education in it?
To properly live a religious life, a Jew must not just rely on the
education of his or her youth but continue to relearn the religion,
and re-understand the Torah as he or she develops and society
evolves. Rabbis and educators also must stop teaching adults as if
they are children simply because they are not yet advanced in their
Jewish learning. We must all raise the bar challenging others, indeed
ourselves, to learn more openly and critically.

Intellectual life is connected to spiritual life in this regard.
Martin Buber explains the Baal Shem Tov's teaching here:

The Baal Shem Tov [the founder of Hasidism
in the eighteenth century] teaches that no
encounter with a being or a thing in the course
of our life lacks a hidden significance.... If we
neglect this spiritual substance sent across our
path, if we think only in terms of momentary
purposes, without developing a genuine
relationship to the beings and things in whose
life we ought to take part, as they in ours, then
we shall ourselves be debarred from true,
fulfilled existence (*The Way of Man*).

We have a precious legacy in our pursuit of intellectualism. As with other aspects of our tradition, true study requires discipline and concentrated attention, and a willingness to resist the constant use of text messaging, computer games, and other distractions. We know from our history that the rewards from these endeavors are great, and we can see around us the risks that come with neglecting them. Jewish intellectualism is not reserved for the elite. Rather, taking ideas seriously is an essential part of living a Jewish life.

7

Hebrew School: A Failed Experiment

Growing up, I spent years worth of Sundays being bored out of my gourd, asked to memorize dates and names, playing games well below my level, and singing songs I did not understand. I was confused by why I was in class with students who were both younger and older than me, many of whom did not show up half the time because of a "conflict" like a baseball game or simple apathy. The lack of commitment from all involved furthered an ambience of disengagement. The only highlight of Hebrew school was the sweet, distracting donuts.

In short, Hebrew school achieved almost nothing for me and unfortunately I'm not alone. Now as my wife and I beginning to think about the Jewish education for our daughter, we have hard questions to ask.

Hebrew Sunday School began with good intentions. Rebecca Gratz, who had previously founded the Female Hebrew Benevolent Society in 1819, created the first Jewish Sunday School in Philadelphia in 1838.

She wanted to create a parallel structure to the Christian Sunday schools already in existence, and believed that by becoming well-versed and observant, Jews would earn the respect of the Christian world. The schools provided employment for Jewish women, and in turn the best female graduates would become the next generation of teachers. Other cities soon established their own Sunday schools on Gratz's model.

Hebrew school today is a way for many parents who do not choose to invest in a serious, comprehensive Jewish education (or are unable to) to feel good that they are giving their child some Jewish experience, and it is often a prerequisite for a child's becoming a bar or bat mitzvah (requiring new jobs and the concomitant costs). Hebrew school today is also, unfortunately, all too often a great way for a child to feel terrible about their Jewish experience. Many synagogue leaders in fact are not even interested in improving the Sunday school. It is merely a vehicle to attract new families to synagogue membership. The Jewish education of our youth cannot be propped up as a superficial means to achieve other organizational goals and benchmarks.

One way in which this manifests itself is in language. Hebrew University professors Sarah Bunin Benor and Steven M. Cohen have conducted interesting research on the linguistic changes that have taken place among American Jews. Hebrew pronunciation in Jewish schools has changed over time. From 1920-1960, pronunciation shifted from a Yiddish-inspired Ashkenazi system to an Israeli Hebrew system, possibly reflecting a rise in Zionism and more Israeli teachers in these schools. As Benor notes: "The use of linguistic features helps Jews indicate which groups they align themselves with and which groups they distinguish themselves from." For example, knowledge and use (or choice *not* to use) the phrase "She's staying by us" [versus "at our home"], which correlates most with Jews from the New York area who have some background in Yiddish, was used by more than half the Orthodox Jews surveyed, while more than 60 percent of non-Orthodox Jews know the phrase but choose not to use it. The statement, Orthodox identity (especially Ultra-Orthodox as opposed to Modern Orthodox) is most likely to correlate with using "SUK-kiss" rather than "soo-COAT" and "shul" rather than "synagogue" or "temple."

While this may appear significant, some Jews merely fall into the fashion (as, for example, people who would say "colored people" at the time the NAACP was founded in 1909, "Negro" during the early civil rights struggle, "black" in the later 1960s, and "African American" or "people of color" later). One baby boomer[52] that had attended Conservative services early in life noted: "When I was growing up, I called it Temple. When my children went to a Day School, I called it synagogue. I now call it shul. I am not sure why," is a similar example.

According to Benor's research, reported knowledge of the Hebrew language correlates strongly with childhood Jewish education. Respondents who attended a non-Orthodox Jewish Day School were much more likely than respondents who attended

---

[52] http://www.bjpa.org/Publications/downloadPublication.cfm?PublicationID=3874

Hebrew school more than once a week to report being proficient in spoken Hebrew (48 percent vs. 9 percent), to have good or excellent comprehension of Hebrew in prayer books (59 percent vs. 18 percent), and to have good or excellent comprehension of Biblical Hebrew (51 percent vs. 14 percent). The differences, of course, become even starker when we compare day school attendees to those who attended Hebrew school only one time a week. One must be immersed in a culture to make sustainable linguistic, identity, and value shifts.

A linguistic trend aside, there is no correlation between attendance in Hebrew school and a sustained commitment to Jewish life. I'd like to say it is better than nothing but I'm not sure anymore. Sometimes the damage of forcing our kids to participate in a boring, out of touch Jewish experience can alienate them forever. Sociologists Steven Cohen and Lawrence Kotler-Berkowitz wrote: "Relative to those with no Jewish schooling, there are no consistent, positive impacts for in-marriage, ritual practices, and attitudes toward Israel associated with attendance at supplementary school for six years or less or at Sunday school for any number of years." They write futher: "This finding is consistent with other research that has shown attending supplementary schools for less than seven years, or attending Sunday schools for any duration, has an impact on joining synagogues but little else." Sunday school is the sole exception for type of Jewish education that is not correlated with a strengthened Jewish identity. Ironically, Christian Sunday School, which Rebecca Gratz tried so hard to emulate, has had its share of boredom. An Internet search for "Sunday School Boring" yields more than 23 million hits.

It's not all bad, though. Here are some things we know do work: day school and summer camp, immersive service learning, Jewish leadership programs, transformative study and travel in Israel, etc. These are powerful experiences with great breadth and depth.

If we do continue with Hebrew schools, then we should take a leaf out of the books of some of these successful programs and at least consider some alternative models:

- Stop pushing "studying Judaism" and start modeling "doing Judaism." One idea would be to make it on Shabbat morning and encourage actual participation rather than on Sunday morning (a less significant day in the Jewish week, and one more likely to present time conflicts).

- Make the program a service-learning experience where contribution is possible and incorporate learning into the service work.

- Lead the Jewish learning in the home (pull together a few students and hire a teacher to come to the house). Judaism should be framed within life context.

- Give kids powerful Jewish experiences that are social, intellectual, and dynamic, and take it out of the "school" context with desks and frontal learning.

- Turn content education into relational learning (strong peer-relationships is highly correlated with staying in the community) and the learning is much richer when integrated into relationships.

- Peer and mentor relational interconnectivity is crucial and not merely for the social value but also to foster a sense of community and a notion that we can (and must) be connected to something much bigger than ourselves. 1-1 relationships are crucial.

- Service (*chesed*) projects cannot be superficial with token symbolism. Kids see right through projects that have no impact.

- Make Jewish learning experiential and include the whole family. For supplemental Jewish education to work, the parents must also be bought in. Families should be empowered to make life choices.

- Do not make the education bar/bat mitzvah focused. And create powerful teen programs that avoid post bar/bat mitzvah dropout.

- Jewish youth must be exposed to serious meaningful and spiritual Judaism that promotes responsibility and engagement. It can be made "fun" but this is not everything and constant games will send the opposite message calling into question the significance of our message.

New approaches are emerging like "A Revolutionary Approach to Hebrew School" called Yerusha. Rabbi Joy Levitt's innovative Jewish Journey Project (JJP), launched in April 2011, is a recent attempt to replace the Hebrew School concept, the current version of which has termed a "failure." Levitt, a Reconstructionist rabbi and executive director of the Manhattan JCC, hopes the new project will offer supplemental Jewish school education for children aged 9-13, and would involve JCCs, synagogues, camps, and other institutions, along with social action groups.

For the 2013-2014 academic year, The Jewish Journey Project (JJP) offered third through seventh grade students courses comprising a "Jewish Passport," leading up to a Bar/Bat Mitzvah in five areas: Torah, God and Spirituality, Jewish Peoplehood, Hebrew, and Tikkun Olam. Students will also be able to take independent study courses. It uses the Manhattan JCC, the 14th Street Y, and Reform, Conservative, and Reconstructionist synagogues in New York in its education, with an approach that does not favor any individual denomination. As of now, 30 courses will be taught as part of the program, seven days a week. But its tuition of $2,200 (with a discount for JCC members) is more than some comparable congregational Hebrew Schools (one has fees ranging from $1225 to $1985). Even the best programs must be made accessible to all. To be sure day schools have their own cost crisis.

The JJP has overcome some, but not all, obstacles. It was funded by more than $1.5 million grant money, including the significant contribution of Michael Steinhardt, who has for a long time been reluctant to fund Hebrew Schools. Six synagogues arc participating in JJP to some degree, but some prominent congregations have refused to join. While some are fearful that this collaborative arrangement may lead people to leave their individual congregations, others hope that it will open up options for students who currently study privately to prepare for their bar/bat mitzvah. In addition, it is an effort to improve the reputation of Hebrew schools. As Ivy Schreiber, director of education at Congregation B'nai Jeshurun in New York, said: "We make the assumption that Hebrew school is a good fit for everyone, and that's not necessarily the case…. we're excited to offer this as an alternative." Some have hope in this slightly tweaked model.

We cannot keep dumping money into an inherently flawed system. Kids can handle one school not two. For a supplemental Jewish experiential education to be successful it should transform children to help them thrive in life, prepare them to make meaningful Jewish life choices, and foster a love for *Yiddishkeit* that empowers them along their life journey.

I'm sure there are some solid Hebrew schools out there, but if there are, they are in the minority. The clergy and staff are stretched very thin and are often not the right folks to be leading. With limited resources, sometimes teenagers or college students who are not knowledgeable of Judaism or trained as educators are brought in to teach. Hebrew school can be a good entry point for those not yet engaged in Jewish life, but it is not a vehicle for sustained Jewish commitment.

The first job for parents is to model Jewish commitment, learning and living and not outsource one of the most primary roles of a parent: to provide one's child with values, structure, community, and education. Most synagogues are not equipped to run excellent programs, yet as long as parents beg their congregations for traditional Hebrew schools (while complaining about their quality) the problem will continue to exist. I have been amazed that numerous parents even view the process as punitive. "I had to go through it so my kids should too." It's necessary pain to acquire some type of minimal and irrelevant type of Jewish identity.

Every child cannot go to full-time Jewish day school (and day schools have their own problems) but Sunday morning Hebrew school can no longer be the obvious alternative. Some towns do not even have a day school and not all families can afford Jewish camp or Israel opportunities. There must be other options accessible to all. Parents and Jewish communal professionals must partner to create more sustainable and considerable alternatives. Judaism is a lived religion. When groups of kids are taken out collectively into the world for experiences, the encounter can be framed through a Jewish lens (with texts and conversations). One need not (and should not) be stuck in a chair for a second school experience to discuss Judaism when they can learn to live it. For some, Hebrew school may work but for the high majority it has damaged the soul cultivating a deep indifference toward (or even disdain for) Jewish life.

Parents must make hard decisions if they're serious about providing the foundation for a committed Jewish life for their children. We cannot simply hope they will love Judaism or enroll them into a program that is likely to fail and cause great frustration for all involved. Most importantly, parents themselves must be invested, supportive, and engaged as well if they wish their children to integrate their learning into their lives. The good news is that some alternatives are emerging and many more are yet to be explored. We must support the day schools and supplemental learning programs that are working hard to employ innovative transformative approaches to secure the future of the Jewish people.

8.)

A Society With Poor Critical Thinking Skills: The Case for Arguments in Education

Researchers have shown that most students today are weak in critical thinking skills. They do poorly on simple logical reasoning tests (Evans, 2002). Only a fraction of graduating high school seniors (6 percent of 12th graders) can make informed, critical judgments about written text (Perie, Grigg, and Donahue, 2005). This problem applies to both reading and writing. Only 15 percent of 12th graders demonstrate the proficiency to write well-organized essays that consisted of clear arguments (Perie et al., 2005).

Critical thinking and argument skills – the abilities to both generate and critique arguments – are crucial elements in decision-making (Byrnes, 1998; Klaczynski, 2004; Halpern 1998). When applied to academic settings, argumentation may promote the long-term understanding and retention of course content (Adriessen, 2006; Nussbaum, 2008a). According to the ancient Greeks, dialogue is the most advanced form of thought (Vygotsky, 1978). Critical thinking and dialogue are often made manifest in the form of argument. Dialectical arguments require an appeal to beliefs and values to make crucial decisions, what Aristotle referred to as endoxa (Walton, Reed, & Macagno, 2008). In all careers, academic classes, and relationships, argument skills can be used to enhance learning when we treat reasoning as a process of argumentation (Kuhn, 1992, 1993), as fundamentally dialogical (Bakhtin, 1981, 1986; Wertsch, 1991), and as metacognitive (Hofer & Pintrich, 1997). Significant differences in approach have emerged as to how best cultivate the skills necessary to form, present and defend an argument. Differences have emerged as to whether the best practices include the use of computers, writing exercises, metacognitive activities, debates, modeling, or frontal instruction. Too many "argument" sounds combative and negative but the use of argument can be constructive and generative.

Epistemological understanding becomes most evident when an individual is confronted with uncertain or controversial knowledge claims (Chandler et al., 1990; King and Kitchener, 1994;

311

Kuhn et al., 2000; Leadbeater and Kuhn, 1989). It is imperative that high school students, of diverse personal, moral and intellectual commitments, become prepared to confront multiple perspectives on unclear and controversial issues when they move on to college and their careers. This is not only important for assuring students are equipped to compete in the marketplace of ideas but also to maximize their own cognitive development more broadly. Longitudinal studies focused on high school students (Schommer et al., 1997) show a positive correlation between educational level and epistemological level. Cross-sectional studies demonstrate that educational experiences influence epistemological development and that it is the quality of education and not age or gender that contributes to different developmental levels of epistemological understanding (Chandler et al., 1990; Leadbeater and Kuhn, 1989). Education is, therefore, key. Argument is a more complex and challenging cognitive skill for students than other genres of reading and writing, such as exposition or narration. It is also more challenging for most teachers who may not have the knowledge or experience of working with argumentative reading and writing (Hillocks, 1999, 2010). In addition, most teachers try to avoid conflict when it comes to learning (Powell, Farrar, and Cohen, 1985).

Many teachers have observed that the frontal authoritarian model of learning bores students sitting in classrooms today. For years, as a student, I was told to take out my notebook and copy what was written on the board. A curriculum in which they are active participants and engaged in democratic, and cognitively challenging for students works better. In the frontal model, teachers provide the questions and answers. In the argument model, the students provide the questions and the answers while the teachers provide the structure, the facilitation, and the guidance. Students gain the necessary skills to be critical thinkers in a complex society with many different agendas, facts, and perspectives.

There are those that argue that too much autonomy is given to students in a student-centered environment. Yet, the risk is much greater with frontal lecture education: that our students master content but do not gain the cognitive, moral, and epistemic development necessary to become autonomous critical thinkers. The choice of reading matter for students is also an important factor.

Students are unlikely to develop critical thinking skills naturally when their class reading assignments consist only of narrative and explanatory texts, as opposed to argumentative texts (Calfee & Chambliss, 1987).

The goal of an argument curriculum is to enhance the development of the responsible citizens and the pedagogical methodology consists of cultivating argument skills, epistemic development, and moral development. School-based nurturing of this development leads to students' autonomous critical thinking and their formation as responsible citizens. We must invest in the education of our youth. They are our future and without a sustainable model of cognitive progression, we will be a society without an intellectual anchor, rudderless against the challenges that face us in perpetuity.

9.)
Developing Cognitive Competence: Learning the Skills of Argument

Continuing from the previous section, we must instill a better appreciation the value of the argument-skills curriculum; over the last twenty years, there has been an increased interest in the study of the skills required for argument. The understanding of arguments has been studied in social psychology (persuasion and attitude change) and in cognitive and developmental psychology (reasoning). There are many ways to know in addition to reason such as through emotion, sense perception or authority. My interest here is in the development of reason. Reasoning consists of the human capacity to establish and verify facts and can be distinguished from intuition, the capacity to acquire knowledge without the use of reason or inference.

Humans have the unique capacity for reason like no other living creatures and many scholars have claimed that the primary function of reasoning is argumentative (Sperber, 2000a; 2001; Billig, 1996; Dessalles, 2007; Kuhn, 1992; Perelman & Olbrechts-Tyteca, 1969). "Reasoning has evolved and persisted mainly because it makes human communication more effective and advantageous," (Mercier & Sperber, 2011). It is through argument that reasoning can be actualized.

Argumentation has been investigated from within a large range of subjects: juror reasoning (Pennington & Hastie, 1992; Kuhn, Flaton and Weinstock, 1994), political science (Finlayson, 2004), economics (Voss, Blais, Means, Greene and Ahwesh, 1986), moral thinking (Anderson et al., 2001; Narvaez, 2001) and media analysis (Limon and Kazoleas, 2005). It seems that very little has been investigated within the domain of religious textual studies. Many have suggested that an appropriate argument curriculum can be applied to all subjects of study.

While contemporary subject theorists consider argumentation to be interactive, social, dynamic and dialogical, consistent with social constructivist perspectives, there is disagreement about the most effective learning approach. To what extent must the cognitive and social processes be integrated? How can it best be assured that students learn to construct two-sided arguments and distinguish between explanations and evidence?

The three primary educational mediums for the development of these argument skills have been: oral, written and web-based discussions. Exercises of oral discourse (Baker, 1999; Chinn, O'Donnell and Jinks, 2000; Mercer, 1996; Reznitskaya et al., 2001) ensure that students are discussing matters face to face. Exercises involving writing an argumentative text (Wiley and Voss, 1999) intertwine writing skills with argument skills. Web-based discussions (Andriessen, Baker and Suthers, 2003; Koschmann, 2003) combine the first two approaches -- partners communicate with one another only through the medium of writing. Some researchers have suggested that in computer-based argumentation, student arguments can often be "shallow and unfocused" and that "discussion threads diverge in multiple directions," (Andriessen et al., 2003).

Another debate has evolved around whether argument exercise should be supplemented by frontal teaching. Kuhn et al. (1997) and Lao and Kuhn (2002) have demonstrated that extended engagement in argumentative discourse, without any other instruction, is sufficient for the improvement of the quality of arguments produced by students.

There is an important practical and intellectual distinction between the experiential teaching approach and the direct instruction approach. Britt (2008) argues for the direct instruction approach (where information is imparted to students frontally and directly with students) and that there should be frontal teaching and training in philosophical language and concepts. Pedagogical supports can be employed to address skill deficits (Larson, Britt and Kurby, 2012). The experiential approach, on the other hand, emphasizes engagement and practice. The choice of one model over another will not only impact how an educator interacts with students but how students engage with the course material and learn. Reznitskaya, Anderson and Kuo (2007) demonstrated how engagement in argumentation was an effective way to cultivate skill development compared to direct instruction. They found that groups receiving direct instruction increased their conceptual knowledge but decreased their procedural knowledge on how to use argumentative strategies. Kuhn, Shaw and Felton (1997) found that

315

sustained engagement in dialogical argumentation significantly increased argument skills.

Engaging in argument can help ensure the development of what has been called a "two-sided" versus "one-sided" approach (Baron, 1990; Nussbaum, 2008; Stanovich and West, 2007; Wolfe and Britt, 2008). A two-sided argument addresses the opposing argument, rather than just arguing for one's own position. It is crucial for more nuanced argument skills that students learn to engage in evidence-based argumentation where they can provide a claim, which is supported by evidence or reasons that support the claim in a principled way. Yet even teachers may also have difficulty explaining how evidence can be applied in high-level argumentative reading and writing (Kuhn, 2005; Langer, 1992; Langer and Applebee, 1987). Many have claimed that most teachers are unprepared to provide instructional support and facilitation for learning argument skills (Applebee, 1991; Hillocks 1999, 2008, 2010; Langer, 1992; Langer and Applebee, 1987; Shanahan and Shanahan, 2008).

In addition to the development of cognitive competence, argumentative discourse can enhance crucial argument skills. Felton and Kuhn (2001) identified that the two primary areas of development in argumentative discourse are "enhanced understanding of discourse goals and application of effective strategies to meet these goals" and have found that engagement in argumentative discourse activities enhances this development. In addition to furthering students' abilities to support claims and draw correct inferences from information (Moshman, 1998), there can be development in argumentative discourse as a social phenomenon (Felton, Kuhn, 2001).

Young adolescents often struggle to attend to opponent's claims and remain focused on their own claims (Felton, 2004; Felton and Kuhn, 2001; Kuhn and Udell, 2003; Udell, 2007). However when instructed to attend to the opponent's argument, students are able to do so (Kuhn and Udell, 2007). Students often fail to identify weaknesses in the opponent's arguments and to "secure commitments" from opponents to be used to support one's own claims," (Walton, 1989).

Adults have greater skills in argumentative discourse than teens do, showing great competency at making counterarguments and "directing and defining the partner's argument with the intent of weakening it," (Felton & Kuhn, 2001). Through normal cognitive development, these skills develop. But students can still be enhanced in growth and these are primary opportunities for development with teens.

Toulmin (1958) contends that arguments consist of a claim supported by grounds, warrants and backing. The problem with the Toulmin model is that it is minimally dialectical and neglects a range of argumentation moves (Reed and Norman, 2004; van Eemereen and Grootendorst, 1992). Nussbaum and Schraw (2007) suggested the argument-counterargument integration for defining a well-developed argument schema and suggested three strategies that could be used to construct an integrative argument: refutation, constructing a design claim (for how a solution should be designed) and weighing (demonstrating how the positive consequences outweigh the negative). In his dialogue theory, Walton (1998) suggests that there are seven different types of argument dialogues depending on whether the goal is to persuade, negotiate, acquire information, deliberate, inquire, and express emotion and grievances, or a combination of these. One learning goal is for students to become more aware of their strategies and goals and why they're choosing the approach they're using. This is part of the goal of metacognitive development. Brown (1997) suggests that incorporating reflective activities into learning helps to ensure that reasoning skills become internalized. While developmentalists have thought about metacognition for some time, the emphasis of study really accelerated in the late '70s, namely with the developmentalist, Flavell (1979). Big strides forward were made in research with the adopting of microgenetic research methods. Microgenetic methods enable the study of the process of "knowledge building," (Chan, Burtis and Bereiter, 1997) and developmentalists today have moved to researching metastrategic knowledge and meta-task knowledge in addition to meta-memory.

Initially, research on metacognitive or meta-strategic knowledge was focused on memory skills (Brown, 1975, 1978); however, more recently, the study of metastrategic knowledge has come to include awareness, understanding, monitoring and management of one's strategic performance of many kinds of cognitive tasks.

In addition to gaining awareness of the sources of one's own knowledge, a learner can gain meta-level control of his or her own knowledge mastery. In addition to students gaining a deeper understanding of material and persuading others with their arguments, it must be ensured that students can generate arguments that incorporate multiple perspectives of an issue. A primary pedagogical tool for the cultivation of argument and reasoning skills is to ensure that reflective activities are included in learning exercises. Nussbaum (2005) has suggested that the giving of "goal instructions" helps to achieve a higher awareness of the learning tasks at hand and can have substantial effects on the argumentation. Theories of experiential learning are relevant to this research project. For example, Kolb (2008) defines his Experiential Learning Theory as "a holistic model of the learning process and a multilinear model of adult development, both of which are consistent with what we know about how people learn, grow and develop," (Kolb, Boyatzis and Mainemelis, 2000, 2). He explains that experiential learning is "the process whereby knowledge is created through the transformation of experience. Knowledge results from the combination of grasping and transforming experience," (Kolb, 1984, p. 41 in Kolb, et al., 2000). This learning process is structured through a four-stage framework including concrete experience, reflective observation, abstract conceptualization and active experimentation. The learning begins with a concrete experience forming the base for the reflective observation. These reflections are the foundation for the formation of more abstract concepts finally leading to the testing of new ideas by the student. Then the cycle begins once again with the search for a new experience.

Another educational approach is to use scaffolded argumentative discourse, breaking up learning activities into different aspects. Kuhn et al. (2008) suggested three techniques designed to heighten and support metacognitive awareness of discourse:

- Working in collaborative pairs

- Integrating explicit reflective activities into a series of dialogs

- Conducting dialogs via computer-supported instant messaging software, which makes them available for reflection.

Argumentative discourse, in addition to argument skill, also demands epistemological understanding (Chandler, Boyes and Ball, 1990; Kuhn, Cheney and Weinstock, 2000; Mason and Boscolo, 2004). Individuals will not be inclined to engage in argument if the positive benefits of such practices are not understood.

One study examined the use of AVDs (argumentation v-diagrams) to further argument and counter-argument integration. Students would draw a "V," write their arguments on the left side of the "V," the counter-arguments on the right side of the "V," and their potential conclusions at the bottom of the "V." Researchers found that students who used v-diagrams were more likely to compromise in their positions and to change their positions than students who did not engage in this activity (Nussbaum and Schraw, 2007). Students who pause to reflect on their position and the position of others are more likely to hold multiple possible positions.

The development of metacognition helps ensure students are more reflective about their reasoning and evidence. In addition to having students develop stronger arguments they can accumulate more doubt that the opposing position is not necessarily false. Kuhn and Weinstock (2002) propose: "the development task that underlies the achievement of mature epistemological understanding is the coordination of the subjective and the objective dimensions of knowing." Creating a balance between the objective and subjective knowing requires that students embrace evaluation through evidence (objective) and a doubt of certainty (subjective). While assertions made are judgments (objective) there is an acknowledgement that reality is not directly knowable and that knowledge is generated by human minds (subjective). By integrating reflective activities on the objective and subjective ways of knowing, we further students' epistemic development. This epistemic development will help students develop as critical thinkers.

This is the key for our future. Ensuring we are building a nation of competent citizens capable of thinking critically at work, at home and in the public arena, is tantamount to the intellectual vitality of society.

Cognitive Conflict: Should Educational Debates Be Competitive Or Collaborative?

There is debate about whether argumentation should be competitive, collaborative or a combination of the two. Others have framed this debate as being about "adversarial" versus "exploratory" discourse. In favor of collaborative learning, Lin and Anderson (2008) explain that "rubbing up against others with different points of view is one of the best ways to bring to light gaps in understanding, inconsistencies in thinking, and my-side bias, and hence, the value of collaborative discussion and reasoned argumentation." Students can collaborate by challenging each other but there are other models of collaboration to consider. Since argument consists both of "product" (propositions and conclusions) and "process" (dialogue about arguments) collaboration can come in the form of discourse (process) or in a shared goal (product). Walton (1999) termed it differently as "information-seeking" dialogue rather than a persuasive dialogue. Wegerif, Mercer, and Dawes (1999) have called collaborative learning "exploratory talk." Reznitskaya et al. (2001) suggests: "collaborative discussion appears to be an effective training ground for the development and internalization of generalized knowledge of argumentation." Felton (2003) suggests that a "process of co-constructing arguments is accomplished through the use of discourse strategies" through "argument construction" and "discourse strategies." Others explain collaborative argumentation as "a social process in which individuals work together to construct and critique arguments" (Golanicks & Nussbaum, 2008; Nussbaum, 2002).

A strong basis for adversarial argumentation can be traced back to Jean Piaget, the Swedish developmental psychologist. Through cognitive conflict, Piaget suggested, conceptual change triggered by disagreement could occur (1963). According to Piaget, a learner constructs knowledge when receiving input from the environment. The learner's mental structures incorporate the new experience (assimilation). If the newly assimilated information conflicts with a previously formed mental structure, then the result is called disequilibrium, which then motivates the learner to seek equilibrium. Reaching equilibrium results in what Piaget called accommodation leading to the development of new mental structures. Through this assimilation and accommodation, the learner adapts to the environmental input received. For Piaget, there are four primary stages of cognitive development: sensorimotor, preoperational, concrete operational, formal operational.

In Felton's competitive argumentation model (debate), there are three skills to argument construction: "producing justifications, producing counterarguments, and rebutting counterarguments." However Felton suggests that the skills of argument construction are learned at a young age and that our educational focus should be on discourse strategies; that is, "to construct arguments competitively in social contexts." Felton and Kuhn (2001) have even developed a system of categorization for strategies in argumentative discourse.

Keefer, Zeitz, and Resnick (2000) claim that collaborative argumentation enables deeper engagements than adversarial argumentation. However, it should be acknowledged that some claim that there is not one correct method (collaborative or competitive) for all students. Rather, each student's personality should be taken into consideration. Nussbaum (2002), for example, showed that "introverts tend to prefer collaborative over adversarial discourse" and may feel more threatened by adversarial argumentation.

While a comparison between the competitive and collaborative models can be quite complex, a more prevailing approach has been put forth. Kuhn, Shaw and Felton (1997) wrote: "In the case of argumentive reasoning, the conflict model of change has dominated, on the assumption that the power of dialogue stems from the discrepancy between viewpoints, creating the opportunity for each member of the dyad to be exposed to new perspectives that might potentially be integrated into their own thinking." Students collaborate through a dialogical adversarial approach to argument. Kuhn et al. (2008) distinguish between the "classical argument" goal (prevailing over an opponent) from "dilemma resolution" (resolving the underlying problem that the two sides address).

To further epistemic and moral development, we must focus more on cognitive development through the cultivation of argument skills. We also must determine the learning culture that will serve as a future foundation for how students view the other in the marketplace of ideas. The choice between a competitive or collaborative learning environment will not only determine the quality of learning but it may also help determine the nature of our future economies and political cultures.

11.)
When Good People Act Evilly: Redeeming A Broken World

In 1971, Dr. Philip Zimbardo, Professor Emeritus at Stanford University, conducted the famous Stanford Prison Experiment,[53] in which students were assigned roles as either guards or prisoners. Alarmingly, the intended 2-week study ended after only six days because of how quickly and wholly the students who were assigned the "guard" positions began acting in authoritative, violent, and frankly fascist, manners. The "guards" inflicted such abuse that the disheartened "prisoners" were beginning to suffer from psychological damage and the environment rapidly became toxic and dangerous. In his experiments and books, Dr. Zimbardo reminds us of the horrifying fact that, given the right situation, most good people can act in terrifying and evil ways:

> Any deed that any human being has ever committed, however horrible, is possible for any of us—under the right or wrong situational circumstances. That knowledge does not excuse evil; rather, it democratizes it, sharing the blame among ordinary actors rather than declaring it the province only of deviants and despots—of Them but not Us.

Professor Zimbardo noted that at Abu Ghraib detention center in Iraq, American soldiers all too willingly adopted the sadistic guard model, torturing and humiliating their prisoners, behaving in a disgraceful and abusive manner that damaged America's reputation around the world. We should not believe that human behavior is entirely determined by circumstance but we should not be so naïve as to dismiss the enormous influence that one's context exacts on one's disposition and character. Susan Neiman explained this point well:

---

[53] http://www.prisonexp.org/

As Arendt's book *Thinking* put it, "The sad truth is
that most evil is done by people who never make
their minds up to be or do evil at all." Focusing on
psychopaths is a good way to forget this, and it
carried more than one risk. In addition to
obscuring how little evil is committed by madmen
(social psychologist Philip Zimbardo estimates it at
2 percent), it focuses on the evils for which
responsibility is hardest to ascribe. Psychopaths, by
definition, are too sick to be entirely culpable. But
the problem, wrote Primo Levi, is "not that evil
men did evil things, but that normal people did
them" (*Moral Clarity*)

Dr. Charles Twagira would seem to be one of the "normal,"
or even better than normal people, as he was the head of the Kibuye
hospital in western Rwanda. In April 1994, Rwandan President
Juvenal Habyarimana's plane was shot down as it neared arrival in
Kigali. Though the assassins were unknown, shortly thereafter, a
group of Hutu (85 percent of the population) extremists launched a
campaign of genocide against the minority Tutsi (14 percent of the
population). Radio broadcasts exhorted people to kill the Tutsi
"cockroaches" as a permanent way to ensure Hutu supremacy, and
approximately 200,000 Hutus armed with machetes and firearms
slaughtered over 800,000 Tutsis (about three-fourths of all Tutsis).
Thousands of Hutus who opposed the genocide were also
slaughtered. This shocking amount of killing all took place within a
few weeks. Dr. Twagira, who was a Hutu, was accused of murdering
the family of a Tutsi man he worked with and accused of refusing to
care for wounded Tutsi people who came to his Kibuye hospital
during the genocide. After the genocide, Dr. Twagira fled Rwanda,
and in March 2014 he was finally arrested in Vire, France, where he
had been working in a hospital. What caused these "normal people"
to engage in such savagery, and then, as in Dr. Twagira's case,
resume normal lives as if nothing had ever happened? How could a
physician treat people one day and then callously refuse treatment to
others and watch them die? Tragically, we have seen this behavior
before, most infamously during the Holocaust. We must be diligent
and fervent in our attempts to understand these complex and
shocking human behaviors; attempting to comprehend the warning
signs for these types of behavior may help in the prevention of
genocide.

One of the most profound ways an individual can come to better understand themselves, and from this self-knowledge become more connected to God, is through prayer. One of the reasons that we engage in prayer is to explore and understand all that is spiritually laden inside of us. From this understanding we become more human, we grow, we connect more deeply with our neighbors, and we seek God more purely. Consider the words of Rabbi Soloveitchik:

> Prayer is a vital necessity for the religious individual. He cannot conceal his thoughts and his feelings, his vacillations and his struggles, his yearnings and his wishes, his despair and his bitterness - in a word, the great wealth stored away in his religious consciousness - in the depths of his soul. Suppressing liturgical expression is simply impossible: prayer is a necessity. Vital, vibrant religiosity cannot sustain itself without prayer. In sum, prayer is justified because it is impossible to exist without it (*Worship of the Heart*, 150).

It is hard to understand the purpose of standing before God and rambling our thoughts, concerns, and dreams; in fact, it sometimes feels unjustifiable. However, Rav Soloveitchik believed that the absolute human need for prayer serves as a spiritual justification. This belief is so relevant today when there is so much at stake and the need for us to be spiritually connected and aware is thus so great. The awareness and connection derived from prayer is at the very core of our aspirations for a redeemed world. Kabbalistic theology teaches us the three crucial stages of creation: *Tzimtzum*, *Shevira*, and *Tikkun*. The Kabbalistic narrative of creation explains that God humbly pulled back from the world and the spiritual vessels catastrophically shattered, or broke, spilling holy light everywhere.

In this theological narrative lays, perhaps, the most significant question of twenty-first century Judaism: What must we be doing uniquely in our own era to re-gather the scattered sparks of light and to repair the world? How will we redeem, elevate, and heal? If we are to accomplish these holy goals we must learn to hold the delicate balance between light and vessel, between oneness and separateness, chaos and order, the infinite and finite, the spatial and temporal and eternal.

Understanding our own capacities for goodness and wrongdoing is a challenging endeavor, but is necessary for mankind to achieve the common understanding essential for progress. However, we are not yet aware of the human potential for good and evil. Rousseau once wrote:

> We know the first from which each of us
> · starts in order to get to the common level of
> understanding. But who knows the outer
> limit? I know of no philosopher who has yet
> been so bold as to say: this is the limit of
> what man can attain and beyond which he
> cannot go. We do not know what our
> nature permits us to be

Though this may still be true today, as Rousseau wrote that it was about his generation, I propose that prayer and spirituality are essential elements in better understanding our behaviors and refining them. It is our responsibility, as religious individuals, spiritual leaders, and members of faith communities, to take the lead in this arena.

The people of the nineteenth century never could have imagined the advancements, or the horrors, that occurred in the twentieth century. Just like those before us we do not yet know what lies ahead in the not so distant future. However, what may come, positive and/or negative, we should not blame the societal ills on the technology that we create and control. Technology has become a favorite target of many philosophers and social commentators, who decry it as an agent of de-sensitivity, social rejection, and de-connection from reality. However, as Neiman explains, we must take responsibility for our technological advancements, recognize the benefits, and watch our judgments:

> But when you think of the risks technology poses,
> presumably you don't mean the technology that improved
> by 50 percent your chances of living long enough to worry
> about them. Nor do you mean the technology that ended
> the days when toothaches were torture and sore throats were
> deadly; when women's lives were exhausted by between
> grinding chores like washing clothes by hand, and anxious
> hours at sickbeds keeping children's fevers down with wet
> rags; when music was limited to people in private concert
> rooms, and art was something you had to take a ship to Italy
> to see. Take stock for a moment: For every high-tech
> advance you find superfluous, there's another you find
> essential. Deciding which elements will enhance our lives
> and which will threaten them is a matter of good judgment
> (*Moral Clarity*, 262).

Psychologists and sociologists have long tried to understand why seemingly good people commit horrible crimes. Apart from unstable childhoods, the impulsive and peer-pressure-driven adolescent years, and varied demographic problems, there appears to be a need that motivation and opportunity must exist in order for people to commit crime. We can see this dependence in even simple mischievous crimes that formerly existed but due to technological changes have disappeared. In the early twentieth century, for example, most cities in America had slow moving streetcars (San Francisco still has a system powered by an underground cable that runs at 9.5 miles per hour). In urban areas, young boys were especially fond of trying to avoid paying the fare by hitching a ride on the front or back of these streetcars, which had small flat areas above the bumpers. Whether due to peer pressure (the fear of being called derogatory names, etc.) boys would commonly run up to the streetcars and hop on; if they slipped and fell off, they risked being crushed; if they stayed, they risked being seized by the streetcar operator or a policeman. Eventually, once the streetcar lines were removed and buses took over, this behavior largely disappeared, as it is nearly impossible to hang on to a moving bus. In San Francisco, the cable cars are so popular that you probably could not hitch a ride if you tried to pay for a spot.

On the other hand, when money is involved, the crimes are more serious and enduring. Money is still at the heart of most criminal activity, as greed remains a powerful force. Recently,

Thomas Rica,[54] a former public works inspector in the wealthy community of Ridgewood, NJ, was found to have stolen $460,600 in quarters from a storage room, in the building where he worked, that was used to hold money from the village's parking meters. Rica, whose $86,000 salary was more than enough to sustain his family, acknowledged that he found the nearby coins (and his access to the room with a master key) too tempting, and pocketed the coins over more than a two year period, a crime that must have taken an incredible amount of time and effort just to carry the tons of coins to his car. A simple Google search will turn up hundreds of similar stories.

While we constantly hear of petty and white-collar criminals, what about notable figures from the past? Interestingly, this behavior can be seen in some of our most famous historical figures. Thomas Edison was lionized during and after his life for his thousands of ingenious inventions, many of which have made life more enjoyable for millions of people. However, even with Edison, a combination of ego (an obsession with controlling the application of an invention) and fear (his financial backer was the formidable J.P. Morgan, who brooked no scruples in the pursuit of money) caused him to embark on a shocking course of evil that is made even more alarming when you consider Edison's fervent opposition to capital punishment.

In the years following Edison's development of the incandescent electric light bulb in 1879, he faced a problem[55]. In order to provide electricity using his direct current (DC) technology, there needed to be power plant located close by (at least every mile) in order to transport the current efficiently, which would necessitate thousands of plants in every city. In the meantime, another scientist and mathematician, Nikola Tesla, developed alternating current (AC), which resulted in the ability to transport electricity great distances without the necessity of numerous power plants (Tesla also developed the much more energy efficient fluorescent light bulb in

---

[54] http://www.northjersey.com/news/ex-ridgewood-inspector-admits-to-stealing-460-000-in-quarters-from-village-video-1.745520

[55] http://www.smithsonianmag.com/history/edison-vs-westinghouse-a-shocking-rivalry-102146036/?no-ist

1888). Edison rejected Tesla's idea out of hand, not realizing (or allowing for the possibility) that it was the superior system.

When Tesla found a backer in George Westinghouse, the AC system took off. Edison, fearing that the competition would overwhelm him and, pressured by his own backer, Morgan, turned to truly evil tactics. Beginning in 1888, he obtained AC dynamos and began to electrocute animals in an attempt to convince reporters and the public that AC was a dangerous technology that would kill people. At first, he killed dogs, but then he moved up to calves and a horse. However, even these disgusting demonstrations were not enough. Edison next arranged for the world's first execution by electric chair, using his rival's AC technology. On August 6, 1890, in New York's Auburn prison, convicted murderer William Kemmler was strapped to an electric chair, and after a 17-second burst, appeared to be dead. However, he soon began to desperately gasp for breath, and the execution was delayed while the dynamo recharged. A second charge was applied for minutes, and Kemmler literally burned to death while the witnesses became physically ill at the horrid, torturous death.

Undeterred after the gruesome human execution, Edison arranged to have an allegedly rogue circus elephant, Topsy, killed by AC at Coney Island in New York in front of the press and thousands of spectators. On January 4, 1903 Edison applied 6,600 volts of electricity to the animal, killing her in minutes. The entire sickening act was filmed and dispersed throughout the United States. Eventually, however, even Edison had to acknowledge that Westinghouse and Tesla had the better system, but not until he had created a truly monstrous invention. To date, only the United States and the Philippines have ever used the electric chair for executions (more than 4,400 through January 2013).

Upon hearing such disturbing tales of good people turning to evil, we might yield to despair about our human capabilities, but that would be a mistake. We have more power than ever before. We constantly fall in order to climb forward (*yeridah l'tzorech aliyah*), but the falls are becoming more intense due to our immense technological capacity. But in this cycle, we must remember we possess the most powerful ability:

Stone is hard, but iron cuts it. Iron is stiff,
but fire melts it. Fire is powerful, but water
extinguishes it. Water is heavy, but clouds
carry it. Clouds are strong, but wind
disperses them. Wing is strong, but the body
resists it. The body is strong, but fear
destroys it. Fear is strong, but wine averts it.
Wine is strong, but sleep conquers it. Death
is more powerful than any of these, but
tzedakah redeems death (*Midrash Tanhuma*).

The most powerful weapon is *tzedakah* (acts of righteousness). It is the way we defy the natural world (breaking from self-interest) and even death (placing our souls in the realm of the eternal). The potential for spiritual and ethical actualization are all around us. We are reminded of the well-known and profound teaching of Reb Menachem Mendel of Kotsk:

It is said that he once asked his
disciples, "Where does God live?"
They were bewildered. "How can the
rabbi ask, Where does God live?
Where does God not live?" "No," said
the rabbi, "God lives where we let
Him in."

Humans can find themselves in situations overcome by pressure. It is through prayer, community, and absolute commitment to justice that we are capable of overcoming temptations for evil and wrongdoing. It is God's promise that we are created with *bechirat chofshi* (free will) and we prove this Divine truth whenever we prevail over the selfish and unjust temptations that have plagued our world since the Garden of Eden.

12

Confirmation Bias And The Ethical Demands of Argumentation

People tend to be one-sided in their perspectives, and this can lead to poor decision-making. Confirmation bias is the tendency people have to favor facts or arguments that confirm the beliefs and positions they already hold. The extreme form of this bias is referred to as "belief perseverance" wherein people hold onto their beliefs even after they've been proven false. Often it is due to wishful thinking or an inability to alter one's emotional attachment to an idea. In daily life, as citizens and as religious people, this tendency is destructively blinding, and we must work to combat it.

A group of Stanford psychologists have showed that subjects maintained their positions on capital punishment regardless of the evidence provided to them. Typically, higher standards are set for evidence that runs counter to one's current position; this corresponding tendency is called disconfirmation bias.

In addition, confirmation bias can be reinforced by only exposing oneself to media that repeats these opinions (and even distortions or discredited conspiracy theories). A 2010 study reported on a poll to determine where Americans gathered their opinions on certain issues and where they got their news. Those who watched Fox News (known for its attendant partisan bias) regularly had more distorted views of reality than those who watched or read other media. For example, among all viewers, Fox watchers were the most likely to subscribe to these demonstrably false views:

- 63 percent believed that the stimulus package created no tax cuts (in reality, a third of the stimulus was devoted to tax cuts for businesses)

- 47 percent believed that the $700 billion bank bailout known as TARP was passed under President Obama (it was passed under President Bush in 2008)

- 31 percent more likely to doubt that President Obama was born in the United States (the disproved "Birther" conspiracy), and 30 percent more likely to believe that most scientists did not believe in climate change (scientists are virtually unanimous in this belief), versus other viewers.

This bias reached absurd lengths on Election Day, 2012. When it was confirmed that President Obama had been reelected, many Republicans refused to believe it because man Fox News commentators had guaranteed that Mitt Romney would win. (Romney himself had not even prepared a concession speech.) Fox commentator (and long-time Republican strategist) Karl Rove embarrassed himself on-air by denying that Obama had won, and another newscaster literally walked him down to an analysis room where he had to be reassured that Obama had definitely won (Obama won the electoral college by 332-206, a decisive margin of victory). This was a case of someone continuing to believe his own partisan wishes rather than evidence in front of his face.

A more tangible example: where would we be if medical diagnoses were predetermined in the medical provider's mind rather than through a differential diagnosis that evaluated all the data and systematically ruled out medical conditions until the correct diagnosis was arrived at? Those who take absolutist positions while ignoring evidence pose a danger to society. Consider a study about jurors: Certainty about verdict choice was associated with the ability to discount alternative verdicts and generate counterarguments against one's own verdict choices, although perhaps not as one might expect. Those absolutely certain were the least likely to demonstrate these skills that involve the ability to consider multiple verdicts and match evidence with different verdict choices, whereas those with high confidence but not absolute certainty were the most likely to have these skills (Weinstock, 2009).

Being absolutely certain about positions is a barrier to critical thinking and full consideration of all facts and evidence. This is an intellectual virtue that the Jewish tradition values and commends. Jewish law mandates that we see the Torah from all perspectives: "Turn it around and examine it for everything is in it" *(Pirke Avot* 5:22). There were many Talmudic arguments between two ideological camps (the School of Hillel and the School of Shammai, for example). The Talmud says that while "both are the living words of God," that Hillel's positions are the ones accepted as authority. The reason given is because they studied the words of Shammai and even quoted them first when presenting their own positions (*Eruvin* 13b).

Challenging our own evidence with evidence from the other side not only keeps us intellectually honest and furthers our argument skill development; it also ensures that we have the humility to move from absolutist positions to more evidence-based evaluative positions. The Jewish community cannot afford to fall victim to an unhealthy civil discourse and should model balanced, open-minded, humble argumentation and learning.

13

The Need for Empowering and Ethical Jewish Outreach

In my own personal religious journey, I was fortunate to have found the right mentors and educators who supported and challenged me, but also never attempted to manage my life journey. They cared deeply about my growth but the steering wheel was always firmly in my hands. I strive to emulate that model in my own leadership and outreach.

Our forefather Abraham is the epitome of Jewish hospitality and outreach. Even when he was advanced in years according to Genesis 18, he would run in order to greet passers-by and offer them food and rest. We, as his descendants, should feel called upon to follow this example: Jewish outreach should primarily be about giving and shared learning; it should not be, as it often is today, about persuasion or coercion.

There are many problematic forms of Jewish outreach that exist today. Outreach must not be designed to make others in the outreacher's own image, but rather to present a broad range of texts, ideas, and experiences and give people the tools to make their own decisions about their Judaism. Diversity makes us stronger, not weaker, and it makes our learning better when we participate in it with people who have a vast array of experiences.

Outreach professionals should educate those who have not had formative Jewish experiences to foster a deeper commitment to Judaism through the study of its traditional texts. The outreach should not cause more divisions and fractures, but help to enhance the unity of the Jewish people by building bridges to connect Jews of different persuasions. Outreach should enrich by making the Torah's wisdom more broadly available. Further, outreach is not only about "one's own." We must bring people of different religions together in mutual understanding and respect by engaging in deep interfaith dialogue. In recent American history, Chabad-Lubavitch was among the first Orthodox Jewish organization in the United States to promote outreach (*kiruv*) as a means of recruiting *ba'alei teshuva*, unobservant Jews who commit to living an observant lifestyle. More recently, in 1987, the AVI CHAI Foundation helped fund two new outreach groups, the Association of Jewish Outreach Professionals

(AJOP) to work within the Orthodox and National Jewish Outreach Program (NJOP) to work within the non-Orthodox community. Over time, the AJOP shifted from having a Modern Orthodox orientation to a more Ultra-Orthodox one, and is now an organization interested largely in *kiruv* and the recruitment of *ba'alei teshuvah*. A report from AJOP's 2007 convention noted that there were now more than 700 non-Israeli organizations represented. Meanwhile, NJOP, led by Rabbi Ephraim Buchwald, has programs in more than four thousand locations that claim to have reached more than one million Jews in the United States (along with other locations and participants in Canada). On the whole, there are estimated to be at most two thousand full-time, and a few thousand more part-time, Jewish Outreach professionals.

The greatest controversy has emerged concerning the struggles of the former *ba'alei teshuvah* who were drawn in through the Ultra-Orthodox (*haredi*) tactic of *kiruv*. Specifically, these former *ba'alei teshuvah* complain that they were not told of the extent of demands that a *haredi* lifestyle entailed. In addition, these individuals shared that they faced discrimination from the haredim, from being ostracized because they were suspected of keeping in contact with their non-*haredi* family members to having their children harassed and discriminated against at school. Finally, it has been pointed out that the *haredi* community might do better by prioritizing supporting the many large families living in poverty who struggle to maintain an Ultra-Orthodox lifestyle, rather than devote so much funding for *kiruv*. Some data tends to support this position. While a higher percentage of Jewish youth affiliate with the Ultra-Orthodox, the data also reveal that only about 40 percent of those raised Orthodox remain Orthodox as adults. Solving internal issues may keep more within the community causing less of a survivalist need to constantly persuade new members. Communities must engage in in-reach and not just out-reach. Further, given the explosion of recent secular-*haredi* tensions in Israel (neither side without blame), we must promote respect and real dialogue as opposed to attempts to merely convert the other into one's own ideological camp.

Some outreach programs are growing and some are closing down. Modern Orthodoxy only has a small program (JLIC) that is effective but only on target campuses. In the summer of 2013, the United Synagogue of Conservative Judaism closed down Koach, the college outreach organization of the Conservative movement. Among other active outreach groups, in the fall of 2012 the Jewish Outreach Institute (JOI) initiated the first sixteen affiliates of its Big Tent Judaism Professional program. The JOI is geared toward attracting many groups formerly ignored by outreach programs, such as interfaith families and anyone else who does or wants to affiliate with Judaism. We need Jews of all convictions engaging in campus outreach to help inspire young spiritually seeking Jews to explore their Jewish roots and to learn to take Jewish leadership.

I was very privileged to serve for two years as the Hillel Jim Joseph Senior Jewish Educator at the UCLA Hillel. This program was committed to building relationships around meaningful Jewish experiences, leveraging social networks for peer-to-peer engagement, raise the bar on relational Jewish learning, inspire and empower young leaders and a culture of Jewish social entrepreneurship. Providing more entry points for deep and meaningful Jewish experiences is Jewish outreach at its best and should be scaled upward.

It must be acknowledged that Americans in general are trending toward a less religiously affiliated life. A Pew Research Center poll in late 2012 found that about 20 percent of Americans listed no religious affiliation, and that 32 percent of adults younger than age 30 were unaffiliated. Thus, there are people who may "feel spiritual" but may not feel a calling for any of the religions they have experienced. They may be receptive to a positive message from honest, accepting, welcoming Jewish outreach workers and enthusiasts who attach no strings to involvement with them and engagement with their Jewish teachings.

We must honor that every individual has infinite dignity and thus should maintain her autonomy in having and owning a distinct spiritual life journey. One dare not overstep this responsibility by asserting oneself aggressively and pushing serious religious and overall lifestyle decisions onto others, least of which the spiritually and emotionally vulnerable. Further, relationships with one's family and friends should be maintained even if transformative Jewish experiences lead a person down a new life path. Mentors must ensure that this policy is maintained, barring any cases of absolutist zealotry from others within the ranks of the outreach world.

Rambam teaches that accompanying another on his journey

is the greatest of all mitzvot related to showing kindness to others *(Laws of Mourning*, 14: 1-3). We must return to our Abrahamic roots of reaching out through love and giving to humbly create more room for others by expanding our tent. Our outreach need not make others just like us; rather we must help others along their journeys and openly be a sympathetic ear and loving supportive voice.

14.)

Celebrating the Joy of Multiple Perspectives

Simchat Torah is one of the most unique Jewish holidays, where we paradoxically celebrate the most intellectual of Jewish activities (Torah study) through the most emotional expression (singing and dancing). What is it exactly that we are celebrating?

There is a practice in many synagogues on Simchat Torah to raise the Torah up backwards (with the writing facing outward toward the congregation) during *hagbah* (the Torah raising). Some explain that this is because of the rabbinic teaching (*Pirkei Avot* 5:22): "Turn it around and examine it for everything is in it."

We turn the Torah around on this special holiday to celebrate the human capacity for (and the Jewish gift of) reinterpretation.

We are reminded during this holiday that, in keeping with the New Year, we approach our learning with new, fresh perspectives. We should bring along all that we have learned from our life experiences and our studies for a year of more advanced perspectives in learning. The Midrash teaches: "God looked in to the Torah to create the world." This is to say that there is incredible creative potential lying in this text and in us. We can emulate the Divine (*imitatio Dei*) through our creative learning.

This celebration of reinterpretation is at the center of our tradition: the Talmud. While one-quarter consists of stories, three-quarters of this premier rabbinic intellectual masterpiece actually consists not of dogmas, but of arguments over interpretations and values. We are not "the people of the book" and we do not read the Torah literally. Rather, we have two thousand years of rabbinic commentary and reinterpretation that continues to evolve, and this provides immense freedom for new insight and creativity.

This spiritual-cognitive exercise can help in many ways. Learning how to see more perspectives can improve one's intellectual (reasoning) and emotional (empathy) potential as well as our civic engagement (giving us a less black/white, partisan worldview).

We are facing a great fragmentation crisis among the Jewish people, exacerbated by a lack of perspective-taking. We should remember that while we have all come from different backgrounds and made different choices about our lives, each of us still owns a portion of the Torah.

I am interested in furthering a living dialogue with diverse people who have intellectual courage and deep respect for alternative ways of living and thinking. In this refuge of intellectual freedom we are building, no one is attacked or criticized for new ways of thinking. Fellow seekers of the truth are able to live with and express uncertainty and doubt on their journey to further a higher understanding and connectivity.

When we dance with the Torah this year, we celebrate our one collective Torah, but at the same time we each also celebrate our different "Torahs," and that is a beautiful aspect of our people and tradition.

15.)
The Value of Reading Novels

I'll be the first to admit that while I love reading fiction I am not a consistent novel reader. I enjoy non-fiction loaded with facts, theories, and analysis. I don't always have the patience for narrative. Given the results of some new research, maybe I should reconsider that. A recent study claims that reading novels makes us nicer and more empathetic psychologists at the New School for Social Research have found. Emanuele Castano, the study's author,[56] said that fiction "forces you as a reader to contribute your own interpretations, to reconstruct the mind of the character." Canadian researchers have also found that reading fiction increases our ability to be empathetic to others:

- A 2010 York University study of 4- to 6-year-old children found that greater exposure to children's literature, but not children's television programs, correlated with children having a greater sense of empathy. The study authors concluded that "engagement with fictional narratives provides one with information about the social world," exposing children to worlds outside their own.

- A 2006 University of Toronto study found that avid readers of fiction were far more socially adept than avid readers of non-fiction: "Comprehending characters in a narrative fiction appears to parallel the comprehension of peers in the actual world, while the comprehension of expository non-fiction shares no such parallels." In addition, the researchers concluded that the ability of a reader to become absorbed in a story was related their ability to feel empathy.

Yet tragically, we've seen a decline of the humanities in America. Given how aggressive and violent our culture can be (have you noticed that many new films are overwhelmingly "action" films, a euphemism for "violence-filled," often with thousands of deaths

---

[56] http://www.newschool.edu/pressroom/pressreleases/2013/CastanoKidd.htm

per movie, often accompanied by one-liners and other inhumane commentary?), perhaps we should be encouraging more reading, novels in particular.

Philip Roth once said:

> The passion for specificity is at the heart of
> the task to which every American novelist
> has been enjoined since Herman Melville
> and his whale and Mark Twain and his
> river: to discover the most arresting,
> evocative verbal depiction of every last
> American thing. Concreteness…is fiction's
> lifeblood. From this physicalness the
> realistic novel derives its ruthless intimacy.

Mark Twain's *Adventures of Huckleberry Finn* illustrates Roth's point. The narrator is a young adolescent boy who, at the start of the novel shares the pro-slavery views of his home state. Gradually, however, as he travels with the runaway slave Jim, he comes to moderate his views (long after the reader has) and eventually assists Jim. It is a moral tale disguised as a children's adventure story.

Novels, when done well, are about life, and introspection upon the depths of human experience. We can all gain from more reflection.

Novels can also focus our attention (and empathy) on a single character. Dickens was a master of the sentimental novel, and while the protagonists triumphed over adversity and evil through their own and other good people's efforts, there was usually a waif who was not as lucky, who succumbed to the harshness of society. The most famous of these was Little Nell, the innocent young girl in *The Old Curiosity Shop* (1841) who faces the villainous Quilp, the ugliness of industrial England, and an otherwise kindly grandfather whose gambling addiction leads him to steal what few resources Little Nell has. As each new chapter of the novel emerged, readers speculated on Nell's fate, and as her condition drew more desperate, Dickens received many letters urging him to spare Little Nell. By the time of the chapter where Little Nell died arrived, Americans flocked to the docks to greet the ships arriving with the latest chapter and inquired whether Little Nell was still alive. Grown men wept when they read the chapter. While Dickens openly discouraged any statues of himself to be erected, there is one of him and the character of Little Nell in Clark Park in Philadelphia, and every year a child is chosen to crown the statue of Nell with a wreath of flowers.

Powerful novels demand that we slow down and process how we are creating and destroying in our lives. The rabbis taught that amidst so much destructive behavior we must stop and reflect upon the world we exist in:

> When the Holy One created Adam, He took him for a tour of all the trees in the Garden of Eden, and He said to him: See how My works are so glorious and pleasant! All of this, I have created for you! Make sure that you do not ruin and destroy My world, for if you do, no one will be able to fix it after you are gone! (*Midrash Ecclesiastes Rabbah*).

Reading can broaden our imagination and our sensitivity toward the human condition. Novels can even affect society. Harriet Beecher Stowe's *Uncle Tom's Cabin* (1852) helped personalize and simplify slavery to many Americans, provided an international boost to the abolitionist movement, and may have literally helped bring about the Civil War. John Steinbeck's 1939 novel, *The Grapes of Wrath*, publicized the plight of the people of Oklahoma who fled from the Dust Bowl and tried to find work in California. As a result, Congressional hearings were held on the conditions of migrant worker camps in California, and some labor laws were enacted to help these struggling Americans. Both novels increased the empathy of readers for the vulnerable and oppressed.

Many novels have endured for their timeless themes. Cervantes' *Don Quixote* has spurred countless retellings that pit romantic idealism versus cynicism, Victor Hugo's *Les Misérables* depicts the human capacity for transformation versus an implacable, harsh interpretation of the law, and many Russian novelists (for example, Tolstoy, Dostoevsky, and Turgenev) explored complex philosophical and theological concepts throughout their works. Needless to say, all impart knowledge of history in their own way. For those not motivated or disciplined to read, perhaps join a book club or start a *chevruta* (learning partnership). We can all use some help in raising our level of empathy and moral imagination.

From Feminism to Masculinism?

I am a proud feminist. I have argued adamantly for increasing funding for girls' education around the world, against wage inequality due to gender, against domestic violence, for women's social entrepreneurship in developing countries, against the problem of *agunot*, among other subjects. I have worked diligently to engage feminist sensitivities into my work, leadership, and interactions. I have become so engaged in the feminist narrative and sensitivities, however, that I have neglected to have any circles of support for understanding what it means to be a young man in the twenty-first century. I have decided now to seek to better understand my gender construction and role as well as my social identity.

One of the most important questions that arises when discussing my male identity is whether there can be a new type of "masculinism" that is not about stereotypical manliness, but about confidently embracing what it means to be a man in contemporary society while also honoring the narrative, journeys, and rights associated with feminism. There are so many extremes when one tries to find a word or image that adequately exhibits this concept. On the one hand, we have the "macho," testosterone-laden image ludicrously and extremely demonstrated by Russian President Vladimir Putin, riding shirtless astride his horse, or taking part in amateurishly staged athletic events where he is the star, which matches his aggressive and reckless foreign policy. On the other hand, we have "effeminate" men who have been disparaged with derogatory names and characterizations. In recent decades, "metrosexuals" enjoy a slightly higher reputation, although their exaggerated narcissistic aspects (their perceived obsession with personal appearance and material consumption) are still not attractive. We could use the word "gentleman" to describe the informed, intelligent, and thoughtfully ideal man, but this word tends to have an upper class, elitist connotation. We need a better term.

While boys have traditionally been afforded advantages that girls and women have not, there are areas where a male's upbringing, emphasizing strength and self-reliance but downplays emotional needs, can be a liability. Recent studies of sexually abused children have found that boys are less likely than girls to report the abuse. Some potential reasons are that boys psychologically cannot understand the experience, considering their inability to cope with a situation where they are helpless and not in control, and, further, that their masculinity requires toughness and discourages them from seeking help. Also, since most abusers of boys (and girls) are male (older boys or men), there is often greater sexual confusion for boys. In addition, people are far more likely to be dismissive of adult female abuse of boys than they are of adult male abuse of girls, and the comparatively lighter sentences of women who abuse boys is a continuing indication of this attitude and approach.

From my perspective as an Orthodox Rabbi, I actually believe very deeply in gender differentiation. I believe that there is unique potential in women's and in men's spirituality and that gender is not spiritually insignificant. I'm aware that much of it is socially constructed (aside from the *limited* biological differences), but I embrace that Judaism, for thousands of years, has found meaning in our different narratives as mother/sister/daughter and father/brother/son. Sometimes, gender differentiation has led to abuse and that should always be rectified. Yet still, other times it positively contributes to a sense of structure, confidence, and healthy self-identity.

What are some of the unique emotional challenges and social pressures that men experience today? How has feminism affected notions of self-identity? What does it mean to explore one's masculinity in the twenty-first century? These types of questions are often demeaned as being feminine on the one hand, or dismissive of feminism on the other.

Moving Traditions, a group that encourages Jews to expand the traditional bounds of gender, recently started a program for teenage boys, "Shevet Achim: The Brotherhood." Through this program, adolescent boys are allowed to spend time in an honest and open "guy space" where hanging out with peers is coupled with serious discussions regarding masculinity and what being Jewish means to them. This program (initiated years after a similar program was developed for girls) was prompted by four research studies of boys in grades 8 to 11 that revealed a serious necessity to address the needs of Jewish boys after their bar mitzvah. Jewish teenage boys comprise less than 30 percent of youth participants in Hebrew high school, youth groups, and camp – this precipitous drop off in youth participation in Jewish activities and community is common for boys after reaching bar mitzvah. Societal pressures advance images of men as physically and sexually aggressive, yet emotionally repressed, and peer pressure often ensures that teenage boys remain alienated and confused. The studies sought to understand why Jewish boys dropped so many of their Jewish activities in their teen years. The findings[57]included:

- The boys identified with and took pride in their Jewish identity, but did not feel that activities after their bar mitzvah were compelling

- The boys' Jewish identity helped them resist mainstream cultural stereotypes. For example, they wanted to achieve academically, felt comfortable showing affection and kindness to others, and showed awareness and concern for the outside world

- With all the pressures of modern adolescence, boys did not want a Sunday activity to be high pressure or overloaded with work. They wanted an easier pace and some time for fun

With these findings in mind, the program was designed specifically to focus on masculinity and it's meaning as the boys move toward manhood. Male educators chosen to supervise the boys-only program must simultaneously interact well with teenagers, and make Jewish ritual relevant and compelling. Additionally, physical activity must be included to maintain the interest of the boys and the spirit of enjoyable competition. Furthermore, the community plays an integral role in the boys' development and is brought in for support throughout the programming.

Whenever I find or participate in a "men's group" it usually means

---

[57]http://movingtraditions.org/wp-content/uploads/2012/08/Engaging-Jewish-Teenage-Boys-A-Call-to-Action-Moving-Traditions.pdf

it has to do with sports, or getting in touch with our "inner caveman," or involves the smoking of cigars or the imbibing of scotch. I know that might resonate with many, but, personally, I'm looking more for a serious community that encourages and supports intellectual and emotional exploration. I do not watch football, drink beer, speak in a demeaning way towards women, particularly "like" cars, enjoy staying in my "man cave," or complain about my blessed family life. For those of us who do not participate in these comically stereotypical male activities, what does it mean for us to pursue our intellectual, spiritual, and moral pursuits as men? How will we be deeply sensitive to the feminist narrative while developing our own distinct identities as men? How will we once again learn to engage Jewish boys in Jewish life without alienating Jewish girls in the process? The search continues...

Middot: Developing Character to
Change the World

Mandela, Lincoln and the Tutsis: A Future Built on Forgiveness

There are hurts so deep that forgiveness of those who did the hurting seems impossible. I have encountered so many who have become alienated from people they love over a disagreement that no longer matters. Neither was able to ask for or give forgiveness and so they parted ways.

The Jewish tradition teaches us, however, that we should emulate God's ways (*halachta b'drachav*), and that God is forgiving. In the *selichot* liturgy each year around the High Holidays, we recite, "*Mochail avonot amo, ma'avir rishon rishon, marbeh mechilah, l'chot'im uslichah l'fosh'im. Oseh tzedakot im kol basar v'ruach, lo karatam tigmol*" – "God deals righteously with all and does *tzedek* (justice), pardoning *chot'im* (careless wrongdoers) and forgiving *posh'im* (intentional wrongdoers)." Forgiving others here is connected to *tzedek*; forgiveness of those who have erred is a fulfillment of justice, an act of healing relationships and society. Part of what it means to be righteous is to be a forgiver: to understand that human beings are fallible and to love others who stumble; God models humility and forgiveness by forgiving us.

Rav Yisrael of Rizhin distinguishes between the *solaiach* and the *salchan*. The *solaiach* is one who forgives when she is in the mood, in an arbitrary rather than intrinsic way. The *salchan*, on the other hand, forgives time after time, as it is a core point of his natural identity as a forgiver. To perpetuate opportunities to forgive and to repair relationships is to be a *salchan*. Some people hurt us so much that we cannot merely forgive them one time; rather, we need to forgive them in your heart time and time again. This helps us not only to heal but also to cultivate a very deep virtue.

This process has another step. As we are obligated to forgive others, so are we commanded not to bear a grudge (*lo titor*). This commandment is in the same biblical verse as the command to love others like ourselves. Forgiving another is about the past; removing a grudge, on the other hand, is about a present sense of indebtedness. To truly love another, we must move beyond entitlement and release our grudges.

How does this apply to our lives? We can observe historic choices of whether to seek forgiveness and its dramatic consequences. To be forgiving is to be courageous, and leaders who try to heal long-standing conflicts often pay with their lives. About a month before his assassination, in his second inaugural address near the end of the Civil War, President Abraham Lincoln famously said, "With malice toward none, with charity for all," but he added that forgiveness entailed much work: "...to bind up the nation's wounds, to care for him who shall have borne the battle and for his widow and his orphan, to do all which may achieve and cherish a just and lasting peace..."

In the past twenty years, South Africa is the prime example of a nation that pursued a path of forgiveness, bolstered by the formidable stature of its political and religious leaders, Nelson Mandela and Archbishop Desmond Tutu. In 1994, South Africa had peaceful elections to elect its first black majority government. Then, in spite of predictions that this government would unleash a vengeful bloodbath against the former apartheid white rulers, the Truth and Reconciliation Commission, chaired by Nobel-laureate Tutu, helped heal the country. Instead of putting all the perpetrators (mostly white) on trial, or granting a general amnesty that would do nothing to defuse the hatred, South Africa tried a different course. Tutu wrote:

> They saw the process of the Truth and Reconciliation Commission, when perpetrators of some of the most gruesome atrocities were given amnesty in exchange for a full disclosure of the facts of the offence. Instead of revenge and retribution, this new nation chose to tread the difficult path of confession, forgiveness, and reconciliation.

As long as the torturers and murderers would acknowledge their crimes and ask for forgiveness, the victims would in turn forgive them, and the state would not pursue further action against them. Incredibly, this tactic avoided the violence that gripped so many other nations. For example, in Zimbabwe (formerly the white-ruled Rhodesia), President Robert Mugabe rejected reconciliation, established an ironclad dictatorship and chose to reward his political allies by violently seizing property even from white farmers who chose to work with the new government.

In the same year, 1994, in Rwanda, the spirit of vengeance ruled. Long-standing resentment erupted in genocidal chaos as murderous bands of Hutus, incited by radio broadcasts, murdered hundreds of thousands of Tutsis by hacking them to death with machetes and clubs, or shooting them at close range. Even Tutsis in churches, hospitals, old age homes and orphanages were not safe. Unfortunately, the world was largely quiescent as nearly one million people were murdered over just a few short months. While today Rwanda is seeking to defuse the hatred through providing basic services to as many people as possible, the wounds have not fully healed. This May 2013, President Jakaya Kikwete of neighboring Tanzania called on Rwanda to negotiate with the Democratic Forces for the Liberation of Rwanda (FDLR), the remnant of the genocidal murderers of 1994, who still engage in murder, rape and torture. This was considered deeply offensive to the Rwandan government, since the call for negotiations came during the 100-day annual period of mourning for the genocide. There are offenses for which forgiveness must wait.

Forgiveness is hard, and sometimes seemingly impossible. Before we decide that we cannot forgive, we should consider the price of not seeking forgiveness, and try to be the *salchan* who follows the command of *lo titor*. As Archbishop Tutu points out, "[r]etribution leads to a cycle of reprisal, leading to counter-reprisal in an inexorable movement, as in Rwanda, Northern Ireland, and in the former Yugoslavia. The only thing that can break that cycle, making possible a new beginning, is forgiveness. Without forgiveness there is no future." There really is no better way to say it than that: Without forgiveness there is no future.

2.)
The Jewish Service Revolution: Challenges and Opportunities

Money may make the world go around, but social media has shown that big ideas can achieve big impact and far reach without any money at all. Running parallel to this, when it comes to Jewish values, philanthropy is certainly extremely important, but we can never neglect the equally important value of service.

Jewish law requires that we give money to those in need (*tzedakah*), particularly that we proactively give ten percent of our earnings to those in need (*maaser*). On its face this obligation relates specifically to money, but in the last century Rabbi Moshe Feinstein ruled that one who cannot donate 10 percent of her net income should donate 10 percent of her time instead (*Even Ha'ezer Vol. 4,* 26:4).

Typically, the Orthodox community has prioritized a discourse and activism of *chesed* (kindness to your fellow), building *gemachs* (borrow clothing and other needs), offering free loans, supporting the mourners and sick, etc. The non-Orthodox, on the other hand, have typically prioritized a discourse and activism of social justice (working to ensure a more just and sustainable society). This has changed and there is now a large and growing Orthodox social justice movement, while the non-Orthodox talk more about *chesed*.

The rabbis taught that acts of *chesed* are even greater than acts *of* tzedakah in three ways: "Acts of tzedakah involve only one's money *– gemilut chasadim* can involve both money, or one's personal service. *Tzedakah* can be given only to the poor *– gemilut chasadim* can be done both for the rich and for the poor. Tzedakah can be given only to the living *– gemilut chasadim* can be done both for the living and the dead" (*Sukkah* 49b).

In *Sefer HaChinuch*, Rabbi Aaron Halevi of Barcelona taught Judaism's philosophy of action:

> Know that a person is influenced according to
> his actions. His heart and all his thoughts are
> [drawn] after his deeds in which he is occupied,
> whether good or bad. Thus, even a person who
> is thoroughly wicked in his heart, and every
> imagination of the thoughts of his heart are only
> evil the entire day -- would he arouse his spirit
> and set his striving and his occupation with
> constancy in Torah and mitzvot, even if not for
> the sake of Heaven, he would veer at once
> toward the good, and with the power of his good
> deeds he would deaden his evil impulse. For
> after one's actions is the heart drawn (*Mitzvah*
> 17).

As American Jews, we are fortunate to be situated in a country with a long history of service. More than a century ago, women such as Jane Addams and Lillian Wald helped found settlement houses that provided free educational, health, and cultural programs for the millions of immigrants who were trying to cope with cultural differences and crushing poverty. Many of those who volunteered for settlement, seeing the enormity of their tasks, later worked for woman suffrage, a living wage for workers, direct election of senators, the peace movement, and other progressive causes.

Service once again came to the fore as the first generation of baby boomers grew to young adulthood. The Peace Corps, which is now celebrating its fiftieth anniversary, was partly a response to the Cold War and partly a means to utilize the enthusiasm for service that had taken hold in this large young generation of Americans.

Even during his presidential campaign in 1960, John F. Kennedy called for a "peace corps" of volunteers to help developing nations, and in response he had received 25,000 letters from potential volunteers. At his inaugural address the following January, President Kennedy famously declared, "Ask not what your country can do for you. Ask what you can do for your country," and followed this up by establishing the Peace Corps by executive order. For most of its history, Peace Corps volunteers worked in countries that invited them to come, and concentrated on education and agricultural aid, although some other areas of assistance have been added. Thus far, about 200,000 volunteers have served in 139 countries. It is one of the great American service stories. The Volunteers in Service to America (VISTA) program was established in 1965 by President Lyndon B. Johnson (and incorporated into AmeriCorps in 1993). While often under-funded and gaining far less publicity than the Peace Corps, VISTA has produced members who were pivotal in the later creation of successful programs such as Head Start and Upward Bound. So far, 140,000 have served within the VISTA program of AmeriCorps. President Johnson's message to the first VISTA cohort aspire service workers through the decades, even today: "Your pay will be low; the conditions of your labor often will be difficult. But you will have the satisfaction of leading a great national effort and you will have the ultimate reward which comes to those who serve their fellow man."

It may appear that service does not generate the same enthusiasm as it has in the past, when government and social movements provided the impetus for service that led to concrete results. Today, youth especially are seen as uninvolved; however, offer a mixed message. According to data compiled by the U.S. Bureau of Labor Statistics, 26.5 percent of Americans volunteered at least once from September 2011-September 2012, with women volunteering more than men. Those between the ages of 35 and 44 are most likely to volunteer (31.6 percent), while those age 20-24 are the least likely (18.9 percent). Interestingly, married people were more likely to volunteer than those who had never married (31.9 versus 20.7 percent), and those with children were more likely to volunteer than those who had no children. From these figures, it appears that efforts to stimulate youth service are needed. Fortunately, there are signs that this trend may be reversing.

In fact, there is now a service revolution occurring throughout the Jewish community. Repair The World, for example, aims "to inspire American Jews and their communities to give their time and effort to serve those in need. We aim to make service a defining part of American Jewish life." Founded in 2009, and operating in five cities, Repair the World already has achieved the following significant results:[58]

---

[58]http://werepair.org/cms/wp-content/uploads/2013/01/RepairOneSheet-Final.pdf%2522%20%255Ct%20%2522_hplink

- 40,000 people have volunteered for local activities

- Helped expand programs for 100 organizations

- Trained 200 Jewish service-learning leaders, and instituted a Fellowship program to continue training future service leaders

- Conducted educational campaigns on college campuses, and started an online resource for academics: RepairLabs.org

- Initiated the first comprehensive Jewish volunteering survey in an effort to determine the best future strategies for Jewish service

Dozens of Jewish organizations offer serious service opportunities and now the Wexner Foundation has started a youth service. The Wexner Service Corps (WSC), a program for Jewish teenagers, began with WSC members helping with the continuing Hurricane Sandy relief efforts. The WSC members learn Jewish texts relating to service, and study the devastating effect of natural disasters and the impact of their service. We, in the Jewish social justice community, look forward to the expansion of this initiative. A lot of serious work is being done to enhance the Jewish commitment to making service an integral part of how we live. Jewish service should be done in distinctly Jewish ways fostered by *middot* (character) education, but we should also encounter the other and stand in solidarity with other communities through our service. Joining hands with other communities should solidify what we are about and also expand what we are about.

We cannot build a future Jewish generation of armchair philosophers and activists. Rather we must be *omed b'poretz* (fighting in the trenches), in touch with society and active in building it brick by brick. It's true that we will often have to allocate serious resources to investing in a culture of service and sometimes it seems that it will be more effective to just allocate that money to the need itself, but we must ensure that we are looking to the longer term, building a future generation that is committed to these causes and deeply in touch with their realties.

While it is important to train young people with the lessons of our own experience, we have to allow youth to experiment and discover the world for themselves, even to make mistakes. They will misunderstand societal problems, and we will question our investments in their growth and our faith in the future, but it is this education that will grant them the wisdom to be courageous moral leaders in the best sense of the term.

Investing in service has not lacked for opposition. Claudia Horwitz, in *What is Wrong With National Service?* wrote, "I have watched national service unfold with disappointment. After much thought and real heartache, I have decided it's just too dangerous to support." This argument neglects reality. What project has ever been perfect from the start? What if we judged the American military performance solely by the Japanese attack on Pearl Harbor? We must obviously allow for mistakes and adjustments.

Lastly, and taking (self-) criticism into account, we must be very cautious with the *how* and the *why* in which we do service to ensure that all are honored and to ensure that we actually help and make a difference and don't just offer exotic tours for those of privilege. Giving time is among the greatest gifts one can give to another. We must foster this commitment. We cannot merely send our youth out by themselves. If we are serious about it, we as adults must also be consistently engaged in service not only to model the commitment to our youth but because it is inherently important.

The Power of Language: Cultivating Positive Emotions

Language affects the heart. When others who speak negatively surround us, it can really affect our mood and disposition. Are we aware of how much negative language there is around us?   A generation ago, psychologist James R. Averill analyzed 558 emotive words with affective meaning (every one that he could find in the English language). He found that 62 percent of them had a negative connotation, versus 38 percent that positive. He concluded that "...in everyday discourse as well as in psychological disquisitions, there appears to be a relative neglect of positive emotions." If Eskimos have one hundred variations for the word for snow, then as Americans negative emotions are our snow. How does this affect us?

A story illustrates the teaching that impressive achievements can be reached without going beyond the surface: A young scholar completed his learning of the entire Talmud for the third time. Full of pride, he ran to tell his teacher about his accomplishment. "Rabbi," he announced enthusiastically, "I've just been through the whole Talmud for the third time." "That's wonderful," replied his teacher, "but let me ask you one question. How many times has the Talmud been through you?" It is an imperative that we learn to choose the input and output of our words carefully. We can rush through them but they will not penetrate us with deep intentionality. We should pause to consider the language we use to describe our world and where we learned it, and truly allow positive hearing and speaking to penetrate our hearts.

Words are powerful. They offer the potential for spiritual destruction or healing. The Torah teaches that we should cultivate positive emotions and use positive speech as much as possible in a transformative and authentic manner. Just as it takes more effort to find a positive than a negative emotional word, so it takes effort to embrace the deep spiritual wisdom of Torah and to allow the holy words to penetrate our hearts. The reward is great.

4.)
The Virtue of Modesty: A Reflection on the Theological
Value of Privacy

In recent years, debates about the right to privacy have emerged stronger than ever. There are always political issues to explore, but we all also have our own introspective work to do to grow in our own sense of modesty (*tzniut*).

Modesty is deeply connected to, but distinct from, humility (anavah), the trait for which, the Torah explains, Moses is the paradigm (Numbers 12:3). The prophet Micah famously calls upon us to "walk humbly" (Micah 6:8), and Proverbs reminds us "to be humble" (11:2). The Talmud teaches that humility is one of the chief virtues of the Jewish people (*Yevamot* 79a), and further, according to Rabbi Elazar bar Tzadok, that this verse is referring not only to our fashion choices but also to our behavior (*Sukkah* 49b).

This emphasis on personal privacy as virtue is a hallmark of the social vision of the Torah and the rabbis. Jewish law prohibits placing a window in one's house that will allow one to see through a neighbor's window. The Gemara learns this from Bilam's praise for Israel's tents, which were set up so that the tent openings would not face one another (*Bava Batra* 60a). This value also informs the prohibition against *hezek re'iyah*, causing damage through sight (*Bava Batra* 2b). Ramban taught that there are three problems with this conduct: *tzniut* (modesty), *lashon hara* (evil speech), and *ayin hara* (evil eye).

First, when one sees what he is not meant to see, there is a sense of shame for both seer and seen and it leads to immodesty for both parties. Second, it can lead to *lashon hara*, one now knows private information that they did not need to know, and they are likely to spread it around. Third, there is an *ayin hara*: Seeing that which one is not meant to see is a metaphysical statement, to wit, that a person's destiny has been altered by what her eyes have taken in.

With this understanding, modesty is not only a legal or moral value, but also a theological one. God is considered the absolute model of modesty, as the Divine is never fully revealed or understood; in this view, God's hidden presence from the world is

360

more of an expression of a value than it is a theological problem. The most unique and special aspects of oneself should often be shared most privately and intimately reserved for those we love most.

Unfortunately, today's discourse on humility and modesty focuses almost solely on dress, particularly women's dress. For example, we have seen recent examples in Israel of ultra-Orthodox men who harass Orthodox girls (let alone the secular majority) for being immodest according to their standards. In the United States, there was a time in the mid-nineteenth century when women were expected to wear dresses that extended to the floor and were many layers thick, making simple tasks such as climbing stairs, doing chores, or crossing a street extremely difficult. However, even the courageous woman suffragist Elizabeth Cady Stanton was unable to withstand the harassment she faced when she wore "bloomers," a shorter skirt with puffy pant legs that extended to the ground but allowed more movement: "People would stare, many make rude remarks, boys follow in crowds, with jeers and laughter, so that gentlemen in attendance would feel it their duty to show fight..." We must learn to extend the virtue of modesty beyond how one dresses, surely not in a way that diminishes the potential of women.

In the modern world, extremists who mask their cruelty behind a veneer of Islam have reached unprecedented levels of oppression through "modesty." Batya Swift Yasgur's book *Behind the Burqa: Our Life in Afghanistan and How We Escaped to Freedom*, details the story of two Afghan women. Under the Taliban, modesty for women was extended to such an extreme that not only was female education forbidden, but women were forbidden to leave their home in most circumstances, and they were forced to wear a burqa, which not only covered everything from head to toe, but also only allowed women to see out of their hoods through a narrow mesh area. The religious police increasingly and brutally enforced the Taliban's edicts. One woman witnessed another woman in a burqa walking close by. Unfortunately, her ankle showed as she walked, whereupon a religious policeman came up to her:

"Hey, Kafir! Infidel! You are exposing
your flesh!" He lashed at her with his
whip. Again and again it descended.
Muffled cries came from beneath the
burqa.... Male passers-by averted their
eyes, women hurried past. When he
was done he spat a curse at her and she
stumbled away.

Eventually the pressure led many women to commit suicide. Isn't it clear that the focus on women's dress should at least fall short of this?

The Jewish value of privacy should be applied to many of the pressing political issues we face today. There are certainly times when collective security may trump the value of privacy, but this trade-off should be considered and then executed only with great caution and deliberation. In America, we have had a long history of legal battles over privacy, from the mid-eighteenth century battle of the British use of general search warrants (the "Writs of Assistance") to recent Supreme Court decisions that allow the police to take arrested (not even convicted) people's DNA samples. In both cases, the authorities tried to use a general search tactic to solve crimes that did not have to be specified, with a risk that the authorities would expand this power as a way to amass more information. Have we switched sides on this issue of privacy? Our actions will determine how much privacy versus security we have.

Our commitment to modesty should affect how we dress, spend, talk, and conduct ourselves in all ways, but modesty is relative to time, culture, person, and situation so we dare not pass judgments on others. In doing so, we must also be cognizant that pressing the idea of modesty may be harmful to some people, especially women, and we should refrain from showing a cruel face to the world in our efforts to encourage modesty. We should live as other-focused people, not self-focused beings. Embracing modesty, humility, and privacy is an attempt to see beyond ourselves. It's a *tzimtzum* (self-retraction) where we create more room for the other.

5.)

One Special Mitzvah and Paying It Forward

What does loyalty and commitment to high quality religious performance mean? In an age of mass consumption, and with a tradition that emphasizes the rigor of 613 different mitzvot, how is one to acquire excellence in observance and spiritual growth?

Rabbi Shlomo Ganzfried, in his *Kitzur Shulchan Aruch* (26:22), taught that it is more meaningful to honor a deceased parent by walking *yashar* (doing good and acting justly) than by saying *kaddish*. He goes on to say that we should honor our parents by committing ourselves to performing a special mitzvah in their honor, and that we should pass along that special mitzvah to our children as well. What a beautiful and powerful idea to own a special mitzvah to honor a loved one and then to continue to pass it through the family.

Rav Chayim Vital, in his magnum opus *Sha'ar HaGilgulim*, argues that the importance of transmigration of the soul (reincarnation) is that it allows humans to seek growth, perfection, and actualization in this and future lives. He argues that one must fulfill the *taryag mitzvot* (all of the Torah's commandments) completely in order to achieve complete *deveikut* (intimacy with the Infinite), and that we must learn the Torah in all its depth and with all the methods available to us. We return to a new life over and over to attempt to fulfill that mission until our intellectual comprehension is mastered. This might provide us with a compelling model for thinking about Jewish continuity through a *Torat Chayim* (living Torah), because our lives are not complete until we have lived the full Jewish experience. In our lives, we each have an important *mitzvah* to perfect (and a teaching to master) before our soul can ascend into its next body.

It is encouraging to see how similar concepts are growing in mainstream American society. We may say "*Tizku l'mitzvot*" after someone has done a mitzvah, wishing the individual the merit to perform another mitzvah. In mainstream society, the term "Pay It Forward" refers to passing on an act of kindness to another (usually unknown) person, in what ideally will be an endless cycle of good deeds. While the term and its concept has been around for centuries, it has been popularized in an unprecedented fashion in the last few years by a popular novel and film, and there are now pay-it-forward organizations that promote the concept through various means, such as passing on a bracelet to the next recipient of each good deed. If we help someone who is going through physical therapy or a lengthy period of unemployment or underemployment, we can make a measurable improvement in her life. In an era that appears to have a perverse, anti-*tzedakah* war on the poor, a virtual return to Social Darwinism, our individual acts can counteract this hostility and preserve a world where we look after and help the poor and vulnerable.

The Mei Ha'Shiloah (Mordechai Yosef Leiner) taught that every soul has its own root and is perfected by a different *mitzvah*, that one should sacrifice to actualize this root *mitzvah* in a way they should not normally act. By taking on one special *mitzvah* to truly cherish and actualize on the highest level possible, and then by sharing it with loved ones and strangers, we are able to transform ourselves and the world around us, in this and perhaps even other lives.

6.)

Honoring Our Parents: Can We Learn From China?

It is well known that millions of elderly Americans are neglected at their most vulnerable time. Jewish law, however, requires in multiple times and ways that we honor our parents (Exodus 20:11, Exodus 21:15, Exodus 21:17, Leviticus 19:3, Deuteronomy 27:16).

The ancient exhortations to honor one's parents endure into our age. As of July 2013, China has required that adult children take care of their parents. The amended Law for the Protection of the Rights and Interests of the Elderly states that adult children must visit their elderly relatives, and they are prohibited from insulting, mistreating, or abandoning them under pain of lawsuit. Wu Ming, the deputy department head in China's Ministry of Civil Affairs said, "Family members should not ignore and isolate the elderly. And they should come often to visit." Today, millions of Chinese workers live thousands of miles away from their parents, families are limited to one child per family, and the tradition values of filial piety have become more challenging to put into practice. But those who fail to take care of their parents will now be fined. This act may be in recognition of the aging of the Chinese population: There will be 221 million elderly (age 60 and older) in the country in 2015, and the percentage will reach about a third by 2050.

In Japan, another country with the longstanding value of filial piety, modern legislation assists families in paying for hired caregivers (although they cannot be family members). Elsewhere, many nations mandate some level of care for the elderly. While the Soviet Union no longer exists, some of its policies survive in the areas it used to control. For example, in much of the former Soviet bloc, the elderly can sue their children for child support, and siblings can sue each other to make sure the money is raised and the burden shared. In Western Europe, eldercare is typically ensured through social insurance programs. The most inclusive policy for the elderly can be found in Norway, where all of the elderly are guaranteed long-term care.

How does the United States, which has traditionally been reluctant in implementing social welfare policies taken for granted in Europe, compare with rest of the industrial world? Currently, nearly ten million adults age fifty and older care for elderly parents, with little governmental assistance. This number has tripled in fifteen years, so now about 1 in 4 adult children provide personal or financial care for their parents. A study conducted by a group of insurance, care giving, and policy think tanks concluded that, taking into account wages and Social Security and pension money, the average adult who becomes a caregiver for an aging parent spends nearly $304,000. In addition, caregivers undergo tremendous stress, and suffer higher rates of cardiovascular disease and alcohol abuse, among other illnesses. On top of this, Social Security benefits here do not increase when personal care costs rise, as they do in some European nations.

One bright spot is that many adults can now take up to twelve weeks off from work to care for an ill parent (or any other family member) without losing their job under the Family and Medical Leave Act of 1993. Unfortunately, this does not go far enough, because this leave is without pay and therefore an unaffordable option for nearly all working Americans. Medicare may help pay for some short-term care, and Medicaid can cover expenses for those with in adequate resources, although these are dependent on individual state requirements, which are constantly under attack today. Currently, as the Medicare website notes, private funds are used for eldercare: "About half of all nursing home residents pay nursing home costs out of their own savings. After these savings and other resources are spent, many people who stay in nursing homes for long periods eventually become eligible for Medicaid." In other words, if you want nursing care as an elderly person, be prepared to lose all your resources. Other programs, such as Meals on Wheels, are also dependent on state funding (with some federal aid that is also under attack), and we cannot assume that it will continue as is in the current atmosphere of austerity. Other options usually rely on independent insurance or health plans that require additional payments.

While the United States remains a wealthy nation, and many can afford their own care, we should heed Jewish law and truly honor our parents. The rabbis tell a story which is codified as law (*Shulkhan Arukh* YD 240:3).

> They inquired of Rav Ula: "How far does
> honoring/dignifying parents extend?" He said to
> them: "Go out and see what one [non-Jew] did in
> Ashkelon. His name was Dama ben Netinah. Once
> the Sages sought merchandise for a price of sixty
> myriads, but the key was resting under his father's
> head, and he did not disturb him.... When Rav
> Dimi came, he said: Once he was wearing a gold
> diadem and sitting among the greats of Rome,
> when his mother came and tore it off him, and hit
> him over the head and spit in his face, but he did
> not humiliate her" (*Kiddushin* 31a).

Even when mistreated and shamed by a parent, many demands to honor parents still remain. To be sure, there are limits:

> One whose mother or father breaks down
> mentally – He must make the effort to behave
> with them in accordance with their condition
> until [Hashem] has mercy on them; but if he it is
> not possible for him to stand it, because they
> have become greatly insane – he may go and
> leave them behind, so long as he commands
> others to treat them properly *(Shulchan Aruch,
> Yoreh Deah* 240:10).

Jewish law wisely and prophetically notes the mental and physical strain that an elderly parent with Alzheimer's disease or dementia can have on a family. However, the law also mandates that we provide some degree of proper care for them. We should not force families to go into bankruptcy in order to avoid placing their parents in virtual warehouses where their parents will be neglected and mistreated.

The thing is that this is not only an ossified, unrealistic demand based on an idealized or no longer extant religious society. We see models for contemporary implementation around the world today, in China, Norway, and beyond. Our parents sacrificed so much for our well being throughout their lives, when we were not able to fend for ourselves. As a society, we must recognize this and provide for them when they are no longer physically independent themselves.

Have We Forgotten Our Seniors? The Mitzvah To Honor the Elderly

In the Jewish tradition, there is a mitzvah from the Torah to honor the elderly (*Leviticus* 19:32). Rashi, commenting on this verse, writes that this mitzvah applies not only to wise elders but applies equally to the ignorant. The Rabbis suggest that although many elderly may have forgotten much of their wisdom in their later years, this does not diminish their value:

> Be mindful of the elderly person
> who has forgotten his teaching for
> reasons that are not his fault, as it is
> said that the broken tablets rested
> with the tablets in the ark (*Brachot*
> 8b).

Rambam states that we must honor the elderly, even if we do not consider them wise, as incontrovertible law:

> We should stand before an old man of
> exceedingly advanced age, even if he is not
> a sage. Even a sage who is young is
> obligated to stand before a sage of
> exceedingly advanced age. Nevertheless,
> he need not rise to his full height, and
> need only show some token of respect
> (*Laws of Torah Study* 6:9).

This is the law found in the *Shulchan Aruch* as well (*Yoreh Deah* 244:1). The Torah suggests that certain levels, and types, of wisdom can be assumed for the elderly; Deuteronomy reads, "Remember the days long gone by. Ponder the years of each generation. Ask your father and let him tell you; and your elder, who will explain it" (32:7). It is even more explicit in the Book of Job: "With age comes wisdom, and length of days brings understanding" (12:12). The rabbis believed that the elderly necessarily had wisdom that we could all learn from (*Kiddushin* 32b).

As the following passage displays, the rabbis elaborate on the impact that age has upon our intellectual and spiritual development:

> [Acher] said: "One who studies Torah as a child, to what can he be likened? To ink written on fresh paper. And one who studies Torah as an old man, to what can he be likened? To ink written on smudged paper." Rabbi Yose bar Yehudah of Kfar HaBavli says: "One who learns Torah from the young, to what can he be likened? To one who eats unripe grapes or drinks unfermented wine from his vat. But one who learns Torah from the old, to what can he be likened? To one who eats ripe grapes or drinks aged wine." Rabi says: "Do not look at the vessel, but what is in it; there is a new vessel filled with old wine and an old vessel that does not even contain new wine" (*Pirkei Avot* 4:20).

We should consider deeply whom we are attaining our wisdom from and how we are balancing out our perspectives. In addition to learning from the aged, the rabbis are clear that we must actively engage and support the elderly. It is written: "We learn that everyone who welcomes in an elderly person, it is as if he has welcomed in the Divine Presence" (*Bereshit Rabbah, Parshat Toldot*). Some explain that this is due to the wisdom and dignity of the elderly. Still, others explain that it is due to their challenges; "Rabbi Yochanan would stand before the elderly Arameans and say, 'How many troubles and experiences have passed over them!'" (*Kiddushin* 33a). Wise or not, this is a vulnerable population that is to be taken care of.

Sadly, in America, today the elderly are often neglected. Shocking statistics reveal some of the economic challenges that seniors face:[59]

---

[59] http://www.nytimes.com/2013/10/06/opinion/sunday/getting-older-growing-poorer.html?_r=1&

.... From 2011 to 2012, the rate of
extreme poverty rose by a statistically
significant amount among those 65 and
older, meaning that a growing number
of them were living at or below 50
percent of the poverty line. In 2012,
this was $11,011 a year for an older
person living alone.

The elderly are unfortunate victims of a perception based on statistics instead of reality. Obviously, in many cities the demands of monthly rent alone exceeds that of an annual income, even for those above the poverty line. Thus, using statistics, it appeared that in 2006 (before the severe recession) fewer than 1 in 10 of the elderly lived in poverty. However, more than 22 percent lived below the 150 percent poverty level (then about $13,000 per year). Then, even more pertinent to seniors, there are healthcare costs that are not factored in to poverty statistics. Taking these costs into consideration, even in a comparatively generous area, New York City let's say, this more realistic poverty rate for the elderly would be 32 percent as of 2006. We must not be slaves to statistics, but should really see and understand the conditions that many of our nation's seniors are forced to cope with in their later years.

Many of those struggling have suffered from long-term unemployment, debt, insufficient savings, and inadequate social security support and retirement savings. This all is exacerbated by the consistent increased costs of living.

Furthermore, there are serious health risks that seniors face as they age, such as the risk for falls and resultant fractures. Indeed, falls are responsible for thousands of serious injuries, disability, and even deaths a year. The combination of decreased bone mineral density and lessening vision leads to an increasing tendency to falls that may result in bone fracture, with hip fractures especially dreaded, as they lead to disability and the necessity for institutional care. Increased urgency for urination (often caused by diuretics and prescription medications) can also lead to falls, as the elderly rush to get to a bathroom before they have an accident. Other health risks such as presbyopia (the inability to see near objects) and other visual problems such as macular degeneration or diabetic retinopathy make seeing and avoiding obstacles increasingly difficult. The inability to reach one's feet (the feet are especially vulnerable to infection, and those with diabetes may be at risk of losing their feet if an infection is unattended) is also a serious problem, and something as simple as trimming one's toenails becomes virtually impossible, or fraught with the risk of cuts and infections.

Unfortunately, the growing elderly population faces yet another threat: abuse and neglect. As people live longer, the quality of life does not necessarily increase with the years. Alzheimer's disease, dementia, Parkinson's, and other disabling conditions often prevent the elderly from taking care of themselves, and caregivers (either family members or eldercare workers overworked in cost-conscious facilities) are often put under tremendous strain, as their relatives/patients often deal with the symptoms of their respective conditions. At times, the result of the caregivers frustration, attitude/demeanor, and workload leads to either abuse or neglect,[60] ranging from physical beatings, sexual assault, neglect (such as allowing patients to develop bedsores by not turning them over periodically, not giving them medication in a timely fashion, or failing to clean their urine and excrement). While these instances are hard to quantify, government sources estimate that hundreds of thousands of the elderly suffer from abuse or neglect annually. It is no wonder that many elderly people diligently try to avoid going to an "old age" home.

We can do our part to help the elderly by ensuring that home therapists visit to ensure that risks for falls is minimized (e.g., by removing throw rugs and excessive furniture), that doctors regularly visit and check on seniors, and, that if a senior is bedridden, that they are regularly bathed and turned so that they do not develop bedsores. In addition, we should all take care of available services. For example, the Program of All-Inclusive Care for the Elderly (PACE) provides qualifying Medicare and Medicaid patients guaranteed services. PACE supplies primary, hospital, home, and adult day care, with nursing, meals, transportation, and social services, provided by an interdisciplinary team of medical providers, therapists, and home and personal care attendants.

---

[60] http://www.aoa.gov/AoA_programs/Elder_Rights/EA_Prevention/whatIsEA.aspx

We can help further by ensuring that Social Security is bolstered and not weakened as an "entitlement." After all, workers pay all their lives into the fund, so they are merely receiving what they have rightfully earned. As of June 2013, the Social Security Administration paid 37 million retired workers an average monthly benefit of $1,269. This amount is clearly inadequate to pay for rent, food, health care, and other expenses. Since more than half of all American workers have no private pension plan, more than a third have no retirement savings, and by 2033 there will be more than 77 million elderly people, our need to provide resources for the elderly will become even more critical.

There are countless ways to honor seniors and they should not merely be symbolic. We can all find more ways to help in a hands-on way and to advocate for their needs in society. The great Rebbe Nachman of Breslov wrote that one can, "Gauge a country's prosperity by its treatment of its elders;" let us ensure our society's greatness by fulfilling our mitzvah to honor *our* elders.

8.)

Conflicts Between God and Parents: Truth Is Chosen Over Truth

One example of how religion commands us to embrace Truth over truth is the requirement to obey God over parents. On the one hand, the *Sefer Hachinuch* makes clear how important it is to honor our parents:

> Among the bases of this commandment [Honoring one's father and mother] is the fact that it is proper that people recognize and bestow kindness upon one who has done him good. A person should realize that his mother and father are the cause of his being in the world, and therefore it is truly proper that he render them all the honor and do them all the service he can.

Yet, Judaism draws a very clear line defining the limits of filial obedience. The crucial Biblical line is found in Leviticus 19:3: "You shall revere his mother and father and keep My Sabbaths, I the Lord am your God." From here we learn that honoring God supersedes honoring parents.

One might think that the commandment of filial piety overrides the commandment of the Sabbath, therefore the Torah writes the Sabbath second to teach that everyone [including parents] are obligated in the Honor of God (*Yevamot* 5b). Maimonides codifies this law and states:

> If a father tells his child to go against the word of the Torah, either to perform a negative commandment or to disregard a positive commandment, even if it be a Rabbinic commandment, a child shall disobey, as it is written: "You shall revere your father and mother and keep My Sabbaths"— [teaching us] that all [including parents] are obligated to honor God (*Hilchot Mamrim* 6:12).

In a sense we learn that eternal truths trump temporal truths. Sometimes people ask us to sacrifice our core values to maintain a relationship. The Torah teaches that we must stick to our principles amidst these trying times. The strongest relationships are those where both parties respect each other's core values and support each other.

Of course, the gifts of parents and God are interwoven. In a profound Midrash, we learn how God and parents partner to create a child:

> Our rabbis taught: There are three partners in (making) a person: the Holy One, the father, and the mother. The father supplies the seed of the white substance out of which are formed the child's bones, sinews, nails, the brain in his head and the white of his eye; the mother supplies the seed of the red substance out of which is formed his skin, flesh, hair, blood, and the black of the eye; and the Holy One gives the child spirit (*ruach*), and soul (*neshamah*), beauty of features, eyesight and the power of hearing, and the ability to speak and to walk, understanding and discernment. When his time to depart from the world approaches, the Holy One takes away his share and leaves the shares of his father and mother with them (*Niddah* 31a).

Each person must express gratitude to God and one's parents for their existence. In the end, our biological features will remain on the earth and only our eternal characteristics will truly remain. Spiritual life is about cultivating those eternal qualities.

9

Sometimes Trying To Help Make Things Worse

Ever try to help and make things worse? You are not alone. Sometimes good intentions are truly not enough. A Talmudic debate explores the importance of good intentions:

> There was a debate: the first teacher held that in order to fulfill a mitzvah (commandment / good deed) one needs the proper intention; Rabbi Gamliel held that one does not need the proper intention (*Eruvin* 95b).

In one passage, Rabbi Shimon declared the wisest person to be "one who considers the outcome of a deed" (*Pirkei Avot* 2:13). St. Augustine once wrote "Good intentions pave the path to hell." We, of course, should truly have good and pure motivations and intentions for our moral work. But more importantly, we must work toward good consequences. Perhaps the most tragic case is when one attempts to help and actually makes things worse for the vulnerable. Consider this tragic case in Haiti:[61]

> Haiti's cholera epidemic, now entering its fourth year, has killed more than 8,300 people and sickened more than 650,000. It is a calamity, though one fundamentally different from the earthquake, hurricanes and floods that have beset the fragile country since 2010. It is, instead, a man-made disaster, advocates for Haitian victims contend, asserting the epidemic is a direct result of the negligence of United Nations peacekeepers who failed to keep their contaminated sewage out of a river from which thousands of Haitians drink.

American food aid is another important example. All too often our aid has helped American business while wiping out local business infrastructure in the area being served. That country then

---

[61] http://www.nytimes.com/2013/10/13/opinion/sunday/haitis-imported-disaster.html?_r=3&

becomes dependent upon U.S. products. Peter Greer, the President and CEO of Hope International, suggests:[62]

> Anyone that's been involved in philanthropy eventually comes to that point. When you try to help, you try to give things, you start to have the consequences. There's an author Bob Lupton, who really nails it when he says that when he gave something the first time, there was gratitude; and when he gave something a second time to that same community, there was anticipation; the third time, there was expectation; the fourth time, there was entitlement; and the fifth time, there was dependency. That is what we've all experienced when we've wanted to do good. Something changes the more we just give handout after handout. Something that is designed to be a help actually causes harm.

Consider some adult reactions to childhood obesity:[63]

> Parents and other adults who are "only trying to help" may do harm rather than good, as a recent study from the journal *Pediatrics* makes clear. More than 350 teens who had attended one of two weight-loss camps filled out detailed questionnaires about their experiences of being victimized because of their weight. It found, not surprisingly, that nearly all heavier teenagers are teased or bullied about their weight by peers. What was surprising was the number of teenagers who said they have experienced what amounts to bullying at the hands of trusted adults, including coaches and gym teachers (42 percent) and, most disturbingly, parents (37 percent).

This phenomenon does not only occur on an international basis, of course. Ever tried to offer a sincere apology and actually made things worse? We must move beyond sympathy. Susan Sontag

---

[62] http://www.forbes.com/sites/jerrybowyer/2013/07/30/your-help-is-hurting-how-church-foreign-aid-programs-make-things-worse/

[63] http://well.blogs.nytimes.com/2013/01/09/feeling-bullied-by-parents-about-weight/

explained:

> So far as we feel sympathy, we feel we are not
> accomplices to what caused the suffering. Our
> sympathy proclaims our innocence as well as our
> impotence. To that extent, it can be (for all our good
> intentions) an impertinent—if not an inappropriate—
> response. To set aside the sympathy we extend to others
> beset by war and murderous politics for a consideration
> of how our privileges are located on the same map as
> their suffering, and may—in ways that we prefer not to
> imagine—be linked to their suffering, as the wealth of
> some may imply the destitution of others, is a task for
> which the painful, stirring images supply only the initial
> spark (*Regarding the Pain of Others*).

The last thing others who are vulnerable need are
overbearing and self-serving advice, or thoughtless help. Rather, we
must start with listening and really understanding what the other
needs.

10

Tevillat Keilim: **Transforming Our Consumption**

There is a mitzvah to take one's new cooking utensils to the *mikvah* (spiritual bath) to give them a spiritual dip (Numbers 31:23). What is the purpose of such a ritual?

The Torah is about transformation. It is about transforming the self (mind, body, soul); it is about transforming our relationships; and it is about transforming society. *Mitzvot* are the primary vehicles we Jews use for accomplishing this holy transformation. Throughout Jewish history, prophets and rabbis have attempted to summarize the 613 mitzvot (the purpose of the Torah) into unique principles:

> Micah came and comprised them in three: 'It has been told you, O man, what is good and what does God require of you – only to do justice, love mercy, and walk humbly with your God,' (6:8). Isaiah came and comprised them in two: 'Keep justice and do righteousness,' (56:1). Amos came and comprised it in one: "Seek me and live,' (5:4), (*Makkot* 24a).

Common in all of these great thinkers and leaders responses is a mandate to embrace life by walking justly and humbly with God. The mitzvot are the instruments to achieve this holy end but they must be performed in such a way as to make us better people

Tevillat Keiliim is about the spiritual transformation of a utensil. In this case, it's not a concrete-transformation but a perspective-transformation, which comes about through spiritual preparation. By taking the time and energy to "make a utensil Jewish" (like a convert who enters the *mikvah*) we intellectually, morally, and spiritually challenge ourselves to think about what it means to own and utilize objects used for the preparation of meals and nutritive consumption. We must ask ourselves, on a daily basis, more thought-provoking moral and spiritual questions about what type of food is worthy of placement upon a utensil that we have transformed into a holy object.

Now that we have "converted" the utensil from the mundane to the holy, we can no longer perceive food consumption as a mundane activity. How were the worker, animal, and land treated in the food's preparation? How will this food affect my family's bodies? Through ethical and spiritual food consumption choices and through blessing, we elevate the food even higher.

When we can collectively actualize and elevate our everyday actions from the mundane to the holy we may eventually fulfill the timeless and beautiful words of the prophet Isaiah:

> At that time, there will be neither hunger, nor war; neither will there be jealousy, nor strife. Blessings will be abundant and comfort within the reach of all. The single pre-occupation of the entire world will be to know the Lord. Therefore there will be wise persons who know mysterious and profound things and will attain an understanding of the Creator to the utmost capacity of the human mind, as it is written, 'The earth will be filled with the knowledge of God, as the waters cover the sea' (Isaiah 2:9).

May we all merit to gain physical and spiritual energy from our meals and let the mitzvah of *tevillat keilim* help to remind us of our spiritual potential while providing the nourishment for actualization.

Conclusion

The world is full of so much injustice, oppression, alienation, and suffering. There are times in all of our lives when we ask ourselves what this life is about. When we are full of despair we sometimes struggle to find the core meaning in our existence. While I am certainly not immune to moments of darkness and despondency, I find myself returning, over and over, to the same philosophy. Life has inherent meaning. The future is bright. We are responsible and capable. We are partners with God to repair a broken world. I believe this is the message of the Jewish tradition.

It is my deepest hope that we can build a society together where the Torah serves as our light to bring God into the world, to bring holiness and light to dark places, and to bring heaven down to earth. We must do personal and national *teshuva* (repentance) to grow together. I serve the Jewish people because I love our people but also because I believe we are, collectively, a powerful vehicle for transformation in the world.

We will not get there with mere sermons and articles. We must act in the world each and every day. This modest book is a reminder of the work that I need to do. My hope is that it can help inspire others to find their path and to actualize their life's purpose. When another finds darkness lets lift them up. When we find darkness let's move toward places of light where others can help us regain our grounding. Together, only together, we can change the world.

Rabbi Dr. Shmuly Yanklowitz was listed in *Newsweek's* "America's Top 50 Rabbis in 2012 and in 2013. He is the Executive Director of the Valley Beit Midrash in Phoenix, AZ. He is also the Founder and President of Uri L'Tzedek and the Founder and CEO of The Shamayim V'Aretz Insitute. Rav Shmuly completed his Bachelors at the University of Texas, a Masters at Yeshiva University in Jewish Philosophy, a Masters at Harvard University in Moral Psychology and a Doctorate at Columbia University in Epistemology and Moral Development. Rav Shmuly is the author of four previous works on Jewish ethics and social justice.

Front Cover Illustration and Back Cover Detail- *The Feast of the Rejoicing of the Law at the Synagogue in Leghorn, Italy* by Solomon Alexander Hart, RA. Oil on canvas. Currently part of the permanent collection at the Jewish Museum, New York. Public Domain Image.

Photo of Author by Avi Dorfman

Made in the USA
Charleston, SC
12 May 2016